Design-Based
School Improvement

Design-Based
School Improvement

A Practical Guide for
Education Leaders

Rick Mintrop

HARVARD EDUCATION PRESS
Cambridge, Massachusetts

Library of Congress Control Number 2015953167

Paperback ISBN 978-1-61250-902-0
Library Edition ISBN 978-1-61250-903-7

Published by Harvard Education Press,
an imprint of the Harvard Education Publishing Group
Harvard Education Press
8 Story Street
Cambridge, MA 02138

Cover design: Wilcox Design
Cover image: iStock.com/StudioM1

The typefaces used in this book are Adobe Garamond and Formata.

To James Romeo, my life partner,
and now spouse in the eyes of the law

CONTENTS

Introduction   1
Design Development and Innovative School Improvement

PART I   **Identifying the Problem**

1   Selecting Problems of Practice   23

2   Defining and Framing Problems of Practice   31
with Elizabeth Zumpe

3   Making Intuitive Theories of Action Explicit   43
with Elizabeth Zumpe

4   Conducting a Needs Assessment   57
with Mahua Baral

PART II   **Developing a Theory of Action**

5   Consulting the Professional Knowledge Base   73
with Mahua Baral

6   Becoming Intellectual Leaders in the Co-design Space   87
with Mahua Baral

7   Understanding the Problem   101
with Elizabeth Zumpe

8   Understanding the Change Process   115

PART III   Preparing to Intervene

9   Designing Interventions   133

10   Making Design Development Research-Based   153

11   Collecting Impact and Process Data   165

12   Making Design Development Studies Rigorous   181

13   Integrating Action Research into Design Development   191

PART IV   Implementing and Iterating Interventions

14   Implementing Interventions   203
     with John Hall

15   Deriving Design Principles   219
     with John Hall

     Conclusion   237

     Appendix   241
     *Getting Started: Key Sources Consulted by the Designers
     Featured in This Book*

     Notes   245

     Acknowledgments   257

     About the Author and Contributors   261

     Index   265

Design Development and Innovative School Improvement

*It may be hard for an egg to turn into a bird. It would be a
jolly sight harder for it to learn to fly while remaining an egg.
We are like eggs at present. And you cannot go on indefinitely
being just an ordinary, decent egg. We must be hatched or go bad.*
—C. S. LEWIS

We live in an inequitable society, and our educational system insufficiently answers to the needs of disadvantaged and marginalized students. Too often, educational systems ignore or avoid problems of inequity or address them superficially. There are several reasons for this failure. Acknowledging problems of inequity often causes discomfort for those who have tolerated the status quo for too long. It stirs up political conflict with those who have benefited from inequities, and it creates value dissonance among those who believe that things are right the way they are. Moreover, equity-relevant improvements in education are complex: they entail technical innovation, moral reorientation, political struggle, motivation, risk-taking, and courage. Thus, efforts to achieve these improvements must consider technical, political, and normative aspects of change, and education leaders who are focused on equity need to recognize their own transformative role.[1]

1

Transformative leaders for equity in education face three interrelated core problems:

- how to *make their organization more effective* so that scarce available resources are used to benefit the students;
- how to enable their organization to *facilitate complex learning* so that all students are exposed to learning opportunities that treat them as intellectually and morally capable persons;
- how to insure that all adult members of their organization *value students equally* so that differences in ethnicity, race, gender, class, sexual orientation, language, immigrant status, or special needs designation do not result in value judgments detrimental to students' dignity, competence, and well-being.

Each of these core challenges entails different dynamics of organizational change. Improvements in *organizational effectiveness* often revolve around coordination, coherence, and follow-through. Improvements in *learning complexity* often home in on capacity building, commitment, and autonomy. *Cultural change for equity* needs to address value dissonance, courageous collegial conversations, and moral leadership.

Equity-relevant improvements are about what schools value, but also about what works. To clarify what their schools value, educators need philosophy and deliberate reasoning. An understanding of what works, however, requires several types of knowledge. For most school leaders, experience and common sense loom large. Fortunately, professionals can also draw from a developed knowledge base on school improvement. But the available knowledge base has its limitations. Studies of effective schools and teaching reveal factors associated with better student outcomes. This body of knowledge, however, does not describe how to create these conditions in challenging environments. Other studies evaluate the effectiveness of certain interventions or programs by rigorously comparing treatment and control groups. These kinds of evaluations, however, leave the challenge of implementing the programs in local contexts as a black box. There is an ample body of case studies that demonstrate how policies or programs were implemented and how changes unfolded within the complexity of educational organizations. This body of knowledge, unfortunately, tends to show how the intended changes did not unfold and tells us too little about how change might unfold successfully in educators' own schools and districts. Finally, a body of improvement theories and how-to guides too often lacks a strong and systematic evidentiary base.

In sum, we know too little about how equity-minded leaders act on their values through practical interventions *and* make them work within their organizations. For this, we need a different kind of knowledge: practical design knowledge. Practical design knowledge is knowledge about what to do or how to intervene when one encounters recognizable problems in one's work. It is design knowledge because it is explicit and spells out the main steps in a sequence of activities and the main content of these activities. It is practical because it is sufficiently concrete so that people can make connections between their experiences of problems and what the design of a solution suggests for them to do. Most teachers are familiar with curricular unit plan documents that show them what and how to teach when they face a specific teaching challenge, for example, how to make students understand a certain concept, such as the "main idea" in a text. These unit plans map main lessons, activities, materials, and perhaps even main prompts or forms of interaction between teachers and students. The interplay of these elements is a design.

But how does a design come about? Sometimes it is the result of trial and error by teachers who tinker with the best way to teach a focal concept. Sometimes it is the result of more systematic research. Sometimes teachers and researchers work together and try out activities, carefully recording how students respond. They engage in what we call design studies or design development studies. These kinds of studies are also useful for the purpose of school improvement, and they are especially useful for thorny problems of improving on equity. Design development marries the values and ideals of visionary leaders with the evidence that their efforts worked. But designs should not be seen as prescriptions. Many educators have heard of, or are familiar with, scripted curricula. They are a form of instructional design that tells users to implement the script with fidelity, step-by-step, glued to the pacing, prompts, and materials of the script. The designs we have in mind in this book are different.

Against the idea of implementation fidelity, the type of design development for school improvement advocated in this book assumes the autonomy of participants. Less concerned about universal effectiveness or broad generalization across large populations of schools, design development of the sort advocated in this book builds on the idea that context sensitivity is the base of all successful improvement, that educational leaders will need to adapt and reinvent for their specific situation, but that design principles can travel. In a nutshell, design development is a systematic and disciplined form of innovative problem solving in educational organizations. It is informed by clear, thoughtful ideas about the adult learning that is needed to accomplish intended results. Design development considers the complexity of specific organizational contexts, employs both the predictive quality of research and the creative power of practical problem-solving, and achieves results iteratively, in trial-and-error fashion.

This book is meant to be a practical guide for educational leaders who strive to contribute to the emerging body of practical design knowledge for school improvement.

A NEW APPROACH TO INNOVATION AND PROBLEM SOLVING

One of the most important competencies of leaders everywhere, but especially of educational professionals serving disadvantaged students, is to make good decisions. Decisions at senior levels in school districts and similar organizations can affect large numbers of people and have far-reaching consequences, but even decisions at a medium-sized school can affect many people. The quality of these decisions is gauged by the degree to which they are informed, reflective, adequate to the situation, effective, sensitive to client needs, and in the service of equitable learning opportunities.

While many decisions are minor and made in a flash of recognizing past experiences in present situations, some are bigger. Some big decisions deal with programmatic directions and strategic orientations of an organization. For example, what should we do about the numerous disciplinary referrals and suspensions in our middle schools; what should we do about widespread bullying behavior in our high schools; how could we upgrade the quality of our principals' instructional supervision so that they are prepared to lead their teachers toward teaching college-ready skills and knowledge? Other major decisions are made at the school level. For example, how can we overcome the exclusion of students with disability from grade-level content, or how can we keep our teachers from over-referring students of color to special education? These sorts of problems recur in many school systems all over the country, and they demand that leaders be innovative problem solvers, programmatically and strategically.

If innovation means the application of new inventions or ideas to existing organizational processes to make these processes more efficient, more sensitive to client needs, or more likely to have better results, then many educational organizations operate in a curious mode of innovation. When leaders sense one of the bigger problems mentioned above, their search for solutions often goes outward. They scan the environment for programs, consultants, or packages that seemingly address the problem. Their preference is to find solutions that carry the label "research-based" or "best practice." Solving the problem then becomes a matter of implementing a package, a script, or a consultant's directions—solutions that have a supposedly proven record of success. Innovation is all about buying the package and, afterward, creating buy-in for it. There is nothing wrong with this *buy and buy-in* mode of innovation if the new program addresses a clear problem, has a record of success, is a good fit with existing beliefs and practices, and is given sufficient attention, resources, and time for implementation.

The drawbacks of this mode of innovation are apparent. Leaders often overestimate the effectiveness of these new programs and underestimate the challenges of implementation in their unique local situations. As attention shifts from one problem to the next, multiple packages accumulate, each with its own set of commands, unique vocabulary, and demands on teachers' time. Incoherence and bad fit with internal beliefs, attitudes, and practices diminish teachers' energy and commitment to learn. The adopted solutions tend to be conventional, rather than innovative or creative. Whether the solutions actually work is often overlooked and seems to count less than whether they give the appearance that the leaders have done their job and addressed the problem.

This book asks educational leaders to think about innovation and problem solving differently. We ask leaders to engage with the design mode of innovation. The design mode goes beyond the simplicity of *buy and buy-in*. It aims at innovative interventions for problems that do not come with a ready-to-buy solution. This mode of innovation begins with the assumption that educational settings are complex; that much of educational change is about adult—and, ultimately, student—learning; and that this learning and its results are emergent, that is, they are not narrowly predictable, but are not completely open-ended, either. In the design mode, interventions are sets of sequenced learning opportunities that are created *iteratively* and repeated through trial and error until a satisfactory outcome has been accomplished. When designers engage in this trial and error, they are acting creatively. But they do not act arbitrarily. Rather, the process is a systematic and disciplined undertaking. What it takes to make it so is the subject of this book.

THEORETICAL AND EMPIRICAL FOUNDATION OF THE BOOK

In 2006, the Graduate School of Education at the University of California, Berkeley, started a new doctoral program for working professionals. From its inception, the Leadership for Educational Equity Program (LEEP) followed the guiding ideas of the Carnegie Project on the Education Doctorate to develop the EdD as a professional doctorate framed around key principles associated with the preparation of "scholarly practitioners."[2] These principles include a commitment to transformative leadership in service of equity and social justice, a focus on analyzing problems of practice and developing meaningful solutions, and a grounding in a knowledge base that integrates practical and theoretical research knowledge. With these principles in mind, LEEP saw the potential of design development methodology as the signature pedagogy for the practice-oriented educational doctorate. Program participants have been mostly school and district administrators, ranging from superintendents to principals, assistant principals, and department heads in public school districts, Catholic dioceses, and charter school units. The program gave my colleagues and me the basis for our experiments with design development in many contexts and related to a variety of problems.

The work is a team effort. As the main author of this book, I was the founding director of LEEP and initiated experimentation with design-based thinking and research from the program's inception. My colleagues and I inherited ideas that Bernard Gifford had developed for an earlier version of leadership development at Berkeley. Cynthia Coburn was a contributor and teacher in the program for the first few years. Her thinking about the connection between research and practice has given us founding ideas. We have benefited from the intellectual commitment of eight cohorts of educational leaders, whose work is acknowledged at the end of the book. Over the years, the core development team has consisted of the program director, four educational leaders (Elizabeth Baham, Annie Johnston, Page Tompkins, and Matthew Wayne), and three university-based young scholars (Mahua Baral, John Hall, and Elizabeth Zumpe). Our work has benefited from the support and critical feedback of over thirty-five members of the Berkeley faculty from nine departments.

Starting in 2006, we tinkered. As behooves design thinkers, we tried many things and failed often. In the last few years, we have become firmer in our knowledge on how to effectively communicate design-based thinking to educational leaders who are, or want to be, transformative leaders for equity. We began a systematic self-evaluation of projects, and our students have graciously allowed us to take a closer look at their progress as they wend their ways through the milestones of developing their research. Because our program is small, the number of students who have completed design development studies is still small, but we make up for it with detailed data collection on the unfolding of their thinking.

The literature on design experiments, design studies, or design development is quite extensive, and in writing this book, my colleagues and I have consulted much of it. Several sources that inspired our thinking deserve special mention.

The initial inspiration came from the work of the late Ann Brown and from that of Paul Cobb and his coauthors.[3] These scholars provided the theoretical underpinnings of design-based research in the learning sciences. Their work emphasizes theory development. Our emphasis, in contrast, is on results: designs that improve schools and school districts or similar administrative units.[4] The work of a team of researchers and designers at the Netherlands Institute for Curriculum Development (SLO) at the University of Twente gave us a theoretical and practical methodology that suited the work of educational leaders charged to improve their organization.[5] Their work has spawned an impressive wave of design research projects internationally. A compelling book by David Coghlan and Teresa Brannick, both of whom hail from Ireland, taught us how leaders could use action research to transform their own organizations.[6] Concurrent with our own efforts at Berkeley, the Carnegie Foundation for the Advancement of Teaching began to develop a major initiative around design-based thinking and continuous quality improvement with the idea of networked improvement communities.[7] This initiative validated and further developed our belief that transformative leaders would benefit from design-based thinking, with potentially far-reaching consequences for larger-scale educational reform and improvement. Finally, we drew inspiration from the work by Elizabeth City and Richard Elmore and their team on instructional rounds, an example of an intervention designed to generate actionable knowledge about instruction in schools and districts.[8]

A DIALOGUE BETWEEN PRACTICE AND RESEARCH

Over the years, one central idea has been recurring in the LEEP design development team—the worlds of research and practice often do not hear each other and do not speak to each other. Universities—ours being no exception—have a way of expecting professionals to live up to the university's presumed superior rigor of knowledge, and practitioners return the favor by questioning the relevance of research for practice. There are many good methodology texts that privilege the voice of the university. Most often, such texts center on abstract exposition of theory and use concrete examples from the practical world to illustrate their points. This book reverses this order. It communicates its message through a concrete narrative with acting researcher-practitioners at the center. Theoretical explications supplement the concrete narrative.

The book is divided into two registers, or styles of writing. In the *concrete narrative,* we describe and observe practitioner-researchers at work. Here, we introduce Christine, Michelle, Eric, and Nora as examples of leaders' problem-solving and design-based thinking. The four characters are composites that exemplify the thinking that goes into design development. The composites represent actual design development studies conducted within LEEP. Many of these studies can be grouped into several types: teacher collaboration and school climate, teacher development and authentic instruction, district and school instructional leadership, and reshaping organizational values and culture. There are some studies, however, that fall outside these types, for example, several studies on using technology or developing tools. In this book, we have concentrated on the main design development studies that focused on core challenges of equity. To facilitate understanding, we present the composite characters' thinking sequentially in the book, and we have filtered out some of the detours, trials, and moves between steps that designers may encounter in real life as they make progress. In the *excursions into theory,* we introduce the theoretical knowledge base and familiarize the readers with relevant academic concepts and discourses. We hope that the concrete narratives and the excursions into theory will, together, provide busy educational leaders with clarity about the power of design-based thinking and design development studies.

There are three ways to read this book. Those who want a graphic idea of design development should read the concrete narrative and skip the theoretical excursions in the first round. Readers who are more theoretically inclined could jump from one theoretical excursion to another and skip the concrete narrative. The theoretical excursions, by themselves, build up the necessary theoretical knowledge base for design development and school improvement. Readers who want to deepen their theoretical understanding can follow up with the basal texts that are cited in the excursions. A third way is to read the whole text in sequence and benefit from the back and forth between practical and academic ways of grasping what design development is all about. Both concrete narrative and theoretical excursions trace the design process as one that begins with the sensing and framing of a problem of practice. The process then moves through the formulation of a theory of action, which consists of a deeper understanding of the problem and the change process. The implementation of interventions is accompanied by research activities that aim to provide data from which design principles may be distilled. These principles are then revisited, altered, or refined in subsequent iterations.

Meet the four leaders whose narratives will give us a concrete idea of what design development is all about. All four of them work in public school districts that serve large numbers of economically disadvantaged students, students of color, and immigrants. But the leaders could just as well be placed in private religious or charter school settings. And the principles of design development addressed in the book apply to more middle-class environments as well.

Two of these leaders, Christine and Michelle, are seasoned principals who have been recognized for the strength of their leadership and have been drafted into helping to craft district-wide initiatives. Christine is an experienced middle school principal known for her no-nonsense demeanor. Her background is math, training that may contribute to her methodical ways of problem solving and her organizing skills.

Michelle, an experienced elementary school principal with a penchant for art and literature, has won many accolades and awards over the years for her work. She is known in the district for her compelling charisma, thoughtfulness, and indefatigable activism on making elementary school an authentic experience for children and their families. She is outspoken about issues of racial equality and immigrant rights.

Eric is an assistant superintendent who is passionate about developing a strong instructional program. After having served as a teacher and then a middle school principal for a few years, he wants to make decisions on instruction at the systems level. This desire pushed him to move into district-level leadership while relatively young.

Nora is a young and newer principal who has focused keenly on her high school leadership. A capable administrator, she believes in the power of procedure, but also wants to be a transformative leader who takes risks for her ideals. In her first years, she has focused steadily on, and has been largely successful with, bringing about a strong commitment to social justice among the staff.

Each of these leaders has different reasons for eventually choosing design development as the mode of innovation even if he or she did not begin with this intention. Christine faces the unique challenge of having to improve on behavioral management in middle schools that are mainly staffed by novice teachers. She is convinced that this staffing pattern will persist in the future. At some point, she concludes that there is nothing powerful enough out there to solve her district's unique problem. She also hopes that her efforts can contribute to problem solving beyond her district, and she imagines herself traveling to these districts and helping them with her new design knowledge.

The idea of design development does not come to Michelle right away. She originally thinks of her advocacy for culturally relevant pedagogy in more conventional ways. When she analyzes her teachers' resistance to her efforts, she discovers that she must find ways to combine curricular and organizational changes to actually make her preferred pedagogy work in her district's schools. She arrives at design development as her answer.

Eric, self-assured and convinced that he knows what to do, stumbles into design development when his first spontaneous attempts at improving instructional supervision do not seem to give him the results he expected. Nora, from the beginning, is excited about design development. She knows that there is so little systematic professional knowledge out there on how to reduce racial and homophobic slurs in high schools that her project must make a difference in creating new practical knowledge that can be applied beyond her school.

EXCURSION INTO THEORY

Design Development and the Science of Continuous Organizational Improvement

Many of us associate the term *design* with the shape of objects, for example, designer clothes, designer furniture, industrial design, or the design of your smartphone. Innovators of design-based thinking like Tim Brown and Tom and David Kelley argue that, in our work and our organizations, we all are, or can be, designers.[9] Designers not only design objects, but can also design forms of human interaction that may elicit as much satisfaction among users as a well-designed object produces. And designers marshal the same creativity, whether the results of their efforts are human interactions or physical objects. Design-based thinking deemphasizes the idea of pressuring or otherwise breaking resistance by potential users of a design. It believes in the power of satisfying human needs.[10] Equity-sensitive designers assume that in human interaction and learning, all participants are motivated to express their needs for competence, autonomy, and community. Designers understand that people's resistance to learning is due to fear, defensiveness, and silence—problems generated by environments that inhibit the expression of basic motivations.[11] Thus, designers are *user-centered*.

Designing interventions for complex problems of practice calls for both intuition and rational deliberation. For some authors, design-based thinking is seen as a "third way" between rationality and intuition.[12] For Donald Schön, reflective practitioners take perceived human needs as their point of departure for inquiry and consider these needs to envision what they want to accomplish.[13] Design decisions around a focal task are made in a mode of deliberate trial and error. In this mode, actors constantly interact with a task-specific environment and judge the quality of their decisions according to a sense of appreciation. That is, a decision intuitively feels right if it aligns with the actors' envisioned end state and their analytical knowledge of how their field works. In designing, *both rationality and intuition are at play*.

Roger Martin suggests that rationality and intuition can be reconciled through a balance of "analytical mastery and intuitive originality in a dynamic interplay" that he calls "design thinking."[14] Similarly, Kelley and Kelley describe design thinking as "the natural—and coachable—human ability to be intuitive, to recognize patterns, and to construct ideas that are emotionally meaningful as well as functional."[15] Design thinking has been characterized in a variety of ways. Martin describes the process as a knowledge funnel, starting with the exploration of a mystery, moving toward the selection of a heuristic, or rule of thumb, and culminating in the development of a more fixed formula or algorithm that evolves from careful study of the heuristic.[16] Brown explains design thinking as an iterative "system of overlapping spaces rather than a sequence of orderly steps."[17] The spaces include inspiration, ideation, and implementation, all of which are constrained by the three criteria of desirability, feasibility, and viability. Kelley and Kelley describe these overlapping spaces of design thinking as a methodology that can be used to meet human needs through a combination of creative thinking and systematic testing of prototypes.[18]

Whether design thinking is an iterative cycle, a funnel, or a methodology, at the core of each model is the assumption that designers do not choose between rationality or intuition, but use both, one intertwined with the other. In Brown's iterative cycle, inspiration necessitates insight and intuition to generate new ideas. It relies on data generated from careful observation of human needs. Development of an inspiration into an ideation requires not only creative thinking, but also analysis and synthesis to search for patterns in the data collected throughout the process. In Martin's knowledge funnel, the exploration of mystery involves "hunches" or "pre-linguistic intuitions," which evolve later into rational algorithms intended to produce systematic and predictable results.[19]

As creators, designers try out novel or ingenious ideas for problems related to human interactions.[20] As researchers, they connect the dots between an unfulfilled human need, an intervention that is constructed with a testable logic, and metrics that indicate to what degree the implemented design helped participants express or fulfill identified needs. Designers embrace the uncertainty of creation, yet they are grounded in the established professional knowledge base related to the problem they have chosen to tackle. Designers are *theory and research based as well as imaginative and creative*.

A design-based approach is appropriate in a work environment that increasingly demands that leaders provide evidence for their decisions and for the results. These results need to be confirmable by participants and verifiable by a community of equity-relevant reformers. Thus, *designs aim at effectiveness*.

In education, designs for improvement should be co-design projects in which interventions are not done *to* people, but done *with* people. Leaders who engage in design-based thinking must themselves be open to learning, experiment, and critique. They need to base their interventions on testable assumptions and evidence that can be disputed by participants. Giving voice to the users of designs, not just to the designers themselves, is a matter of fairness and justice.[21] Thus, *designs are co-created*.

In sum, design development is imaginative, theory and research based, user-centered, context-specific, created cooperatively, emergent, iterative, and dependent on results.

At the heart of design development is a notion of continuous quality improvement through iterative, evidence-based cycles of inquiry. Several models have been developed around this main idea, design development being one of them. Total quality management, often attributed to the work of W. Edwards Deming, is another such model. It was pioneered by Japanese manufacturing industries in the postwar era.[22] Following in the Deming tradition, ideas of "improvement science" have spread in recent years from manufacturing to service industries, such as health care and education.[23]

Mindful of the complexity and local specificity of change, the improvement-science approach melds pragmatism and science. At the heart of the approach is disciplined inquiry that builds on existing research, practical design knowledge, and simply good ideas from change efforts across organizations. Ideas are tested in short, rapid cycles of trial and error, resulting in design prototyping. Each cycle begins with a diagnosis of a specific problem, explicit goals, and a plan of improvement steps that are subsequently implemented. The effectiveness of these steps is tested in small populations, and implementation, evidence of progress, and results are assessed. Deming's "plan-do-check-act" cycle, later referred to as the PDSA or "plan-do-study-act" cycle, embodies these steps.[24] The participants are cross-role teams, ideally representing all relevant actors from various layers of the hierarchy related to the problem at hand. The purpose of the inquiry is explicitly *not* to push the participants to expend more effort or to exhort "bad apples" to increase the output of existing systems, but to learn how to change systems so that routine processes lead to better results.[25]

Scientific principles are evident in the systematic data collection that guides and accompanies the learning process. Teams demonstrate improvement over time by quantifying their targets and developing metrics to chart progress and assess results. Evidence may be based on multiple quantitative and qualitative sources.[26] On a larger scale and depending on the data richness of the specific industry, statistical procedures capture quality, for example, by calculating error and variation of production output. One such approach is called Six Sigma.[27] On the pragmatic side, continuous improvement builds up inventories of increasingly standardized change concepts or strategies that can apply to many situations.[28] On the scientific side, more rigorous design development studies build up knowledge of transferable design principles and promising learning activities.

Thus, quality improvement informed by principles of improvement science incorporates knowledge from both practice and research to examine improvement activities in local contexts.[29] The research may produce findings that can be disseminated and applied to other settings by distilling standard practices attached to clearly defined problems.[30]

In *Learning to Improve: How America's Schools Can Get Better at Getting Better*, Anthony Bryk and his coauthors describe how improvement science can be applied in education organizations.[31] The authors outline six distinct principles for this work. The approach to design development studies we have developed in this book lives and breathes these six principles.

First, those engaging in an improvement-science approach to organizational change should "make the work problem-specific and user-centered." Here, Bryk and coauthors emphasize the need to diagnose and frame the problem by actively learning what and how strategies work. The problem solvers should focus on what needs to be solved and for whom. Emphasis is placed on the users, and the problem should be framed from their point of view.

Second, improvement science projects should "focus on variation in performance." Problem solvers should understand and appreciate the differences of performance and should develop solutions considering the context—"what works, for whom, and under what conditions."

Third, to do improvement science, problem solvers must "see the system that produces the current outcomes." They should fully understand how an organization currently functions; they need to recognize its hidden complexities and use this information to develop a theory of practical improvement.

The fourth principle is the need for data. As Bryk's group explains, "we cannot improve at scale what we cannot measure." Data should be collected continuously, and feedback should inform improvement by tracking the practices that take place. But in education, there are often multiple practices influencing the outcome. Thus, data should show "causal cascades," or how each practice influences another practice that in turn affects something else. Data should reflect the specific processes or markers that are influencing change, along with whether they are achieving the intended outcomes.

Fifth, disciplined inquiry drives improvement. Using a sequence of inquiries or small experiments, interventions should be tested and the results from each test should inform subsequent tests. Once an intervention is tested and used in one place, designers can then scale it to other contexts by engaging in new cycles of improvement, a process the authors call "adaptive integration."

The sixth principle is the need to "accelerate learning through networked communities." This principle speaks to the need for an organized scientific community of partners to spread and scale robust practical knowledge.[32]

As outlined in this book, design development is one version of continuous quality improvement. Design development builds up practical design knowledge for educational leaders in problem areas for which the field demands rigorous and imaginative innovation.

When leaders switch from buying and implementing programs or packages as their mode of innovation to a design mode, they begin by asking some basic questions:

- What exactly is the behavior I am trying to change?
- What causes the behavior; what forces, factors, or circumstances keep it in place?
- What must people learn or unlearn to curtail the power of these circumstances and to change the problem behavior?
- How do I generate the desire or motivation for people to learn in my organization?
- How do I generate the required new knowledge and skills, given what is available in my organization?
- What kinds of activities, tools, or structures elicit or foster that kind of learning?
- What assets can I draw from for the change process; what constraints do I need to reckon with?
- How do I open up new opportunities or spaces to act?
- What can I learn from the existing professional knowledge base on my problem?
- What can I learn from the conventional "solutions," if they exist?
- Where is my creativity and ingenuity needed?
- Where do I enter uncharted territory?
- How will I know that what I am trying out has worked?

As the four educational leaders in this book—Christine, Michelle, Eric, and Nora—systematically go through the design development process, they will answer these questions. Throughout the book, we show how they arrive at their answers.

OVERVIEW OF THE BOOK

The book follows the basic steps in design development. The four leaders' narratives will illuminate these steps with concrete detail. All designing begins with the *selection of a problem of practice*. Not all problems lend themselves to design development. Most important, not all problems educators face are problems of practice. More about this in chapter 1.

Once a problem of practice is selected, it needs *framing and defining*. Because the field of education is so complex, most problems of practice encountered by educational leaders are ill-structured. How to handle ill-structured problems and keep problem solving manageable is the topic of chapter 2.

Educational leaders are busy people. When they think about problems, they rely primarily on their best intuition. They use intuition to make causal connections between the way they see the problem and possible remedies. That is, they have intuitive theories of action in mind. Most often, intuitive theories are implicit. Leaders act on them without being clearly conscious of why they, the leaders, did what they did. Intuition is also a powerful source of creativity, an indispensable asset for promoting change in highly complex organizations. Educational leaders develop designs by *making intuitive theories of action explicit*, the subject of chapter 3.

As powerful as intuition may be, it can also be misleading in its fuzziness. There are two ways to challenge intuitive theories of action and make them more analytical: needs assessments and consultation of the research and professional knowledge base. *Needs assessments*, discussed in chapter 4, help educational leaders confront their assumptions with data drawn from the workplace. *Consulting the professional knowledge base* and translating this knowledge into designs (chapter 5) requires educational leaders to develop and refine intellectual leadership.

Partnerships with institutions that generate or disseminate new knowledge, such as universities, play a special role in advancing intellectual leadership. The *role of intellectual leadership* is discussed in chapter 6.

After conducting needs assessments and a thorough review of the professional knowledge base, designers are ready to develop a theory of action for their intervention. This task divides into two steps. First, designers develop a deeper *understanding of the problem* (chapter 7) by looking at their focal problem's symptoms and its causes. Second, designers need to know how to lessen the power of these causal factors; to motivate people to engage in change; and to rearrange existing beliefs, attitudes, or practices or to foster new ones. Thus, they need a better *understanding of the change process* (chapter 8).

After having gained a deeper understanding of the problem's symptoms and causes and the change process, designers may still face areas of uncertainty. But even if there is little uncertainty, the sheer complexity of intervening in the organizational life of schools often requires a good dose of creativity and risk taking. We show in chapter 9 how designers move from the theory of action to *designing interventions*.

By treating an intervention as a research project—recording the project's design, implementation, and results with data—leaders will know with relative certainty whether the intervention actually worked and why it worked or did not. Thus, in *making design development research-based*, designers not only plan and implement an intervention, but also generate valuable data for future interventions (chapter 10).

In essence, the data collection stream consists of two types of data, *impact data and process data*. The difference between baseline and outcome is captured by impact data. The process that presumably has led to the outcome is captured by process data. How to avert getting bogged down by the data from typically complex equity-relevant projects and how to manage both impact and process data are the topics of chapter 11.

Rigor is a cornerstone in all research endeavors. We show in chapter 12 how designers *make design development studies rigorous*. The rigor of a design development study may be jeopardized when educational leaders wear multiple hats. Action research is a method that has been developed expressly to facilitate research rigor when researchers are directly involved as actors in the processes they are studying. Chapter 13 shows how to *embed action research into design development.*

Once designers have planned their interventions and associated data collection procedures and instruments, they are ready to implement. We examine issues of *implementing interventions* in chapter 14. Finally, how designers distill from their design iterations specific lessons that can transfer to new iterations or other situations by *deriving design principles* is the subject of chapter 15. Figure I.1 summarizes all the basic steps in design development.

In moving through the fifteen chapters, the reader engages in a sequence of problem-solving steps, roughly following what John Bransford and Barry Stein coined *the IDEAL model*: identifying, defining, exploring, acting, and looking back.[33] The model is a useful organizing tool. Cycles of inquiry frequently used in education follow a similar logic. But the reality of designing is different. In Schön's conceptualization, reflective problem solving in professional practice is a conversation within a design space between designers and their tools, types, images, metaphors, artifacts, and concepts.[34] As designers try out solutions, these "materials" talk back to them. In education, the material is social interaction, and the "back talk" mainly originates from people.[35] The design space shifts as different frames are tried out. The conversation moves back and forth between attempts to understand the problem and imagined solutions or changes. Imagined solutions

FIGURE I.1   Design development logic model

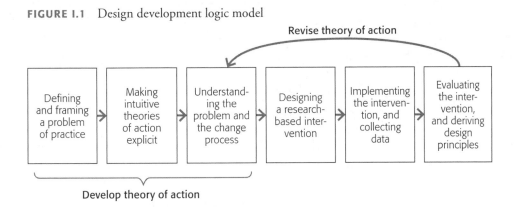

influence how designers frame and define the problem, and vice versa. Innovative solutions may be the result of innovative problem framing, perception, and definition. Designs are the result of reflection and artistry, rather than rational information processing. Even though we describe the process here as sequential, in reality design thinkers skip around, and steps are repeated to enhance clarity.

Identifying the Problem

1

Selecting Problems of Practice

For the most part, equity-relevant educational leadership in disadvantaged environments is severely constrained by inequitable conditions maintained by decisions made elsewhere and not subject to easy solutions at the local level. Leadership at the local level is largely about making the best out of rather adverse circumstances. But this does not mean that leaders cannot advance toward more equitable services or learning opportunities in the sphere the leaders influence or control. They do this by examining a *problem of practice*, a problem for which a remedy is urgently sought that can be locally implemented. This definition of a problem of practice undergirds design development thinking. Just as there are many questions, only some of which are researchable, there are many problems, only some of which are actionable.

Problems abound in schools, districts, and other educational settings. So how are leaders to determine which problems to focus their energy on for the purpose of design development? In this chapter, we ask a set of questions that help bring suitable problems of practice into focus:

→ What are the urgent problems in our organization?
→ What are our spheres of influence within the organization, and which problems are within that sphere?

→ Which problems can be addressed within a specified time frame of a design development study and within the resource and capacity limitations of our organization?

→ Which problems are strategically connected to the goals of the larger organization or administrative unit (such as a school district)?

→ Which particular practices happening in the organization right now are indicators of this problem?

PRACTICES

Problems of practice deal with *practices* that are entrenched in leaders' own organizations. What professionals do in their work is not arbitrary. It has regularity, recurrence, routine. People move and speak in predictable ways. At the level of micro-interaction, for example, most educators automatically smile when a child finds the right answer after much struggling. Most educators frown when a young person is rude to them or to classmates. Smiling and frowning are practices that have specific meaning in given situations. Teachers' ways of micro-interacting are so predictable that students watching a teacher can infer his or her mood even when the teacher tries to conceal it, or they can tell a teacher respects or cares for them. Some practices are less micro-interactive and more formal, for example, the ways a school organizes the assignment of students to honors or remedial classes, the procedures the school uses, the words that accompany the justification of the assignment when colleagues talk with each other, the words the school uses with students or parents to explain the decision. Much of what we do in educational work settings consists of myriad practices applied to specific situations, and people repeat these practices whenever they think a situation calls for them. Instructional practices are a small part of these practices.

In the spirit of the times, many equity-minded educators, when asked to name their most urgent problem of practice, answer, the achievement gap. But the achievement gap is not a problem of practice. The gap is the result of many different practices that educators engage in. A problem of practice is identified when some of these specific practices are recognized, named, and selected out of the many that together cause the achievement gap. The four educational leaders we encounter in this book tended to begin with broad problem statements: "I want to narrow the achievement gap"; "I want to make the system more just"; "I want to overcome the pernicious effects of race and class"; "I want to create a respectful climate"; "I want to make a difference in the way teachers teach marginalized students of color." These statements are expressions of the leaders' broader political, prosocial, and service commitments that fuel their educational engagement. In each instance, these broader commitments attach themselves to specific practices. For example, educators might tend to exclude disruptive students through referrals and suspensions rather than including them with pedagogical measures. Or educators might deliver lessons that contain little reference to culturally diverse experiences of their students; schools might tolerate bullying behavior; or teachers might emphasize drill and practice in their classrooms, neglecting complex learning and students' authentic intellect.

EXCURSION INTO THEORY

Problems of Practice

In his work on instructional rounds, Elizabeth City, Richard Elmore, and their team suggest selecting a particular type of problem that they call a problem of practice.[1] Problems of practice revolve around focal or core practices that need improvement within organizations. In the area of instruction, a core practice might be how to make lessons more effective, in contrast to more peripheral concerns (e.g., nicer bulletin boards) or more isolated aspects of the work (e.g., strategies for how to call on students). Problems of practice are always collectively owned problems of the organization. Through communication, members of the organization may reach a shared understanding of what practices should be the focus. Problems need to be made sufficiently specific to practically guide the improvement effort. Problems of practice are high leverage.[2] They entail "actions and changes in structures [that] can lead to significant, enduring improvements."[3] While tackling high-leverage problems of practice can lead to systemic, meaningful change, it is often not apparent which problems within the organization have the highest leverage.[4] Thus, selecting the right problems of practice is challenging but potentially productive in launching organizational improvement.

The educational literature sometimes uses the term *practice* to mean "instructional practice." The way we use the term here connotes a wider spectrum of phenomena: mental and bodily routines of everyday work life that are specific to organizational fields, such as education. They could be repetitive actions, habits, speech patterns, or mental operations that participants in a given field of work perform. When these practices become deeply entrenched, taken for granted, and mutually reinforcing of each other, we may call them *habitus*.[5] When a person enters a new field, let's say as a novice teacher in a public school, he or she learns the habitus that prevails there and, by doing so, helps reproduce the structures that order the field of education, with all its humanizing and dehumanizing tendencies.

ORGANIZATIONAL PRACTICES

With a focus on leadership, problems of practice deal with the way adults deliver services. Improved quality of services increases the chance that students will have better learning opportunities. But we do not study students directly, because educational leaders may have an indirect or a mediated effect on student learning.[6] Educational leaders must go through adults in the system to accomplish this effect. For our purposes, therefore, problems of practice focus on the effect leaders have on practices of service delivery to students and families. Students and parents may tell us indirectly whether educational professionals improved their services.

In identifying a problem of practice, the question is not one of what educational leaders are interested in or what captures their fancy. The question is, what are the organization's most urgent development problems for which new solutions or improved approaches are needed? Suitable problems of practice are burning issues in the organization—issues for which people in leadership positions at all levels want answers. Thus, in finding the problem of practice to address, we should be less concerned about our individual interests (though these are still part of the equation) and more concerned about a need that is felt or articulated in our work environment. As mentioned previously, design development projects require resources and therefore should be reserved for the vexing problems of practice that really need a remedy. These projects must be worth the investment of several iterations of planned and careful intervention and data collection. Even if the leaders can only conduct one iteration, the problem of practice should be big and urgent enough in the organization that others would want to follow up with subsequent iterations.

SHORT-TERM AND LONG-TERM PERSPECTIVES

Problems of practice are local, but they are often embedded in larger structures of the education system of a given state or country. Issues such as how to decrease the number of students receiving disciplinary measures, how to decrease the occurrence of racial or antigay slurs, how to increase the complexity of writing instruction in a highly prescribed learning environment, or how to ensure that all students are algebra-ready in ninth grade involve local practices. But these issues may also involve societal structures or forces, such as racism, sexism, de-professionalization, stratification by social status, or stereotypes about ability. Overcoming these structures takes time and requires large-scale action that mostly surpasses the scope of design development described here. But dedicated educators can lessen the effect of societal structures or forces in the spaces they influence.

In addressing a problem of practice, we should capitalize on all the forces moving toward humanizing education that we can, but we must also be realistic. Some big problems may be worthy causes for a professional career, but are not actionable within the span of time-constrained improvement efforts. This means we need to focus on a problem of practice within certain feasibility constraints. Instead of overreaching, we can focus on a circumscribed problem for which we can provide useful new remedies within a short time frame and at a workable scale. For example, if the big problem is how to make work teams in schools commit to closing achievement gaps, then the actionable problem of practice may be how to motivate and help a ninth-grade mathematics team develop a program that articulates grade-level instruction with remediation. Or, if the big problem is how to make instructional supervision and leadership more effective, the actionable problem of practice may be how to help principals give good feedback after informally observing an instructional sequence of fifteen minutes.

As leaders narrow their problem of practice, actual practices become more defined in terms of observed or perceived behaviors, and desired behaviors or states become more concrete and circumscribed by the short time frame of the change project or intervention. The actual formulation of aims or goals for the design comes at a later stage, when designers have enough information about the beliefs, attitudes, practices, and capacities of people who will participate in the project. We begin with broader aspirations and make them increasingly more precise as we go through the design process. In chapter 2, we show how our four leaders narrow their focal problems of practice.

STRATEGIC ORIENTATION

Design development projects should be articulated within the larger strategic goals of the organization within which the projects are to take place, assuming the organization has formulated such goals. Up front, most changes take an additional investment of time, energy, and intellectual and material resources. And if the organization does not prioritize the change project, it is likely to get short shrift or be quickly washed out, unless there is strong bottom-up enthusiasm. Only when projects are connected to a district's or school's broader strategic goals and commitments will they be likely to spread or scale up if they prove to be effective. Moreover, in line with the organization's strategic orientation, a whole sequence of smaller projects may be spaced out over time and may, in conjunction, create bigger emergent results. For example, after learning how to give good feedback after an informal observation, instructional supervisors may want to tackle how to connect informal feedback to formal evaluations of teaching or how to connect observation criteria to rich professional learning in professional communities or work teams. Or, after creating a seamless differentiated curriculum, our ninth-grade mathematics team might tackle how to spread its new practices to other work teams in the school or the district.

Most change in education is incremental, and—especially if it goes below the surface of established routines, taken-for-granted beliefs, or entrenched political interests—even incremental change is hard. For leaders who are passionate about equity and justice, problems of practice described as *actionable* here may seem small. But consider that we, as educators, have a poor track record of preserving our own and our colleagues' precious energy for change. Instead, we often create change overload and program churn. We must guard against this waste. This book asks professionals to think hard about the connection between their intentions and the human and material resources at their disposal to meet their goals. When we make this connection and colleagues notice that we not only have strong values and ambitious goals, but also keenly understand how to effect change, given people's resources, knowledge, and energy, we can become transformative.

PRACTICALITY AND SENSITIVITY TO CONTEXT

Design developers support schools or districts by responding to urgent problems of practice that pose a *design challenge in a specific context*. We know from a long series of implementation studies that no matter how effective a designed intervention may be, if it is not practical in a given context, it will not have a sustained impact on routine practice. This is especially true for work environments that are strained, turbulent, resource-scarce, or otherwise challenging. Practicality is sensitive to context in several dimensions:

- The designed intervention itself must be practical. That is, the participants must be able to implement it in a given organizational context. Time, space, political will, and the participants' priorities together make the sequence of planned activities a probability.
- The new practices that the intervention fosters must be within the "zone of proximal development," a concept from the learning sciences that teachers may be familiar with when they gauge the appropriate difficulty

of their curriculum for students. Something similar applies to adult learners. That is, the required investment in learning must not surpass the knowledge, skill, time, energy, and resources of the participants and must be within the bounds of their capacity to stretch to what Elizabeth City and colleagues usefully call "the next level of work."[7]

- Given that deep and lasting change in educators' practices requires the active engagement of adult learners, creating motivation and commitment needs to be a deliberately designed component of interventions.
- The designers themselves must have sufficient skill, time, and resources to carry out the intervention.

CHAPTER SUMMARY

In this chapter, we described some of what educational leaders need to know when identifying a problem of practice in the organization. We showed that a design process is best suited for a problem that can be described as follows:

- *Urgent for the organization*: the problem arises out of a perceived need.

- *Actionable*: the problem exists within the educator's sphere of influence.

- *Feasible*: the problem can be addressed in a limited time frame and with the resources available.

- *Strategic*: the problem is connected to the goals of the larger organization (such as a school district).

- *Tied to a specific practice or set of practices*: the problem is narrowed to specific practices that have a good chance of improvement.

- *Forward looking*: the problem stretches toward the next level of work.

2

Defining and Framing
Problems of Practice

with Elizabeth Zumpe

Imagine looking at a painting for the first time. You notice the physical boundaries of the painting, the picture frame, and the canvas. But the picture may not make sense to you until you use imaginary frames *within* the painting to see the meaning of the picture. You try to grasp the main scenery, theme, or action it depicts: "I see. This painting is about men and women exerting themselves in hard physical labor tilling the soil . . . There, off to the side, are overseers . . . They threaten the workers with physical violence . . . These workers are . . . coerced." You interpret the central scenery by putting an imaginary frame around it. Only if your frame puts overseers, positioned off to the side, inside the main scenery will you interpret the painting as a depiction of coerced labor. The main scenery is not always in the physical center of the picture, but once you have recognized the main scenery, it becomes the center, and the other motifs, let's say a beautiful forest right next to the field, revolve around it. You may also recognize that the painter could have extended the picture a lot farther. But the canvas limits what is being shown. Our imagination may go beyond what is on the canvas, but the painter made a selection and decided on boundaries.

In this chapter, we show that picturing the problem of practice is similar to seeing a painting for the first time. Canvas, colors, and lines may look familiar, but central scenery, peripheral motifs, frames, and boundaries need to be grasped before you understand your problem. Different ways of seeing the picture may lead to different views of what the problem is all about. In the painting example, some observers may not notice the overseers or may block them out and then assume that the painting is about farmers at work instead of the power of coercion. In this chapter, we look at four educational leaders, Christine, Michelle, Eric, and Nora (figure 2.1). Their narratives illustrate how leaders come to picture their problem. A theoretical excursion provides more detailed explanations on what the literature says about problem solving and the types of problems that leaders encounter in education settings. This chapter helps us answer the following questions:

→ What are the boundaries around our problem of practice?
→ What are people's main actions or practices that define what is in the center of our problem?
→ What are the frames that help us understand the broader meaning of the main action?
→ How does our way of seeing the problem shape how we think about its solution?

FIGURE 2.1 Four educational leaders and their problems of practice

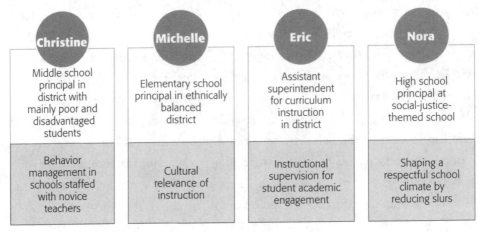

CHRISTINE'S PROBLEM OF PRACTICE
Behavior Management in Schools Staffed with Novice Teachers

Christine works in a district that has encountered a recent surge in referrals and suspensions in the middle schools that mainly serve socioeconomically disadvantaged students. She is a principal of one of those middle schools, and the district asks her to join and lead a task force that can investigate this issue across the middle schools. She and her colleagues wonder what might cause this observable pattern. They find that the increasing teacher turnover has left some schools almost entirely staffed with novice teachers. Hiring novices has coincided with the recent upsurge of discipline problems. Christine's task force settles on novices as the main cause of the problem. This understanding becomes the launching pad for the task force, which consists of Christine, some of her principal colleagues, some counselors and teachers on special assignment, and a district administrator, to search for a remedy.

Christine and her task force are charged with finding a suitable approach that helps bolster first- and second-year teachers' classroom management skills. So they begin by looking in the professional knowledge base for reports on the many programs and workshops on classroom management for novices. They also find guides and studies in the field of teacher education on how novices develop good management skills. The team wonders if the district's problem would be solved if it bought or adopted an established approach.

Christine thinks about her own experience as a novice teacher. She remembers training programs that helped her become more effective. But then it hits her: back then, she was one of a few novices in the midst of experienced teachers at her school. This is not the case for the novices in her school now. Instead, she, as the principal, must rely on a few experienced teacher leaders in the midst of many struggling novices. In other words, the district's problem is organizational, not individual. By initially assuming that the problem was one of novices needing more training, her district task force had used an inadequate framing of the problem. Now she thinks, while individual-level classroom management workshops are useful, they can't do much without organizational backing.

Her new way of seeing the problem opens up a whole new perspective. She wonders what organizational structures, rules, routines, and support are minimally needed to back up struggling novices. What collegial interactions are needed to bolster shared norms in the midst of schools that are disorderly? How might her task force put together something that will move schools in the district in the right direction, given the skill levels of the teachers?

MICHELLE'S PROBLEM OF PRACTICE
Cultural Relevance of Instruction

Michelle is an experienced elementary school principal in a school district that serves African American, Hispanic, and white students in fairly equal proportions. The faculties in most of the district schools, including Michelle's, are overwhelmingly white. Standardized test scores document a large achievement gap between students of color and white students. Michelle is concerned about this achievement gap and believes that the district needs some thorough reorientation. She observes that in her district (her school being a case in point), nobody talks about the cultural relevance of what and how they teach. Michelle has been a member of a group of educators called Educators for Social Justice, a group that has read texts about culturally relevant pedagogy (CRP). She has come to be convinced that CRP is a necessary part of closing the achievement gap.

For Michelle, both the problem and the solution are clearly aligned. The problem is the achievement gap, and through her reading, she has learned that this gap for students of color may be associated with low expectations and deficit thinking (the blaming of students for their presumed failures) on the part of white teachers who lack cultural sensitivity or cultural competence, issues that CRP addresses head-on. When the superintendent convenes a district equity committee that is charged with bringing CRP to the district, Michelle is drafted for the committee. The committee decides to contract with charismatic speakers who are to inspire faculties. Lists of culturally relevant texts are compiled, and materials are distributed. The committee compiles lists of culturally relevant texts and distributes these lists and samples of culturally relevant material to each school in the district. Every school is charged with setting up an equity committee that organizes conversations and classroom walkthroughs. Michelle is elated.

ERIC'S PROBLEM OF PRACTICE
Instructional Supervision for Student Academic Engagement

In Eric's capacity as the assistant superintendent for curriculum and instruction for his school district, he is responsible for the principals' professional development. Creating a strong instructional program district-wide is also one of his particular passions, so he recognizes instructional leadership of the principals as an important issue. He has noticed that principals do a poor job of giving useful feedback to teachers after instructional observations. First he thinks that his principals rush too much. In his mind, he begins to design a remedy: "I've got to formulate a new policy, teach principals better communication skills, and give them a protocol that they can fall back on when they get overwhelmed by too many tasks all at once."

Then, after talking with a few principals, he realizes that they are not rushing; the principals avoid conferences, or try to get through them as fast as possible, because the conferences make them feel uncomfortable. Eric wants to know where the discomfort is coming from. So he accompanies some of the principals through classrooms and engages them in informal conversations about what he and they saw. As he listens to the principals commenting on the observed lessons, he thinks, "If these principals know how to distinguish between good and not-so-good teaching, they certainly can't explain it to me. And therefore they can't explain it to their teachers." Eric decides that this situation needs to change.

He thinks about his own principal preparation program and several instructional supervision books he has read. He realizes in his leadership preparation program, he learned about supervisors' communication skills. But somehow it was assumed that the soon-to-be principals knew what good instruction was and could explain it to their teachers. "I need to look elsewhere," he thinks.

So he asks himself, "Where did I learn the skill to look at instruction and figure out what's good or not so good?" He was fortunate to have been enrolled in a strong teacher education program and to have had a good mentor teacher when he was a student teacher himself. So he figures that he needs to draw from this experience for his professional development with the principals. He remembers that his teacher education program included watching videos and using an observation tool with which he and his classmates analyzed instructional sequences and then discussed their observations. He decides that this is now the way to go for his district.

NORA'S PROBLEM OF PRACTICE
Shaping a Respectful School Climate by Reducing Slurs

For Nora, the problem is clear. As a high school principal in a social-justice-themed high school, she is discouraged to realize that despite all the school's efforts to highlight the school's emphasis on fairness and cultural sensitivity, too many students treat each other with disrespect. So she has assembled around her a group of engaged teachers who want to improve the climate. They have made bullying the leitmotif of a six-week campaign during which the students engage in conversations and various classroom projects. Nora feels that this approach has helped, but she is appalled by the racial and homophobic slurs that students continue to hurl at each other. The bullying project seems to have made little change in these speech patterns. How should she go about this—another bullying project for students, now with a focus on slurs? Nora and her leadership group feel that they have reached a certain saturation point with their students. Nora is fond of "management by walking around." And on one of her walks in the corridors of her building, she observes that teachers, many of whom are passionate about social justice, stand by idly when they hear slurs nearby and do not intervene. In an instant, her problem shifts from a student problem to an adult problem. She becomes convinced that she must somehow encourage teachers to take action when they witness slurs.

EXCURSION INTO THEORY

Problem Solving

According to Allen Newell and Herbert Simon, problems are solved within a particular task environment or, as described by David Jonassen, a task domain.[1] For example, a task environment for educators would be the administering of a school or the teaching of a classroom full of students. To the problem solver, the task environment is a given structure that generates numerous tasks. Most of these tasks are carried out as unproblematic routines of day-to-day work. These tasks become problems when problem solvers perceive a tension between a current state and a desired state, or between a perceived need and a desire to increase the possibility of the need's being met. Problem solvers face an unknown: not only does the solution require search, but the problem itself is not apparent.[2] Problems are not simply passively received from the environment; they need to be actively perceived and constructed by the problem solver in what Newell and Simon call "the problem space"—the mental capacity that problem solvers expend on thinking about the problem.[3]

Problem Space and Solution Space

In the problem space, problem solvers make mental representations of tasks, needs, goals, and the situation at hand. They aim to categorize a problem and thereby reduce its complexity by emphasizing the relevant aspects of the situation and ignoring the less relevant aspects.[4] They do this by using abstractions, typifications, or schemas that help thinkers see order where randomness of behavior would otherwise prevail.[5] Problem solvers need to define and frame the problem to focus and structure their thinking and to function within their capacity to process information.

Problem solvers make a mental representation of a problem by holding four things in their minds: the initial state of the problem; the desired or goal state; a set of allowable operators, that is, the concepts, constructs, principles, rules of behavior, and so on that apply to the domain of practice or the task environment; and a set of constraints, that is, the givens of a situation that a chosen solution strategy needs to reckon with.[6] Condensing and organizing this information into concise verbal descriptions or visual models helps problem solvers keep in mind the complexity of a problem space. Doing so also helps in the search for solutions and in assessing the usefulness of the chosen strategies.

Problems in a Given Task Environment

According to Newell and Simon, "the structure of the task environment determines the possible structures of the problem space."[7] For example, if the task is to teach a classroom of students, the environment is structured by the spatial organization of school buildings; the number of students taught by, usually, one teacher; the normative expectations of students to be respected and of teachers to be able to control the class; and so on.[8] These conditions are givens, constraints, or assets that problem solvers cannot ignore or change at will. When a problem arises, the problem space—that is, how this problem is represented in the problem solvers' minds—must reflect the structures of the task at hand and the environment that the problem is embedded in. Classroom-related problem spaces need to reflect the conditions of teaching listed above and many more.

The problem space is not merely a mirror of the objective task, but is a subjective selection of relevant information and knowledge that define the problem. How the problem space becomes constructed will have repercussions for the kinds of solution paths, operations, or programs that the problem solver will choose. In other words, the construction of the problem space shapes what Newell and Simon call "the solution space," the mental capacity that problem solvers expend on thinking about solutions.[9]

Types of Problems

While the exact terminology used by various authors differs, the literature on problem solving, broadly speaking, distinguishes between well-structured or well-defined problems and ill-structured or ill-defined problems. A well-defined problem is clearly circumscribed. The constructs, rules, and constraints are clear, and the search for solution strategies converges on a clearly defined solution of the problem, as in solving a mathematical equation, solving a puzzle, or completing comprehension or application assignments in a textbook.[10] Solving a well-structured problem converges on those operations that, in a step-by-step fashion, reduce the discrepancy between current and desired states, for example, when problem solvers overcome puzzlement and find their way out of a maze.[11]

An ill-defined problem lacks a convergent solution strategy. There is no simple right or wrong per se. In ill-defined problems, all aspects of problem construction are challenging. Problem solvers need to clarify how to name the problem, how broad or narrow the problem is, who the stakeholders are, what its current symptoms are, how it is categorized, what the desired or goal states might look like, and what operations or actions are possible. The constraints of the situation are often fuzzy as well.[12] Ill-defined problems do not speak the clear language of textbook assignments or controlled experiments. They do not exist without problem solvers as diagnosticians, analysts, and spokespersons. They need definition. But domains, such as the professional domain of education, generate stocks of problems that are repeatedly encountered, named, recognized in practice, and described in the knowledge base.[13] Some well-known problems in the educational domain are how to increase student academic engagement, how to narrow the achievement gap, how to motivate teachers, and how to create a respectful climate.

Most problems encountered by educators in their domain of practice are ill defined.[14] But some are more fluid than others. For example, School X finds that hallway security has recently declined during passing periods. Problem solvers swiftly ascertain that because many teachers fail to stand at their classroom doors, students pass through the hallways largely unsupervised. Teachers who do not show up at their posts claim that they are distracted by similarly important tasks, and those who do show up complain about free-riding among their colleagues. The goal is clear: there can be no compromise on safety. The means are clear: supervision is required. The constraints are clear: no personnel other than teachers are available to get the job done. The solution converges on a simple rule and its enforcement: all teachers must be on guard. But around this rule, exceptions may be permitted if they do not end up violating the main expectation. Exceptions could be that standing guard may alternate by odd and even room numbers, teachers may use good judgment and complete other tasks occasionally, but not without expressed gratitude to the neighboring colleague who filled in, and so on.

The relatively well-defined structure of this problem contrasts with a much more uncertain and opaque problem space, as in the aforementioned case of rampant bullying at a high school. Because there is no one operation that would alleviate bullying, it is hard to find clear technical solutions. In all likelihood, behavior management, the reinforcement of school norms, and direct counseling for main offenders may have to play together. Different sets of actors, including parents, may play a role. Ownership on the part of students is key. It is not clear what rules, concepts, or principles apply to the problem and guide the search for solution strategies. As to goals, because problem solvers are not clear on what bullying actually is, they are similarly unclear on which desired state can be a solution. Can the solution be "no bullying," since we do not know exactly what constitutes bullying? The solution strategies are widely divergent; many approaches may lead to a remedy. But will there be one that solves the problem? Answers to these open-ended questions will depend on the problem solvers' definition of this ill-structured problem. Most big problems in education are of this ill-structured type, while the simplicity of the earlier hallway-monitoring problem is rare.

Problem Definition

How do problem solvers define problems? Assuming that problem solvers are aware of the problem because they pay attention to symptoms, cues, or tasks that indicate a tension between what is and what ought to be, they draw from prior knowledge, experience, and the domain knowledge base, in this case, the domain of education or of school improvement.[15] Several cognitive operations may be employed. Problem solvers recognize rules or general principles that apply to the way they see their current problem. They draw similarities or analogies between patterns encountered in their current problem and patterns experienced previously. If no patterns are readily available for matching, problem solvers may engage in means-ends analysis. This type of analysis breaks down the currently encountered, complex patterns into more manageable chunks, which consist of concepts, rules, or principles that may have known solution strategies attached to them.[16]

For example, it is Monday morning and a child comes into class fatigued and irritable. The teacher knows this Monday morning pattern, and when the child misbehaves, she knows without much thinking that it is best to soothe the child and leave her alone so that the girl has the space to recover from the stress of the weekend experience. In another example, the teacher has a child in class who, no matter what he has tried (praising, incentivizing, sanctioning), will not do his homework. He has called home, only to hear that the child's parents feel helpless about this situation. The teacher cannot solve this problem without breaking it down into chunks. He looks first at cognitive aspects (e.g., is the work too hard?), then social-emotional aspects (e.g., is the child afraid of failing?), and, finally, family relationship aspects (e.g., does the child respond to stresses in the family?). As a teacher, he may have solution strategies for the cognitive and social-emotional aspects related to schoolwork. Family relationship aspects may require a referral to a specialist. Many technical solutions to this problem come into view.

But by breaking down the complex problem into its components, the teacher has created in his mind means-ends relationships on which he may be able to act.

Problem Framing

Many problems in education are not unlike those encountered in politics and policy making. In both areas, problem solvers need to have an opinion, make a judgment, and defend this judgment against possible alternatives.[17] Thus, problems in education not only are ill structured in a technical way, as we saw earlier, but also in a normative way. Assumptions of appropriateness, worldviews, ideologies, and self-interests shape what problem solvers consider desirable, their perception of facts, and their interpretations of evidence. These broader cognitive and normative orientations are expressed in frames: key words, key concepts, key propositions. Normative frames connect the problem space to broader contextual and institutional meanings.[18] For example, as described earlier, Michelle adopts CRP as the technical solution. Many other technical solutions were possible, but Michelle's assumption that the achievement gap is about ethnicity and culture and that white teachers are causal agents in creating cultural insensitivity frames her thinking about the cause of the problem and its solution. In thinking about her problem in this way, Michelle applies beliefs that are widely held not only in her Educators for Social Justice group, but also in educational institutions at large, if not in whole segments of society.

The terms *problem frame* and *problem definition* are sometimes used interchangeably in the literature. Here, following Donald Schön and Martin Rein, the term *frame* is reserved for the broader political and normative assumptions that go into the construction of the problem.[19] Frames are often contested, as they communicate the potential causes of the problem, who is responsible for the undesirable states and remedies, what solutions are appropriate, and how solvable the problem appears.[20] Going back to the earlier example of the achievement gap, framing the gap as a problem of oppression and liberation versus one of effectiveness and underperformance fundamentally shapes both the problem space and the solution space. In the oppression and liberation frame, problem solving is directed toward movements in which teachers and students are change agents. In the effectiveness and underperformance frame, managerial solutions may consider teachers and students the recipients of resources, demands, or incentives. Thus, ill-structured problems in education require not only careful definition, but also framing and a keen awareness of one's deep assumptions that generate these frames.

Christine, Michelle, Eric, and Nora encounter ill-structured problems in their task environment. All four are school or district leaders who are charged with shaping how adults deliver services to students. In each case, the four professionals actively construct their problems. The nature of their problem is not patently obvious until they apply certain frames and definitions that "jump at them" in light of their experience and keen observation. For Christine, the problem of behavior management takes shape when she begins to define her problem in individual *and* organizational terms. Michelle has a clear moral frame in mind when she perceives her teachers in racial and ethnic terms. Eric's problem definition is still quite fluid, while Nora's view of the problem has shifted from the students to the adults in her building. In subsequent chapters, we will show how these leaders' problem definition and framing shapes the way they go about devising solutions or remedies.

CHAPTER SUMMARY

In this chapter, we described how leaders define and frame their problems of practice. We made the following observations:

- Setting boundaries around a problem is about knowing what one can safely leave out of the picture without losing its meaning.

- Defining a problem is about finding focal patterns of action that one can interpret as meaningful by matching them with prior experiences or understanding.

- Framing a problem is about understanding the focal patterns of action in relationship to a bigger picture: one's ideas about who or what causes the patterns, who is responsible, and who ought to make changes.

3

Making Intuitive Theories
of Action Explicit

with Elizabeth Zumpe

A theory of action is a prediction of how to address a problem of practice. For example, "My plants are not growing; what do I need to do to make them grow?" We can think of the theory of action as an if-then statement: "If I water the plant every other day and put it in the sun, it will grow." But wrapped inside that if-then prediction is an assumption about what's causing the problem. The prediction about the plant may turn out to be incorrect if it is an arid-climate plant that needs little water or a shade-loving plant that prefers less sun. If we know nothing about plants, we have no idea about what to do. We have no intuition. When we go to the store, we read the plant's label: this is a shade-loving plant that needs water once a week. Without this information, we would be lost. But most of us are not that clueless about things we do in everyday life and on the job.

Everyone walks around with intuitive theories of action through which a person makes causal connections between behaviors and outcomes. Most often, these causal connections are made tacitly; that is, people are barely conscious of doing so. For example, when people enter a public space, they try to look friendly and agreeable. Why? Well, they just do. But on second thought, they know that an angry face makes others uncomfortable, while a friendly face will not. People

43

do not have to know about mirror neurons to explain this observation; they just know, intuitively, that one person's face has the power to trigger an emotional reaction in someone else. They know it is something about the connection between visual cues and emotional reactions—that is their *intuitive theory of action*. And this intuitive theory is implicit. Later in the book, we will show how an intuitive theory of action gradually shifts to an analytical one.

In this chapter, we mainly do two things. We contrast the concepts of intuition and heuristics with the concepts of rationality and analytics, and we show what role intuitive theories of action may play in educational leaders' intuitive problem solving. We address the following questions:

→ What is intuition?
→ What role does it play in people's understanding of the world?
→ How is intuition different from a systematic analysis of problems?
→ How do people make intuitive connections between what causes a problem and what changes it?
→ What is an intuitive theory of action?

HEURISTICS AND INTUITION

Most people have pretty good intuition about their work; otherwise, they would not have had the success that has come their way. People experience repetitive cause-and-effect relationships in their work. They have experienced what works and what does not. When people see a behavior that poses a problem, they just know by association what might work as a remedy. They associate a pattern of behavior that they perceive as problematic with a set of actions that they ought to take. These kinds of shorthand decision rules, called *heuristics*, are necessary for quick decisions.

For example, a common heuristic that seems to come naturally to educational leaders is the so-called PD heuristic, or the professional development heuristic. When educators apply the PD heuristic, they name a problematic practice by describing what is *not* there and then assume that a workshop matched to that absence will provide the remedy: "When in doubt, PD." With the PD heuristic, educators tacitly entertain an intuitive theory of action without explicitly stating it: "What we lack is new information and training." And this intuitive theory is often, indeed, correct, but not as often as people think. That is because with the PD heuristic, educators treat the learner as an empty vessel that they need to fill with their own professional development.

Teachers who have a superficial understanding of student learning use the empty-vessel intuition as well. They cover new content without being clear about the students' preexisting understanding, ways of thinking, and misconceptions that need elaboration, refinement, or challenge before deep learning can happen. For example, students who have never heard of the industrial revolution do not, of course, know anything about it. But they may have preexisting notions of industry, revolution, and the role of technology and science in economic development. And filling students with the new concept will do little if the teacher does not, in the process, recognize that in all likelihood, all the revolutions the students had looked at previously were political revolutions, most notably the American Revolution.

Learners, student or adult, are not empty vessels. If a teacher intuitively believes that the problem is that students do not know anything about the industrial revolution or that they "need to learn" about the industrial revolution (since they presumably do not know anything about it), he or she treats students as empty vessels. If we approach a problem this way, our problem is the absence of our solution. The teacher's solution, in this case, is covering the industrial revolution.

When educational leaders treat adults as empty vessels, the leaders may fall into the same trap faced by a teacher introducing the industrial revolution. Confronted with achievement data that show English language learners lagging behind native speakers, they may have identified a consultant that has a specific set of engagement strategies for English language learners on offer. After covering the strategies in a professional development session, the leaders expect the teachers to know and apply these strategies. When the leaders afterward make their rounds through the classrooms to check, they find that the strategies are not used widely. The problem has now morphed into the failure of teachers to adopt the leader's solution, and the remedy for that is often "more PD." In the leaders' shorthand thinking about the problem, adults learning new things on the basis of what they already know and practice is left out of the picture.

If a teacher thinks that students in all likelihood know that revolutions are about sudden shifts in political power between those in control and those who want more freedom and self-determination, he or she can state the problem differently: students already understand revolutions as political revolutions (e.g., the American Revolution, which freed the colonists from British control). The teacher now needs to extend this understanding to the understanding that technology and economics can create revolutions as well. Below, when we describe Michelle's intuitive theory of action, we give a concrete example of a leader thinking shorthand, and in her intuitive shorthand thinking, she treats her teachers as empty vessels that need culturally relevant pedagogy.

The daily flow of work rarely allows practitioners to address problems in their full complexity. In most situations, leaders only have time and energy for the kind of problem solving that is done quickly, using shortcuts: "Strategy X has always worked for me when I have encountered situation Y, so let's do X." Or when under pressure, a leader might think, "People whom I trust tell me that Strategy X or Program Y has promise or has been shown to work, so let's try it." But these intuitive ideas are often not the best ones for making important strategic decisions about new directions, new programs, new organizational structures, or new professional development initiatives. This is because intuition, and the associated heuristics, can often be misleading.

EXCURSION INTO THEORY

Decision Making, Rational and Intuitive

The standard decision making model assumes that humans base their decisions on choice. They base their choices on their preferences, their knowledge of alternatives for action, their knowledge of the consequences of their actions, and a rational assessment of what maximizes desired outcomes.[1]

Bounded Rationality

Decisions are thus a matter of rational choice. Yet even if they have the intention or desire to do so, people do not make decisions that are "wholly rational."[2] Complete rationality would require that people be able to consider an infinite number of alternatives and have a perfectly complete and accurate understanding of the situation at hand. Both of these requirements are impossible, given the limits of information processing capacity and human cognition.[3] Thus, even when people try to make a rational decision, they actually act with what Herbert Simon calls "bounded rationality"—people do the best they can to make what seems to be the best decision with the information at hand in a given situation.[4]

The idea of limited information processing capacity that underlies the concept of bounded rationality is reformulated in dual-process models.[5] In these models, fast, relatively spontaneous, and effortless processing of information is contrasted with slow, rule-bound, and effortful deliberations, the former relying on intuition, the latter on rationality. Intuition produces understanding that can only be backed up with fuzzy empirical verification and associative justifications. Rationality applies sequential logic, measurement, and analysis. Intuitive reasoning gives "first answers" to choices or problems, while rational reasoning may follow up with verifications. Most everyday decisions are made quickly. Short time spans do not allow actors to think long term through possible alternatives to actions and their consequences. Intuition is called for.

Intuition

There is a cognitive and expressive-emotional side to intuition.[6] Cognitively, intuitive judgment relies on heuristics. Heuristics are rules of thumb that abbreviate the decision-making process. These quick-and-dirty approximations enable individuals to lump problems into manageable pieces.[7] Heuristics operate with categories, rules, or whole patterns, for example, "Disadvantaged students bring to schools social adversities that cause discipline problems that require vigilant classroom management" or "White teachers over-refer black students to special education because of a racial dynamic that needs to be disrupted with information, awareness of moral wrongdoing, and sanctions."[8] A heuristic might arise from practices that have repeatedly worked in the past. Patterns from previous experiences are matched with analogous present situations. For instance, past years' budget allocations may guide decisions about the current year.[9] Heuristics are an integral part of human thinking, and the myriad decisions people are asked to make cannot be carried out without heuristics that economize human cognitive capacity.

Heuristics, however, are associated with a number of biases. These biases create misperceptions that can lead to erroneous decisions.[10] Heuristics sway decision makers to judge the likelihood of an outcome with systematic cognitive bias. A few examples: when people stereotype another person, they simplify their thinking, believing that the individual who is a member of a particular group will most likely behave according to the general characteristics associated with this group. Or when people assert that they have "always done it this way," they associate the uniqueness of a given situation to a well-rehearsed pattern. Accessibility of information is key in decision making and problem solving. What is fresh in our minds will more readily be seen as relevant for a specific decision or problem than will distant memory. In applying these types of heuristics, decision makers judge the likelihood of an outcome not according to careful analysis of the situation, but according to "the ease with which the mental operation of retrieval, construction, or association can be carried out."[11] In this case, decision makers are likely to rely on experiences that are more easily brought to mind—a tendency that biases them to emphasize analogies and neglect the possibility of outcomes less frequently encountered in the past.[12] Decision makers swiftly take a perceived symptom of a present problem (e.g., teachers fail to attend meetings for the common planning of curriculum) and infer that it represents a pattern (e.g., teachers avoid scrutiny; they need to deprivatize). This pattern becomes associated with a set of conventional strategies that worked in the past (admonition and monitoring) or are currently being sold by solution advocates (developing professional learning communities).

Notwithstanding the cognitive biases of heuristics, Stephen and Patricia Davis point to a side of intuition that emphasizes emotional-expressive qualities.[13] These qualities, they believe, are especially useful when situations call for novelty, flux, and creativity. Intuition, being subconscious, may create sudden clarity that eludes actors who engage in more systematic means-ends analyses. Intuition "is knowledge constructed whole-cloth in a sudden shift from the subconscious to conscious awareness."[14] As such, intuition can be experienced as a "sudden flash of insight" that is "accompanied by an emotional feeling such as certitude, excitement or fear."[15] Intuition presents actors with "judgments or choices before consciously considering them."[16] Intuitive thinking is essential when people need to respond to situations for which they have no existing frames of reference. When leaders are challenged to go beyond conventional strategies and develop novel approaches, intuitive thinking is at a premium. But as with heuristics, actors can go wrong with intuition of the more expressive kind, as strong emotions in a decision situation can distort people's view of reality, and thoughts from the subconscious mind may merely represent wishful thinking.[17]

Thus, for good decision making in complex organizations, both rational analysis and intuition have their place. A desirable path would use both: *think fast* to gain the benefit of insight from intuition and heuristics, and *think slow* to check for bias and error and guard against the tried-and-true, but untested, conventions that uphold the status quo.[18]

When decision makers tackle problems in the practical world, intuition is the first, and most precious, source of insight. Intuition bounds people's thinking, structures and simplifies the complexity of their undertaking, generates their aims, and makes connections between causes and effects. Most often, as we have shown, intuition guides people in tacit ways within the rapid pace of the workday. But some situations can be puzzling. They make us stop and think. We marshal our practical knowledge base, experiences, the things we learned in professional settings, and our current insights and think hard about the problem and its solutions. We make our intuitive theories of action explicit: we frame and define the problem and the behaviors that indicate the problem to us, and we imagine a desired state to be attained; we try to better understand the problem's symptoms and its causes. And we try to figure out how to change people through a deliberate process that we believe will produce the desired state, which is often rather fuzzy and aspirational to begin with.

CHRISTINE'S INTUITIVE THEORY OF ACTION

We showed how Christine and her task force have come to frame and define their problem with discipline in their district's middle schools as an individual *and* organizational problem. From an individual perspective, the cause of the problem seems clear. First- and second-year teachers, it is almost an axiom, have a lot to learn about classroom management. So as a solution, a few classroom management professional development workshops surely cannot hurt. Then there is the organizational aspect of the problem. This is trickier. The team brainstorms a whole slew of ideas and ends up settling on three of them. Administrators, the team believes, have to be more vigilant about rules and their enforcement; there needs to be more emotional support for students who repeatedly break the rules; and there need to be instructional assignments for all the students who are sent out of class so that they will not fall further behind. Individual workshops, schoolwide rules, and support for students make intuitive sense to the team, and these measures would presumably go some distance in addressing the problem. The team's intuitive theory of action follows a specific logic. They look at what the teachers, administrators, counselors, and detention supervisors can do as one next incremental step that may improve the situation. The team, in effect, triages the problem by formulating for the district an action plan that lists these strategies.

MICHELLE'S INTUITIVE THEORY OF ACTION

Michelle has framed her problem of practice as the need for teachers to embrace culturally relevant pedagogy. In her theory of action, she intuitively connects the broad problem of the achievement gap and the racial makeup of her students and teachers with what she is convinced is a best practice for this situation. Michelle is surprised when teachers in her school are cool to the equity committee's initiative. She senses reluctance when her enthusiastic presentation of the new project is met with cautious reserve. She begins to suspect that the teachers' reluctance may be evidence of their deficit thinking and cultural insensitivity. In the district equity committee, she defines her problem as "teachers resist CRP" and her solution as "overcoming teachers' resistance to CRP." In other words, in her intuitive theory of action, Michelle *defines the problem as the absence of her solution.* Rather than naming an existing practice that was problematic and that needed elaboration, refinement, or challenge, she named a desired practice that was absent.

The problem with this kind of thinking about change as filling an empty vessel is that soon, the leaders are surrounded by "resisters." Adults, even more than children, do not learn things for which they cannot see the purpose. To see the purpose, they need to connect the leader's desired change—what the leader sees as an absence—to what already exists in their thinking and practice, and they need to generate the motivation to do something about it. Pointing out to adults that their problem is that they ought to do what somebody else has identified as their need is not a powerful motivation theory.

A different way of seeing the problem emerges when Michelle discusses it with her assistant principal, Grace. Grace has been the actual nuts-and-bolts instructional leader at the school. Grace cuts to the chase: "You can't expect teachers to have courageous conversations and engage in deep interpretation of culturally relevant texts when you ask them to follow a skill-based prescriptive program with fidelity and when you pressure them on results from weekly quizzes and quarterly benchmarks. You can't expect teachers to suddenly think outside the box when the district has discouraged that for years." Michelle is stunned: the assistant principal is telling her that, far from bringing the solution, Michelle is part of the problem. She swallows, but she does hear what Grace has to say. For the moment, Michelle decides to suspend her fervent belief in the CRP solution and to reassess the situation by gathering more information about what the teachers in her school are actually doing that is problematic.

Michelle is puzzled. She feels that she must shift her perspective. But what is she missing in her thinking? She settles on observing her teachers' practices and better understanding the causes of why they act the way they do.

ERIC'S INTUITIVE THEORY OF ACTION

Eric's problem of practice revolves around instructional supervision. We showed earlier that his problem definition shifted as he located the causes for the problematic practices first in the principals' failure to prioritize classroom visits and then in the principals' lack of competence. When he thought about the needed changes or why his imagined changes would do the job (i.e., his understanding of the change process), he intuitively drew from his varied experiences. And one powerful experience in his teacher education program stuck out. He remembered watching videos and using an observation tool with which he and his fellow students analyzed instructional sequences, followed by discussions about their observations.

Eric's intuition tells him that the cause of his problem is that principals have a hard time analyzing lessons and giving feedback. He intuits a solution: "If I review videos and use an observation tool with the principals, then they will learn how to become better instructional supervisors." Note that when Eric thinks about the changes he needs and his intuitive understanding of the change, he thinks in shorthand. He thinks of tools, materials, and activities as the things that drive his outcomes. There is nothing wrong with that, as this is how most people think when they intuitively consider teaching somebody something new. People think of what *they* must do to make another person learn and change, but they often think only fleetingly about what should go on inside the target person's mind. Instead of learning *by* doing, people use the heuristic that learning *is* doing. Of course, activities can help people learn, but what exactly are they supposed to learn while engaging in the activity?

Following this intuitive theory of action, Eric's intervention is to bring the principals together five times for a workshop. During the workshops, he plans to expose the principals to videos of classroom instruction that will be analyzed with an observation tool that he borrowed from an evaluation program currently touted as effective by his district. Halfway into the intervention, Eric notices that what he has designed is not working. Sure enough, the principals watch the videos with the observation tool in hand, and while watching, they check off whether the teacher stated the lesson objective, had good time on task, used a variety of strategies to ensure equitable participation, and so forth. But Eric is dissatisfied. The observation tallies just do not add up to what Eric now realizes is most important to him: students' academic engagement with the content. His problem definition has shifted yet one more time.

Eric now realizes the limitations of his intuitive theory of action: his framing of the problem was fuzzy. He started with "they don't observe," then moved to "they don't want to observe," and finally to "they don't know how to analyze lessons." Now he realizes that this framing of the problem was still too vague. He ends up with "they don't know how to recognize students' engagement with ideas."

As the frames around his problem of practice change, different behaviors that Eric considers problematic come into view. With this changed view, his learning goals for the adults, or the desired end states, shift as well. He realizes he needs a precise definition of the beliefs, attitudes, or practices he wants to change and a precise definition of where he wants to end up.

He wonders what was missing from his (intuitive) understanding of the change process that prevented him from predicting the limited effect his intervention had. After all, he chose activities that had worked for him. He asks himself what it was about those activities that had been so effective for him. In thinking about this, he realizes he has left something out of the picture: what kind of learning was supposed to take place during these activities? For the principals, the task seemed clear: they were to note and rate the occurrence of discrete teaching behaviors. But this is not what Eric wanted. He wanted them to analyze lessons more deeply.

In his intuitive theory, the key drivers of the principals' learning were the observation tool, the videos, and the space for professional conversations. Eric pulled the car out of the garage and drove it, but he was not clear on what the passengers were supposed to see while they were riding. His passengers donned their administrator hats and saw only objects that needed to be checked off. He, however, wanted them to see a dynamic interactive system between teachers and students around instructional material. What kind of learning will now have to take place to shift that perspective? Eric realizes that his understanding of the change process lacks a good grasp of what kind of adult learning will need to take place, which is at the core of change.

NORA'S INTUITIVE THEORY OF ACTION

For Nora and her school leadership team, framing and defining the problem came relatively easy. They worked in a school in which social justice was taken as an explicit guide for action. They had focused on bullying behavior among students, and they were now going to tackle homophobic and racial slurs in their school by addressing adult behavior. They formulated as their desired state that adults will intervene when they hear slurs in the building.

But now Nora is faced with a huge challenge. She is a capable administrator and she has firm moral commitments, but she does not know what to do. She knows intuitively that addressing slurs is slippery territory, and she is, yes, scared. For a moment, she considers contracting the services of an acclaimed reform organization that has as its specialty "re-culturing schools for equity." But in the end, she and her leadership team decide that they want something homegrown, designed by themselves, and with the potential to deeply influence their school's culture the way they see it. They do not think that implementing an externally developed package will do this, but they are nevertheless going to draw from the wisdom of this reform organization.

In a brainstorming session, the team sketches its intuitive theory of action. The team members begin by trying to understand what explains their problem. They think about what they know about slurs, both personally and professionally, and what they have witnessed in terms of slurs at the school. They settle on the following intuitive understanding of their problem: "Slurs have the potential to hurt because they put people to whom slurs are directed into an inferior position. Slurs are an expression of something bigger than the school. They reflect the value judgments we make about certain groups in society." The team also senses that because slurs are so common and ingrained in the everyday culture of schools, people are not even aware of what is going on even though they probably all feel that they are committed to social justice.

What to do about it? The team members settle on awareness, commitment to social justice, and intervention strategies as the building blocks of their intuitive understanding of the change process. Their theory of action is as follows: If they create adult awareness of the pervasiveness of slurs in their school, reaffirm that the school, as a social justice school, cannot tolerate the problem, and develop ways to approach students when they use slurs, then adults will feel inclined to step in and take action.

As adults regularly take action, the culture of the school may shift. But Nora worries. Will the social justice theme of the school be powerful enough to get her faculty through the dangerous territory of racism and homophobia?

CHAPTER SUMMARY

In this chapter, we explained how a theory of action begins—intuitively. We discussed the following points:

- Intuition produces understanding that can only be backed up with fuzzy empirical observation and associative justifications. Rationality applies sequential logic, measurement, and analysis.

- When leaders are challenged to go beyond conventional strategies and develop novel approaches, intuitive thinking is at a premium.

- When using intuition, people rely on heuristics, that is, rules of thumb that connect present patterns of behavior to prior experience and knowledge.

- An intuitive theory of action combines, in a fuzzy, creative way, what a person knows or understands about both a problem's causes and the drivers that move the change process forward and that may improve on the problem.

- Most often, problem solvers develop their intuitive theories of action implicitly and semiconsciously. People awaken their intuitive capacities and problem-solving skills by making their intuitive theories of action explicit.

4

Conducting a
Needs Assessment

with Mahua Baral

Design-based thinking is innovative problem solving that is user-centered. In this chapter, designers become further aware of and challenge their intuitive assumptions. They get their feet wet in data collected from the users by conducting exploratory needs assessments. As they ask questions, observe other people in their work, and look at artifacts, designers attempt to define behaviors in observable or perceptible terms. Observations or perceptions give them the evidence needed to question their intuition and quick heuristics. Designers need to ask two questions:

→ How should we describe the behaviors that are focal for our problem of practice?
→ How can we make sure that our assumptions about our problem can be backed up by evidence?

Christine, Michelle, Eric, and Nora are facing urgent problems of practice. They respond, as people usually do in these situations, with an intuitive theory of action based on preexisting knowledge and experience. Such intuition about cause and effect, and means and ends, is a necessary starting point for addressing any problem. Each of these educators goes about his or her problem differently. In the previous chapter, we showed how all of them strive to find the right kind of boundaries, definitions, and frames around their problems as they make their intuitive theories of action explicit. The four educators differ in the next steps they take. Some move directly to action. Some begin to explore how people actually behave; others think hard about the learning they want to bring about. Some feel certain about their intuition, but can't completely ignore some nagging doubts.

Christine's district task force jumps directly from its intuitive understanding of the problem into an action plan for novice teachers, counselors, and administrators. The action plan spells out one new activity that each set of actors—teachers, administrators, and counselors—can undertake to improve the situation immediately. The task force believes that the urgency of the situation demands immediate remedy and results.

Of the four leaders described here, Michelle is the most committed to her solution, so much so that her problem becomes the absence of her solution. And her understanding of the change process is all about overcoming teacher resistance to her solution. But while she may be a fervent believer, she is also blessed with a healthy appreciation for evidence. So when she is made to stop and think, she elects to take a closer look at her teachers' beliefs, attitudes, and practices.

Eric's problem definition is in flux as he acts on his intuition. Intuitively, he remembers what he used to do when he learned about instruction, and his recalled activities become the drivers of his district's professional development for principals. But he is dissatisfied with what these drivers yield, and he realizes that he has been fixated on activities when he should have thought about adult learning.

Nora's leadership team feels that their theory of action is intuitively apparent. Slurs are rampant and adults do not step in when they hear them. The adults need to be made aware of their lack of intervention, reminded of their commitment to social justice, and taught some straightforward ways of approaching students when they as adults hear racial or homophobic slurs. But Nora is uncomfortable: is doing all this really so easy?

EXPLORATORY NEEDS ASSESSMENTS

Designing begins with a perception of a problem, something that designers have encountered and believe needs changing and improving. In education, we sometimes start by looking at indicators such as test scores, grades, disciplinary referrals, referrals to alternative services, dropouts, and the like. Or we might look at student behavior. For example, we may notice a lot of students in the hallways during instructional time or frequent fights. At other times, we listen to teachers' complaints about, or justifications for, things the teachers deplore. Finally, we observe behavior directly or solicit other people's beliefs, dispositions, or explanations. From all these data, we can form judgments about a focal problem of practice.

Before jumping into exploring the knowledge base for a problem of practice and thinking about designing interventions, designers need to check if their assumptions are correct. Local needs assessments aim to question assumptions regarding the problem of practice. Designers also use these assessments to find out what assets they have at their disposal to move people to change or adopt new practices. Exploratory needs assessments should occur concurrently with the formulation of the intuitive theory of action so that intuition and exploratory data speak to each other. These early explorations can be rather informal, yet designers should get their feet wet in reality. What should they look at?

When Christine, Michelle, Eric, and Nora were formulating their initial problems of practice, they started out with statements of this type:

- *Christine*: We have too many students spending time out of class for disciplinary infractions, and these children miss out on instruction. Novice teachers have difficulties controlling their classrooms and don't use good classroom management strategies. When many novices are in one school, the school gets out of control. Administrators, counselors, and teachers need to work together. Everybody needs to do his or her part.
- *Michelle*: Teachers have low expectations and approach their students of color with deficit thinking and do not teach in culturally relevant ways.

- *Eric*: Instructional supervision has to get better in this district. Principals are not motivated to visit classrooms. We need to mandate classroom visits.
- *Nora*: We are a social-justice-oriented school. We can't tolerate so many slurs, because slurs hurt our students. Teachers seem to close their eyes to rampant slurs. We need to do something about it as adults in this building.

Busy educational leaders are expected to know the answers, rather than asking the questions. Not surprisingly, given this expectation, leaders often develop problem statements for which there is really little to explore. Look at the problem statements above closely: if a problem statement names an intention, a problematic behavior, its causes, and the solution—all blended together in one statement—then there is no point in conducting a needs assessment, since all the answers are already there. Or they are assumed to be there. And it would be rather difficult to decide which data to collect since many of the statements already contain the leaders' judgment or opinion on something that is unobservable. When that happens, their statements are of *high inference*. Actually, the leaders' initial problem statements are really more like intuitive theories of action. To move from intuition to analysis, designers need to untangle these problem statements. In the exploratory needs assessment, designers are mainly aiming at naming the beliefs, attitudes, or practices that are problematic. They try to stay away from jumping to conclusions about solutions. Designers want to describe what they can see or hear. Statements that contain observations or perceptions are *low-inference statements*. Once designers have a good description of the problematic state or behavior, they are in a better position to name the desired state or behavior that they believe they can reach within the time frame of the design.

EXCURSION INTO THEORY

Needs Assessments

Needs assessments are used to identify problems, priorities, causes, and resolutions to make improvements within an organization.[1] This systematic process helps organizations determine "the best way to portion out the available resources, including time, money, and organizational efforts, to meet all the demands—the needs—that compete for them."[2] Through a systematic process of data collection and analysis, needs assessments help organizations set priorities and identify the actions necessary for a desired result.[3] Many books provide guidance on needs assessments, describing various models that organizations may use to better identify and understand problems.[4]

There are basic principles of needs assessments common in all approaches. As described earlier, these assessments are *systematic* ways to make and *justify* decisions. The assessments can be *scalable* to meet specific needs of different projects, can be *replicable* so they can be used in multiple organizations, and can provide a *systemic* view of the various social systems within an organization.[5] Needs can be defined as gaps in results or as perceived discrepancies between a current and a desired condition.[6] And thus needs can be assessed in three ways: *proactively*, to identify areas that need improvement; *continually*, to inform, monitor, and justify whether decisions are leading to desired results; or *reactively*, to search for new strategies, tactics, and approaches in an aim to improve.[7] A needs assessment should actively involve all stakeholders, including those who provide and receive services.[8] The assessments are often used as a preliminary process to plan improvements and thus should focus on examining identified gaps or wants from the perspective of those who are receiving the product or service.

Needs assessments, a critical element of design development studies, help researchers question assumptions and collect data to inform the solutions and interventions best suited to address a specific problem of practice. In literature on design research, needs assessments are described as "mini-studies" and can be conducted in a variety of ways using various methods. Local needs assessments do not necessarily have to meet the same level of rigor that full-fledged studies do; rather, these assessments may be more exploratory.

LOW-INFERENCE OBSERVATIONS OF BEHAVIORS

Fortunately, many of the beliefs, attitudes, and practices (in short, behaviors) that we, in the field of education, consider problematic are perceptible. The behaviors can be observed, or learned about, through conversations. If possible, isolated behaviors should be grouped into larger patterns. But this step is still at the level of perception. In this first round of needs assessment, designers should stick with direct descriptions of behaviors and should not yet make any further inferences about what causes the problem. Elizabeth City and colleagues provide a useful discussion of this step in *Instructional Rounds*. They introduce a "ladder of inference" that begins with description and moves through assumptions to conclusions. "If you start at the top of the ladder," they say, "it's hard to go back down—the other rungs are missing."[9]

Yet, there are limits to direct observation or low-inference description in understanding human behavior, and social scientists are all too familiar with these limits. A practice or behavior is observable, but observers often do not know what it means without knowing the actor's intentions, which are sometimes unacknowledged, subconscious, or concealed. Likewise, people can only learn about another person's beliefs through communication with the person, but all people act strategically when they talk with others. People are well aware of how they need to present themselves selectively to others to look good in other people's eyes.

The situation with attitudes is even more difficult. Attitudes (e.g., inspiration, motivation, commitment, sympathy, fear, hostility, dislike of certain people, pretense of agreement, racism, sexism, homophobia) can only be inferred through speech or actions, and given the uncertainties with speech and action, attitudes can often only be ascertained through relatively higher inferences. In everyday life, people help themselves with these high inferences by trusting their intuition and reading subconscious cues, such as facial expressions. But in design thinking, we need something more robustly verifiable for problem diagnosis. So, for all those high-inference states of mind, designers need clues of more low-inference behavior that people can actually display. One cannot ask a person directly if he or she is defensive. Such a question would probably raise a person's defenses. One cannot ask a person directly if he or she stereotypes other people. In research, we help ourselves by asking indirect questions about something more concrete: ideas, feelings, or narratives that hint at underlying attitudes that we are interested in, or we may observe people's actions and ask them about seeming contradictions between statements and actions. So in the case of stereotyping, we may ask a teacher to simply describe his students, his assumptions about their behavior, and the frequency with which the teacher encounters this type of student. In the case of defensiveness, we may ask teachers what troubles them in their job and then find out who or what, in the eyes of the teachers, is at fault for those troubles. This is called *operationalizing*. We may operationalize defensiveness as "teachers naming many external sources for problems over which teachers may have some internal control. These sources tend to be seen as aggressive, and they thwart teachers' professed good intentions." Thus, operationalizations make abstract, high-inference constructs (e.g., being motivated, being engaged, being defensive) concrete; they bring observations down a rung on the ladder of inference. In everyday life, people operationalize when they say that a seemingly small gesture or action can "speak volumes." What they mean is that the gesture or action stands for a more encompassing, more "voluminous" attitude.

For example, when Michelle listens to teachers frequently stating what their students cannot do and what they lack in terms of readiness to benefit from the teachers' instruction, she infers *deficit thinking*. In this case, these teachers' statements operationalize deficit thinking. Or in another example, a person's display of voluntary effort in staying after school to watch videos of lessons in conjunction with his or her expression of belief that this activity is meaningful or rewarding would help operationalize high intrinsic motivation to learn how to become a better instructional supervisor (which is Eric's desire to instill in his principals).

The exploratory needs assessment, as a first step, should focus on searching for low-inference, or operationalized, ways to describe beliefs, attitudes, and practices that show that designers are on the right track in defining a problem of practice. (This assessment, by the way, also helps designers define concrete, testable changes captured by impact metrics that pick up on these concrete behaviors. More on that in chapter 11.) The exploratory data collection should result in a low-inference statement of the problematic behavior that designers want to tackle. We now look at how two of the four leaders, Christine and Michelle, deal with needs assessments. As for Eric and Nora, we showed that Eric skipped a needs assessment in the beginning and jumped right into action. Nora and her team, on the other hand, determined that they wanted to tackle slurs by changing a straightforward problematic behavior: when teachers hear slurs, they do not intervene. Toward that end, the leadership decides to fan out throughout the building and surreptitiously tally whenever they hear students using slurs and whenever teachers within earshot do, or do not, intervene. These low-inference data confirm their conjecture: teachers for the most part do not intervene.

CHRISTINE'S NEEDS ASSESSMENT

As described earlier, Christine and her district task force have developed an action plan based on their intuitive conjectures of what novice teachers need and what each set of actors in the organization might do to improve on student discipline. They have skipped needs assessments and relied on the certainty of their experience.

When the new plan is put into action, however, it produces unforeseen outcomes. Principals report that the number of students sent out of class has actually increased. Christine and her task force are puzzled. They decide to visit schools and conduct an exploratory needs assessment. They pick two schools.

They first visit the counseling offices. There they find that the counselors can in no way handle the caseload that the teachers generate by sending out students. The team estimates that the counselors can only handle at most one student sent out every other period by any given teacher in the school. This estimate assumes that the number of severe cases has to remain very small. The problem cannot be remedied through the counseling office.

Then the team talks to the teachers who send out relatively large numbers of students. Not surprisingly, these teachers are mostly novices. The teachers with the numerous student referrals report that the new stress on behavioral rules has made them feel more vigilant about rule infractions. The teachers feel that since the students are now sent to the counseling office with assignments, it is up to the office to ensure that the assignments are completed and that disruptive students are served. The classroom management workshops offered by the district are seen as useful by the novice teachers. The teachers' relationships with the administration, however, are problematic. The administration has required teachers to reduce the number of students sent out of class. A referral statistic with the names of teachers attached has appeared on a bulletin board in the teachers' lounge. Teachers feel pressured. Frustrations run high.

The task force discovers that many teachers feel isolated and left alone with discipline problems, and sending students out is the valve that alleviates the pressure. Grade-level teams (GLTs) are for the most part not functioning. Joint responses to difficult, but not severely disruptive, students are rare. Often, students receive conflicting messages from different teachers. Teachers display defensiveness when the conversation moves to difficult students. When teachers get together in teams, they process trivial tasks and often relate to each other with tension. It is only December, and many novice teachers are already contemplating leaving at the end of the school year.

The findings from this initial round of needs assessment substantially reframe the problem. The focal need moves from classroom management and triage to a more medium-term development of functioning GLTs that should collectively tackle many non-severe disruptions and shore up mutual support through difficult times. Christine and her group now name their low-inference problematic behavior in this way: The teachers rarely talk with each other about students that they share within the grade level, but when they do, they offer one another only superficial suggestions. Although the teachers are skeptical about the efficiency of working together, waste time on trivial tasks in grade-level meetings, and sometimes relate to each other with tension, they also deplore their isolation and lack of support.

MICHELLE'S NEEDS ASSESSMENT

Let's return to Michelle, the elementary school principal who has become a strong advocate of culturally relevant pedagogy as her remedy. How has she described her problem of practice? She began by looking at test score indicators and saw a wide achievement gap between ethnic groups in her district. She has associated the achievement gap with low expectations and deficit thinking on the part of mostly white teachers who she thinks might lack cultural sensitivity or competence. She has jumped from an indicator to a possible cause. In her intervention, she wanted to address the possible cause—deficit thinking—with professional development that raises cultural competence. As described earlier, when her intervention fell on deaf ears, she was at first baffled, then she felt confirmed in her assumption that teachers did not seem to care. But when confronted by her assistant principal, she took a step back and decided to look more carefully.

Michelle's reasoning is not implausible, but from a design development viewpoint, she skips a few steps that she would need to frame and define her problem of practice correctly. The achievement gap is a huge problem in the United States and elsewhere. But she will have to realize that the gap is not a problem of practice, but the result of many practices, and this result is indicated by a measurable achievement gap. Indicators point to problems, but are not the problem of *practice*. No designed intervention can close the achievement gap directly; educators can only change beliefs, attitudes, or practices that may eventually be registered on the indicator. School and district leaders have the strongest influence on adults, not students. So leaders' problem of practice should focus on beliefs, attitudes, or practices of adults who are members of, or associated with, their organization.

Back to Michelle. After talking to her assistant principal, she decides to begin her needs assessment by observing classrooms. She still entertains her idea that there is something culturally remiss with the teachers, but she also looks for evidence that her assistant principal could be right and that her problem of practice is related to the way teachers teach the prescriptive literacy program.

Her observations focus on one thing at first: how teachers relate to students when they teach. She finds that, exceptionally strong teachers notwithstanding, teachers in her school basically follow the script of the program. They assign the texts and use the prompts from the program. They are, for the most part, friendly to the students, encouraging them to participate and giving them space to work with the material. But after working awhile on specific assignments, the teachers move on to the next item in the program, leaving quite a few students confused and behind. When Michelle talks with teachers afterward, they complain that many of their students cannot keep up with the program. The teachers are frustrated with the lack of progress; they feel they themselves are trying hard and are doing their best with the students they have. And they wish there was more support from the parents and the district.

The problematic behavior that Michelle believes she needs to address has now become much more low-inference and concrete than her initial intuitive understanding, which focused on teachers' unwillingness. She now describes her low-inference problematic behavior: Constrained by the pacing of the prescriptive curriculum, teachers move forward without checking for their students' understanding of the material. The teachers seem less concerned about the relevance of the material for the students' cognitive or cultural needs and more concerned with coverage. Defensively, they justify this neglect by pointing to the missing support of parents and the district.

PRELIMINARY DESIGN CHALLENGE AND DESIRED STATE

The design challenge follows from two steps: a good low-inference description of the beliefs, attitudes, or practices considered problematic and a statement of the desired state or behavior. Initially, the desired state is a rough estimate of what sorts of changes are realistic for the duration of the designed intervention. These types of designed interventions typically run for about three to six months, perhaps with some follow-up activities beyond this time frame. As designers continue thinking through their projects, the desired state they aim at and the design challenge may be revised along the way. Formulating and refining a succinct design challenge is one way to making a design development study more and more precise.

The preliminary design challenge of Christine's task force, which is concerned about novice teacher's behavior management abilities, may be formulated this way: "Our design challenge is to move teachers in GLT meetings, within a three-month period, from rarely and superficially addressing the emotional and behavioral management needs of disruptive students to making conversations about students with discipline problems part of their regular routines. Grade-level teams will lessen skepticism about working together and will efficiently process tasks. The sense of isolation should give way to a prevailing sense of hopefulness and collegial support."

And Michelle and her district committee, concerned with the cultural relevance of instruction at their schools, may state their design challenge as follows: "Our design challenge is to have elementary school teachers who are teaching district-adopted literacy programs move, within a three-month period, from feeling constrained by the pacing of the prescriptive curriculum to being guided by it. In the planning and delivery of lessons, teachers' rushed checking for their students' understanding should give way to materials and instructional strategies that enable children to exhibit comprehension and interest. An increased ability to reach students and a reemphasis on the teachers' autonomy should lessen teachers' defensiveness in blaming parents and the district for unsatisfactory results."

CHAPTER SUMMARY

In this chapter we have examined how exploratory needs assessments clarify what focal practices make up the problem, and how evidence helps educational leaders, as designers, move their intuitive theory of action toward more analytical precision. Precision is the result of the following:

- Identifying and describing low-inference behaviors (beliefs, attitudes, or practices) that can be observed or communicated through speech.

- Becoming aware of the inferences one makes about the focal beliefs, attitudes, and practices that make up one's problem of practice.

- Formulating low-inference problematic and desirable behaviors that result in an increasingly precise design challenge.

PART I SUMMARY

We have shown that design development is a form of innovative problem solving. Part I of this book follows the famous dictum "If I had an hour to solve a problem, I'd spend fifty-five minutes thinking about the problem and five minutes thinking about solutions."[10] In the first four chapters, we have described how educators should think hard about the problems they should choose for design development, and we have narrated how four representative leaders have gone about doing so.

Leaders in organizations must locate the chosen problem of practice in their organization's needs for creative problem solving. They need to make sure, to the degree possible, that the chosen problem is embedded in their organization's strategic approach to improvement.

We have shown that problems in education are mostly ill structured and that they require framing, and defining. We have described how our four leaders have begun to tackle this task.

As a first approach to a problem of practice, designers rely on their intuition as a powerful source of insight and creativity that they command, or rather that naturally comes to them as experienced practitioners. The power of this source is further enhanced when designers make their intuition explicit to themselves. They embrace their intuition, but as they recognize assumptions and biases in their intuitive theories of action, designers challenge these theories, refine them, and make them more analytical. By pulling apart a complex problem of practice through logic and evidence, leaders become more analytical and discover how the problem's components are interconnected.

We have discussed how needs assessments are a first step in searching for this evidence. Needs assessments have enabled the four leaders described in this book to question their assumptions and to narrow their scope of work.

Apart from needs assessments, consulting the knowledge base is a another big step forward in bolstering one's logic. Of course, designers could have started reading sources from the literature right away, searching here or there. But not until they have a clearer picture of what they are after—that is, after they have taken the steps thus far—does the exploration of the professional knowledge base become efficient. The knowledge base is rarely organized according to the users' wishes and needs. Rather, designers are tasked with assembling a knowledge base from varied lines of inquiry to address their design challenge. If the professional knowledge base held ready and solid answers in stock for a problem, why would people need to go through the trouble and develop innovative designs and conduct research? They could just implement a known solution.

Developing a
Theory of Action

5

Consulting the Professional Knowledge Base

with Mahua Baral

In the flow of the design development process, designers now need to put their intuition on a firmer ground with the help of knowledge accumulated through educational research and the systematic documentation of professional practice. The task we are describing in this chapter expects educational leaders to relish intellectual challenge and to learn how to become knowledgeable readers of educational research and reports from practice. In this chapter, we describe how leaders identify various areas of the knowledge base that are relevant for their specific design challenge, access sources in these knowledge areas, and make sense of conflicting information from these sources. In consulting a knowledge base, leaders need to ask the following questions:

→ How do we move from a reliance on intuition alone to a good logical base for our design?
→ What exactly is a theory of action?
→ How do we make a theory of action more analytical?
→ How do we access the professional knowledge base?

→ How do we create a conceptual order among our sources to establish a robust base for our design work?

FROM INTUITION TO ANALYSIS

We launch our forays into the professional knowledge base from the intuitive theory of action. The intuitive theory gives designers two kinds of ideas: ideas about where they should begin the search for sources from the knowledge base and assumptions about the problem and the change process—assumptions that leaders might need to challenge. The goal is to gradually move from intuition to a theory of action that rests on analysis. As we said earlier, this transition requires that designers recognize the components of a complex problem and make connections among its parts through good logic and evidence. Theoretical concepts, research findings, and solid reports of practical applications help designers in this endeavor.

A theory of action consists of five main parts: (1) problem definition or framing; (2) the goals or aims of the action (chapters 1 through 4); (3) an understanding of the problem's symptoms and causes (chapter 7); (4) an understanding of the change process; and (5) an understanding of the organizational context within which the change is to unfold (chapter 8). As designers begin to study the knowledge base relevant to their problem of practice, they try to fill these five conceptual bins of the theory of action. They ask themselves several questions:

- What am I learning about how to frame or define my problem of practice?
- What can I expect to accomplish?
- What am I learning about the problem's causes?
- What am I learning about possible change processes that may improve matters?
- What am I learning about the contexts in which knowledge about my problem has been generated; how do these contexts compare to my own?

EXCURSION INTO THEORY

Theory of Action

The distinction between theory and theory of action was originally suggested by management scientist Chris Argyris, who drew from the work of Kurt Lewin.[1] Argyris observed that managers or leaders of organizations need knowledge that regular social science is poorly equipped to deliver. According to Argyris, regular social science aims to predict a causal relationship between a set of factors and an outcome. The relationship that emerges is meant to be generalizable, that is, valid across a variety of situations.[2] Science enables generalizations in two ways: by operating with concepts that are defined in abstract terms that can be applied to any context and by employing research designs that disconnect data collection from the specifics of contexts, for example through random sampling.

Concepts are defined as variables when they differ in quantity, but not quality across contexts. For example, once a concept labeled *academic expectations* is defined as the "belief that future academic success will occur with high probability," this definition should ideally apply across all situations, and it is assumed that when the concept of academic expectations is used, it stands for the same belief across the varied contexts. But that belief may vary in strength depending on individuals or contexts explored in a study, and we may say that individual *x* in context *y* has high or low academic expectations. In reality, the literature in the field uses a variety of definitions of a particular concept. It is therefore standard practice in solid research to define one's main terms.

Causality becomes decontextualized, and thus generalizable, in experimental and quasi-experimental research designs. When researchers arrange an experiment in the behavioral sciences, they specify in detail the setting in which subjects are to act. Experimental settings can sometimes differ quite a bit from natural settings. Then the researchers assign individuals randomly to treatment and control groups. In quasi-experimental designs, people cannot be randomly assigned to treatment and control groups, but data may be collected from random samples of subjects from a wide variety of contexts that could also be randomly selected. Statistical procedures allow for contexts to be controlled for. The purpose of what Argyris calls regular science is to describe a phenomenon, explain the causal relationships among variables, and, in the process, generate a theory.[3]

Scientific Knowledge for Leaders

Scientific knowledge for managers or organizational leaders is similar to the type of science described above, in some respects, and is different in others. The overall aim of organizational leaders is to be effective, that is, to translate intent into results through actions. They need generalizable knowledge that predicts means-ends relationships across contexts. They also need theories that define, describe, and explain relationships between treatment and effect. But this knowledge is not sufficient. Organizational leaders cannot control their environment, as in an experiment. Nor can they ignore the context of their actions, as in quasi-experimental designs. Knowledge resulting from highly controlled or contextually unspecific research endeavors does not help leaders in their main task: *creating the conditions*, in the first place, that are examined by science with description and explanation, and doing so within the likely dynamics of their organizations. Argyris sums up leaders' main work: "In a theory of managing, explanation, generalization, and testing are all in the service of creating managerial actions."[4] For example, when research on effective schools finds after the fact that educators' high academic expectations contribute to student achievement, organizational leaders need to know how to create a culture of high expectations before the fact.

Argyris suggests that leaders need *actionable knowledge*, namely, knowledge that can support practicable actions in specific organizational contexts.[5] Actionable knowledge is generated in one context, but is made relevant for other contexts. Theories of action are the appropriate vehicle for generating, testing, and corroborating actionable knowledge. Actionable knowledge is empirical (what works) and normative (what leaders value), as improving an organization hinges on managers or leaders acting on their intent, vision, or judgment *and* producing intended outcomes. Thus, theories of action connect the values and intentions of leaders with their understanding of problems at hand and their knowledge of effective processes of change in given social contexts.

CHRISTINE'S CONSULTING OF THE KNOWLEDGE BASE

In this chapter, we detail how Christine consults the knowledge base, and in later chapters, we will describe how Michelle, Eric, and Nora deal with their knowledge base in a more cursory way. As discussed earlier, for Christine's task force, the rampant discipline problems in the district's middle schools came to be framed as an individual problem of competence in classroom management *and* as an organizational problem of grade-level team dysfunction. As for the individual aspect of the problem, the task force felt that there were many workshops and consultants out there that the district could contract with. But the taskforce also thought that the development of GLTs (Grade-level teams) in schools with a majority of novice teachers was something new that warranted design work, a problem that the district just had to solve. Incidentally behavior management is a problem that goes beyond one district. It is an issue in many districts that have middle schools that serve disadvantaged students and have high numbers of novice teachers and high attrition among them.

Within her task force, Christine is in charge of examining the knowledge base. It makes sense for her to begin her search with the literature on professional learning communities. That literature, she finds, is vast and varied, and there is no way that she can consume it all. And she does not need to. She consults the literature to improve on her understanding of the problem and the change process, but she does not need to review the literature, in the traditional sense of conducting a comprehensive review. She does not need to have a full command of published research studies and professional wisdom in her field. But she does need to understand the broad theoretical contours of her problem and its possible remedies. And she must make sure that her intuitive assumptions are justified by what the knowledge base for her problem suggests. If she can find consistent findings or views across theories, research studies, and practical applications related to her problem of practice, and if these views are consistent with her own assumptions, then she may conclude that her assumptions are justified. If she finds inconsistencies, she may need to further calibrate.

A high degree of consistency in the knowledge base is often missing. More often than not, inconsistency prevails. Researchers conducting studies within different theoretical traditions can come to very different conclusions that may contradict each other, even though the researchers are studying the same phenomena. Reports on practical applications sometimes omit or brush over important complexities of research findings. And actionable knowledge, or research knowledge that is directly applicable to the change process related to specific problems of practice, is often sparse.

As Christine delves into the research literature on professional learning communities (PLCs), she soon finds that it gives her some broad concepts that explain the structure and functioning of PLCs and that a wide variety of practical how-to guides are available. However, none of this literature seems to speak to her specific situation of nonfunctioning GLTs due to the staffing constellation at her schools. And there are very few suggestions on how to move these groups from point A, their problematic state, to point B, a state of better functioning and higher competence in behavior management. To better understand this challenge, Christine reads literature on work-team development. Here she finds lots of interesting material that describes how groups of coworkers charged with a common task may grow out of conflict and dysfunction and develop over time to become mature work teams.

Now she needs to connect this literature to the specific conditions and tasks that she is facing. Her situation, she had reasoned in her intuitive theory of action, will require some sort of socialization process between the few senior leaders and the many novice teachers on staff in her middle schools. It will also require some direct learning of new classroom management skills at the individual level. She discovers a literature on both of these topics, and she incorporates these sources into her knowledge base. In reading the research on PLCs, work team development, and organizational socialization, she comes to thoroughly question her assumption that her intervention could be a straightforward sequence of how-to workshops for the novice teachers. Rather, given the volatility and tenuousness of group development, especially in the organizational context of the schools she is dealing with, she would be better off conceptualizing her intervention as a way of developing leaders, in her case senior teacher leaders. These teacher leaders would be equipped, through information, inquiry, and support at the district level, to direct, and ride out, the unforeseeable ups and downs of group dynamics at the school level.

Mindful of the main components of a theory of action, Christine notes what each source tells her about framing or defining her problem, setting aims and goals, identifying the causes and symptoms of her problem, and understanding the change processes and the contexts in which the change processes studied in the literature occur. For example, when she begins reading about PLCs, she learns that norms of privacy shield teachers from each other so that they are left alone with their challenges (understanding the problem's causes). She learns that PLC development is facilitated when teachers follow protocols that help them get organized to process work more efficiently (understanding the change process). The literature helps her learn that full-fledged PLCs are characterized by shared norms and shared commitments to students (clarifying her aim: where the change process might end up). Finally, she discovers that PLC development seems quite challenging in urban schools with the characteristics that resemble her situation (understanding the context). For each source, she tags the text accordingly and writes a brief memo.

As she amasses the sources for the knowledge base, she also realizes that some concepts are more useful than others in precisely capturing the kinds of behaviors she is aiming at. For example, she discovers that the term *community* is used pervasively in the literature on PLCs. A lot of material comes up when she searches for this term, and authors define the term very differently. To her, the term seems opaque. She also discovers that in research on work-team development, the term *community* does not play a central role. Instead, interpersonal dynamics, group self-organizing, and task processing are in the foreground. In one of Christine's key sources, she finds a very useful typology on the depth of teacher collaboration.[6] The source makes a distinction between swapping stories, general help and assistance, sharing, and joint work. This source is also used in studies by other researchers. The idea of joint work seems a robust concept and makes a lot of sense to her as a good definition of what she is trying to accomplish in her GLTs.

At this stage of searching the knowledge base, Christine is not yet ready to formulate a full-fledged theory of action. But step by step, the picture becomes clearer and she relies less on intuition and more on firmer analysis. Christine feels much more certain about her understanding of the design challenge after reading up on the various areas of her knowledge base. But it also becomes clear to her that there are still blind spots in her knowledge base (e.g., the dynamic between novice and senior teachers around the focal task of classroom management)—areas for which she cannot seem to find sources. It will be up to her to fill in the gaps through the trial and error of designing and to orchestrate the various components of her intervention with creativity and aplomb.

SEARCHING FOR SOURCES

As a first step approaching the search for sources, designers identify what broad areas of the literature to access, what concepts and terms to search for, and how to search for key sources on databases (such as ERIC, Google Scholar, JSTOR, or iSeek). The designers' intuitive understanding gives them some ideas, and they rely on their hunches to provide initial search terms. After selecting a database and typing in key terms, they skim the list of sources to identify pieces that may be most useful to them. There are several things they can look at when reviewing sources. The number of times an article or a book has been cited provides some indication of how influential a source has been to the larger education research community. The titles of sources, their abstracts, and the key words associated with them paint a picture of what the literature includes. As designers read an abstract, they can identify whether they want to look at a source more carefully or if it lies outside the scope of the research area. Publication type, authors' names, and year of publication may also shed light on what to expect from a source and how relevant it may be, given the current time and context.

In searching an area of the literature, one could pursue two strategies, either specific or general searches. Both are useful. In a specific search, researchers look for a narrow fit between their problem of practice and the sources that may come up in databases. For example, if Nora, addressing the issue of rampant slurs in the hallways, wants to know how to conduct difficult conversations about race, she can type in this request as a search term and, with a little exploration, find that there is a literature under the search term "courageous conversations." Now she can use this term for further searches in related areas. In a general search, researchers find a broader area of knowledge, say, instructional supervision, and since this is definitely a core concern of Eric's, for example, it makes sense for him to get an idea of the main concepts, findings, or controversies in the field, accessed under this search term. In many cases, education leaders may benefit from looking at literature outside of the field of education, such as sources in the fields of sociology, social psychology, or management. As leaders find sources, it is important to keep them organized and to categorize them into broad areas that are most useful for the project. Several citation management systems, such as Zotero and Mendeley, are available to help designers keep track of sources. There is a variety of different programs, and the best one depends on the user's personal needs and preferences.

CREATING CONCEPTUAL ORDER IN THE KNOWLEDGE BASE

When designers explore the knowledge base, they will be confronted with an array of sources that at first sight are all over the place. Knowledge can be acquired from a range of sources: news magazines, practical guides, scholarly books, peer-reviewed research journals, online research reports, theoretical treatises, and all sorts of other useful materials. There are some simple criteria for tackling the knowledge base and creating conceptual order across the sources: classification of genre, identifying the topic, robustness of research, and empirical and theoretical consistency.

As designers review each of the sources they have selected, they classify the *genre* of the text. They separate sources that deal with theory, empirical research, and review of research studies. Then there are digests of research knowledge for practitioners, practical wisdom, opinion, newsmagazine articles, and so forth. The former set makes up the peer-reviewed research base. Though all sources are useful, the research base is privileged, and practical wisdom ought to be backed up by a research base whenever possible. To be sure, designers should include all types of sources, but should note the character of the sources that supply the main insights for their theory of action.

As designers look across sources, they ask, do the sources talk about the same thing? That is, is the topic the same? Often, authors use the same terms, but mean very different things. Several studies on goal setting might use the same language of "goals," but in one instance, the research may be on performance goals and, in another, on learning goals. This obviously makes a big difference.

Sometimes, authors use different terms, but mean very similar things. For example, in Christine's search on PLCs, she finds studies that mention ethics of care, commitment to service, and commitment to students. When she looks at how the authors define these terms and what empirical phenomena the studies refer to when they use the terms, she finds that these terms connote similar phenomena. It is therefore important to look below the surface of search terms and key words and study the definitions and meanings of the terms used in each source. Once designers have established that sources talk about a similar topic, they can group them together and look across the sources' findings, conclusions, suggestions, or recommendations. This exercise also helps designers define their own topic or make their understanding of the problem of practice more precise. As the designers' focus becomes clearer to them, they come to distinguish between sources that provide core insights and those that should be treated as more peripheral.

How robust is a knowledge base? How much can designers trust its findings and insights for their own design work? They look at the array of sources that they have previously identified as on topic and central. A knowledge base is robust if it includes the following elements:

- established, widely accepted theories;
- a good number of strong empirical studies;
- review articles that condense multiple empirical studies;
- studies differing in their methods: both in-depth interpretations of qualitative data and generalizations through statistical analysis of quantitative data;
- solid reporting on practical applications of research.

These criteria represent an ideal. Given the complexity of designs, knowledge areas tend to be multiple; and the knowledge base is rarely robust in all areas. While research knowledge may be more systematic and evidence-based than practitioner reports or wisdom, social research knowledge is far from uncontested. As a result, one stand-alone study does not establish a robust research base. Designers just need to be clear: weak areas of the knowledge base make for more conjectural theories of action and more room for trial and error, or room for error in their design iterations.

Once designers have established the topical identity and robustness of their sources, they search for *consistency* across sources. First they look at empirical findings whenever applicable. What behavioral patterns (beliefs, attitudes, practices) do the sources report? Are these patterns consistent or inconsistent across the sources? If there is inconsistency, the designers need to figure out why. Perhaps the studies asked different questions; used different theoretical or conceptual models to guide data collection; or used different measures, variables, analytical procedures, or interpretive codes. Sometimes, literature reviews contained in the original sources, or actual review articles, may explain consistencies or inconsistencies in empirical findings.

When sources such as empirical studies and review articles report on behavioral patterns, they usually also give theoretical explanations for these patterns. The explanations may consist of theoretical concepts and the relationships between these concepts. Sometimes these relationships differ qualitatively (e.g., high expectations for disadvantaged students are the result of proactive leadership or are the result of teachers' views of race and class oppression). Sometimes the relationships differ quantitatively (e.g., proactive leadership plays a large or a small role).

As to the consistency of empirical findings and theoretical explanations, several scenarios are conceivable. A set of sources may register similar empirical behavioral patterns that have consistent explanations. This would be quite strong consistency. Or there may be inconsistent behavioral patterns across sources, but the inconsistencies make sense seen through the lens of common or overarching theoretical explanations. Or a set of sources may have neither consistency in empirical behavior patterns nor consistency in theoretical explanations. In this case, the array of sources may be quite inconsistent and the whole field of research about a given topic may be plagued with rival empirical methods, explanations, and theories. This level of inconsistency is not unusual in social research. If designers encounter such inconsistency in their relevant knowledge base, they need to establish reasons for this rivalry. Perhaps the research is conducted within different paradigms, that is, often-unacknowledged deep assumptions about the nature of human beings and society. Or the research may have been conducted within different empirical research traditions, some of them admitting evidence that others would consider unscientific (e.g., autobiographical research). Designers need to be clear about their reasons for preferring one school of thought over another.

Christine begins by reading the practical literature on how to develop professional learning communities. She finds that the sources stress consensus, unity of purpose, and shared norms and values. Then she comes across sources that criticize this consensus view and stress the importance of conflict. Interestingly, the pro-consensus sources find empirical evidence that group cohesion is beneficial, and the pro-conflict sources find conflict beneficial. Each set of sources provides plausible theoretical explanations. This is puzzling to Christine until she latches on to literature that studies the role of conflict in work-team development. With this literature, she has a theory that explains under what conditions conflict is productive and under what conditions it is unproductive. What looked like inconsistency to her beforehand has now been explained through an overarching theoretical explanation.

As mentioned before, the professional knowledge base, and especially the research base, is rarely comprehensive enough for designers to understand a problem of practice fully. They may need to stitch together their knowledge and infer from related phenomena. But in the end, designers need to be clear on what they do *not* know after reading all their sources. An elemental condition of designing is its uncertainty and unpredictability. There comes a point at which designers need to jump into this uncertainty. That next step into uncertainty is unavoidable. Actually, design development studies are made for this uncertainty. Problem solvers design their intervention with the best possible theory of action and then learn from the intervention itself about what works and what does not.

CHAPTER SUMMARY

In this chapter, we showed how education leaders need research and professional knowledge to make their theories of action more analytical. Conceptualizations of research studies, theoretical models, empirical findings, explanations, and solid reports of practical applications are the foundation for good logic and strong evidence. Toward this end, designers must take the following steps to consult and exploit a professional knowledge base:

- Challenge assumptions by searching the literature for consistent findings and theories.

- Search for sources by identifying broad or specific areas to examine, using key search terms and phrases, and exploring a variety of databases.

- Sort through sources, and create conceptual order within the knowledge base. Classify genre, group literature by similar topics, and identify consistency among behavioral patterns and explanations across sources.

6

Becoming Intellectual Leaders in the Co-design Space

with Mahua Baral

Accessing the research and professional knowledge base requires expertise in reading sources, analytical skill, and the ability to communicate insights from the knowledge base to co-designers. Some of the co-designers may be less involved in the theoretical side of the design work or may be on the periphery of the design project altogether. For example, some decision makers need to be informed, but are not directly participating in the project. Design development calls for what we call *intellectual leadership*. Research-practice partnerships are an organizational arrangement that facilitate intellectual leadership. In this chapter we therefore address the following questions:

→ What does it mean to be an *intellectual leader*?
→ How does an intellectual leader support a *co-design* situation with his or her colleagues?
→ How can *research-practice partnerships* foster intellectual leadership and design work?
→ How can co-design teams and partnerships *distribute responsibility* for intellectual leadership?

INTELLECTUAL LEADERSHIP

Several decades ago, the critical theorist Henry Giroux developed the concept of teachers as intellectuals.[1] We extend this concept to the role of leaders in design work. Intellectual work, according to Giroux, overcomes the "separation of conceptualizing, planning, and designing from the processes of implementation and execution."[2] Bringing these two sides together avoids treating people as mere instruments to reach goals set by those higher in the organizational hierarchy or by policy makers. Intellectuals are knowledgeable in their field and understand how their field connects to the larger world. Intellectuals are creative, inquisitive, and critical. They insist on thinking not only about what works, but also about what they value. They have the courage to use their own judgment and to resist organizational authority when it is used to produce inequity and injustice. While intelligence can coexist with a lack of freedom, intellectual work is bound up with democracy, as intellect is not possible without using one's mind freely.

When intellectuals become leaders, they communicate the fruits of their thinking to others and bring about thoughtful collective action. Equity-relevant designs encourage innovative problem solving and enable groups of people to learn new practices in a democratic way. These designs organize people as self-determined subjects, not as managed objects. When people think about leaders in educational organizations, they categorize the leaders according to their leadership styles and approaches to their work. While the literature values transformational leaders for their ability to motivate others, charismatic leaders for inspiring others through charm and personality, and instructional leaders for their acumen in managing the instructional program, design development requires intellectual leadership. It is not by accident that in the previous chapter, Christine seems to be acting with little assistance from her colleagues on the district task force. Among her colleagues, the heavy lifting in accumulating the knowledge base is left up to Christine, just as it is left up to Michelle, Eric, and Nora in the other narratives. It is actually quite conceivable that co-design teams have two or three of these intellectual leaders, but however many individuals fulfill this role, co-design teams are communities of practice in which peripheral participation in intellectual work is legitimate and expected.[3]

CO-DESIGN RELATIONSHIPS

The best equity-relevant designs are co-designed by a team with manifold expertise and experience. Equity-relevant problems in education are complex and multidimensional, so that any one individual is not likely to have the specialized knowledge needed to understand all of the elements of a design intended to address such problems. Also, designs speak to contextual needs, and it takes the combined insights of various actors within an organization to amass the necessary practical and context-specific knowledge to get a full picture.

For example, Christine, whose schools are staffed with novice teachers inexperienced in behavior management, chairs her district task force. The group consists of participants in various roles: a district administrator, some principals, some counselors, and some teachers on special assignment. All members of her group have engaged in making their intuitive theories explicit and all have taken responsibility for parts of the ongoing needs assessments. As the intellectual leader, Christine has the expertise to access the professional knowledge base. She summarizes her insights for the team and shares certain key readings with the team. While she is admittedly the expert in the knowledge base, she enables her team to participate in formulating the theory of action for the design. The team will go on to design the intervention together, with the benefit of each member's creativity and experience.

Michelle's co-design setup for addressing the issue of culturally relevant instruction is different. She operates partly in her school, where her assistant principal is a critical friend and her teachers increasingly become co-designers, and partly in the space of her district equity committee. She does not chair this committee, but as an intellectual leader, she contributes in a major way to the committee's thinking. The actual co-design work, however, is not done in the equity committee. Instead, it is Michelle and two other principal colleagues who have committed to this endeavor. Michelle is the one feeding this smaller co-design group of principals with ideas from the knowledge base, but all three principals, together with select groups of teachers at their school sites, are engaged in thinking deeply about the design.

As the assistant superintendent for curriculum and instruction, Eric is responsible for the professional development of the principals in his district. He runs the monthly principals' meetings and organizes the principals' professional development days for his district. Sometimes he conducts the sessions himself, sometimes he contracts with external consultants, and sometimes he pulls in internal district staff with special expertise. For his design work on instructional supervision, he acts on his own part of the time. For the work on instructional rounds and for the coaching of principal-teacher conferences, he brings in an experienced coach from within the district. This coach, however, is more a critical friend than a co-designer, as she isn't actually part of the design itself and doesn't make or carry out decisions about the intervention. Unlike the other three leaders, Eric is having difficulty making his project a co-design experience for the participating principals. He is used to being a lone actor, and the relationship of authority he has established with his supervisees creates distance.

Among the four leaders, Nora's situation is unique. Her design is being developed for one school only, her own. But from the beginning, she involves a teacher leadership team in her project on slurs. Most of these teachers do not have the time, and many of them have no inclination, to engross themselves in the knowledge base on slurs and cultural change for equity. They look to Nora for intellectual leadership. Even though the chairing of the team alternates, Nora is the undisputed informal source of most of the team's analytical thinking. But all members' voices are strong nevertheless. When analysis needs to mesh with experience and creativity, team members speak with equal voices. And it is agreed from the beginning that in many planned activities for the intervention, Nora, as the principal of the school, will remain in the background.

In sum, design development is most productively done in co-design teams. Equity-oriented design development eschews the division between design experimenters setting up a treatment and participants as objects of observation. Rather, in most instances, the participants become co-designers. As co-designers, they are included as knowledgeable actors who understand the purposes, goals, and logics of the ongoing design work. They contribute their ideas to the development of the design and are deemed capable of critiquing it. But intellectual leadership is indispensable. Design development is highly sophisticated and requires expertise in accessing the research and professional knowledge base. Moreover, a successful design relies on the determination of leaders to think for themselves and trust their own judgment. Intellectual leaders go beyond so-called buy and buy-in and insist on innovative problem solving that works in their situation and serves the participants' needs for learning.

RESEARCH-PRACTICE PARTNERSHIPS

Intellectual leadership does not grow in isolation. It is a matter of partnerships between budding intellectual leaders in the sphere of practice and organizations that can nurture and support this type of leadership. These organizations could be universities, especially educational leadership programs, or other entities that generate or deal with professional knowledge. Regardless of organizational form, it is most important that the partnering organization values and furthers intellect. That is, organizations must strongly support independent judgment, critical appraisal of one's goals and actions in light of the bigger picture, and acquisition of knowledge that is serviceable beyond the narrow instrumental purpose of training people how to implement solutions designed by others. Leaders need to acquire knowledge and competence in the domains of problem solving, innovation, design, and research methods, but also in domains related to organizational learning and change, at the individual, group, and systemic levels. The previous chapter, on consulting the professional knowledge base, has given a flavor of what is involved.

EXCURSION INTO THEORY

Research-Practice Partnerships

With the momentum of the US Department of Education's Institute for Education Sciences (www.ies.ed.gov) dedicating funding to research-practice partnerships, and the Carnegie Foundation for the Advancement of Teaching (www.carnegiefoundation.org)

advocating the use of improvement science within networks of researchers and practitioners, a growing body of educators are experimenting with the use of partnerships in reform efforts.[4] Partnerships between researchers and practitioners are seen as mutually beneficial exchanges, with both groups benefitting from working together.[5] In a 2013 white paper synthesizing the state of scholarly thinking about research-practice partnerships in education, Cynthia Coburn, William Penuel, and Kimberly Geil categorize partnerships into three types: research alliances, design research partnerships, and networked improvement communities.[6] In alliances, researchers conduct research for a given district and give advice based on their findings. Design research partnerships engage in co-design with the aim of developing innovative approaches to change. Networked improvement communities are networks of multiple districts conducting short and rapid plan-do-study-act (PDSA) test cycles to continuously study and improve solutions to focal problems of practice.

In co-design, the "abstract space for experts" (the expertise of designers) and the "concrete space for people" (the expertise of users) converge in a space Yanki Lee calls the "realm of collaboration."[7] In this realm, participants may play different roles, depending on their varied expertise; the participants are both the agents of change and the subjects who are studied.[8]

Elizabeth Sanders and Pieter Stappers distinguish between co-design and cocreation.[9] In their view, cocreation refers to "any act of collective creativity, i.e., creativity that is shared by two or more people," and co-design refers to a specific type of cocreation in which "collective creativity is applied across the whole span of a design process." Co-design brings together "the creativity of designers and people not trained in design working together in the design development process."[10] Co-design partnerships are often characterized by a "fuzzy front end," during which the team explores the parameters of their collaboration.[11] Popular in the field of business, the co-design approach has been advocated as a promising approach to improvement in other sectors as well.[12]

For education, research on all sorts of partnerships is in its initial stages.[13] Partnerships need to bridge different norms, incentive structures, and timelines for products prevalent in the worlds of research and practice.[14] Practitioners, under time pressure, want answers to problems. Researchers want to produce time-consuming, high-quality research. Case studies of co-design efforts have shown how relevant authority, status, and social hierarchy are in team interactions, and how artifacts (e.g., data documents, videos of instruction, articles) can span boundaries across roles within the organization and between the worlds of research and practice, create common referents, and generate a shared understanding between practitioners and researchers.[15]

DESIGN DEVELOPMENT IN PARTNERSHIPS

Intellectual leadership is a high aspiration. It entails determination, hard work, and time. Many schools and districts value teachers and administrators as reflective practitioners, and intellectual leadership is prized. Yet, sometimes school or district decision makers may be overburdened and lack the time or the energy to cultivate intellectual leadership even if they are willing. The buy and buy-in mode of innovation consumes far less energy, time, and intellectual resources than does design development. And conventional approaches to innovation may be suitable at times because strong programs and expert external consultants are available. But other times, conventional approaches are unavailable or seem doubtful in their effectiveness. Here design development is indicated.

Design development is not meant to replace other forms of innovation. But design development studies will broaden the intellectual heft and innovative capacity of educational leaders and decision makers. For all its ambition, however, design development has to remain practical within school and district contexts. And toward that end, designers need to think about how to distribute intellectual leadership across multiple actors in partnerships between research and practice. When these types of partnerships aim at design development, they in effect become *co-design partnerships* (CDP), a term we will use from here on.

Earlier, we stated that CDPs could be forged by universities or an array of other organizations as long as the partnerships foster intellectual knowledge, innovative problem solving, and design-based thinking. For example, organizations specializing in designs for identified problems of practice could establish partnerships to improve their designs or to learn how to tailor their designs to unique local needs. Other organizations, specializing in design development methodology, could help professionals think through problems and could specialize in the research component of design development. Many versions of partnerships with varying ways of distributing the responsibility for intellectual leadership are conceivable (see also this chapter's "Excursion into Theory" section). Since we the authors are university based, and since, of the many knowledge-focused institutions in society, universities are primed to value intellect, we will discuss three types of CDPs for which we have gained firsthand experience—partnerships between districts and universities. We call them consultative, mediated, or integrated CDPs (figure 6.1).

Consultative Co-design Partnerships

In the consultative CDP, university researchers work directly with school and district decision makers. The practitioners in the partnership are expected to be reflective about their work, but the heavy lifting of intellectual work is done by university researchers. The researchers help practitioners frame and define their focal problem of practice and, by accessing and condensing the knowledge base,

FIGURE 6.1   Three types of co-design partnerships (CDPs)

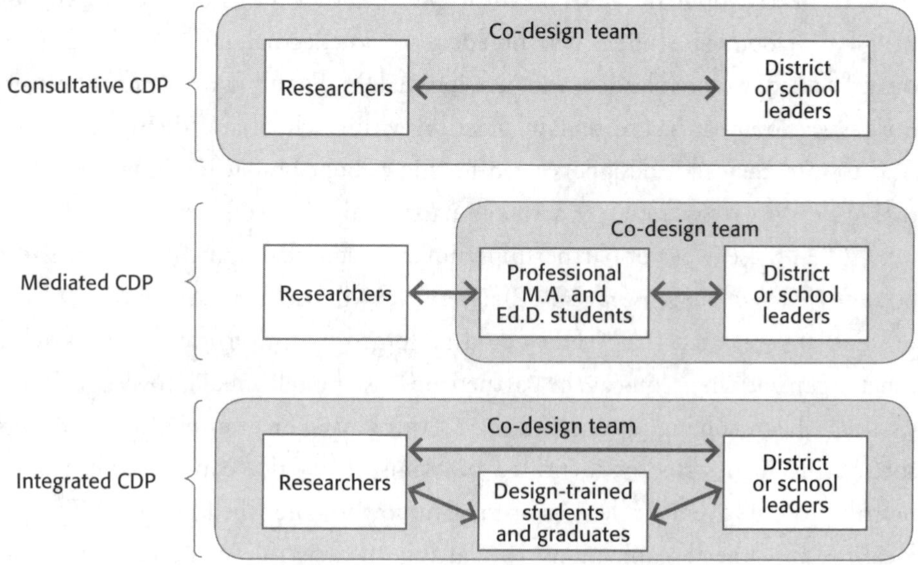

help practitioners move from intuition to an explicit theory of action. District practitioners are involved in designing the intervention and implementing it, while university researchers conduct the data collection that accompanies the implementation process. In the consultative mode, roughly speaking, researchers contribute research expertise and a penchant for analytical thinking, whereas practitioners contribute their practical knowledge and the strength of their intuition. The partnership aims at three things: developing design iterations that help solve a burning problem of practice, satisfying the researchers' scientific curiosity, and enhancing the reflective capacity of both partners.

Mediated Co-design Partnerships

In the mediated CDP, the university trains a cadre of practitioners from a variety of local systems in problem solving, design development, research methods, and various other domains related to equity-oriented school and district improvement. Scholarly practitioners learn how to consult the professional knowledge base, as described in chapter 5. Moreover, they have the opportunity to interact with like-minded colleagues from other local systems and with researchers, professors, or other skillful instructors and to engage in intellectual inquiry. University-based leadership programs at the master's and doctoral level are well equipped to fulfill this function. But mere participation in deep inquiry will not enable individuals to rise to the level of intellectual *leadership*.

For their design development projects, students in these programs—often principals or lower-level administrators in central offices—rely on research know-how available through the university, and they use their leadership skills to form, nurture, and facilitate co-design teams in their own local systems. They in essence become the intellectual leaders for these co-design teams, and with their new capacities, these leaders may influence the mode of innovation in their local systems or districts. Local systems benefit from the intellectual capacities of the university in a mediated way, through the cadre of trained designers and the involvement of researchers in the designs. Researchers open up, and become more responsive to, the problems of practice initiated by local systems. The partnership is mediated through graduate students enrolled in leadership programs. As intellectual leaders, these individuals bridge the two worlds.

The majority of designers whom we have worked with, including those whose work we drew from to create the composite narratives for this book, do their design work within this type of partnership. These individuals joined the professional doctoral program at the University of California, Berkeley, already as distinguished leaders in their organizations. They work with academic advisers and are supported by a small group of staff trained in design development methodology. Most important, through their doctoral program, they form a network of local leaders, competent in design-based thinking and design-based research methods. At a certain tipping point, they may become a critical mass of leaders who, with concerted effort, push their local systems into a new mode of innovation and problem solving. The limits of the mediated type of partnership is that the professional graduate students work closely within their design network, but may be a rather isolated voice in their district.

For practical reasons, small and short-duration design teams, with one lone practitioner-scholar providing the theoretical and research expertise, are rarely able to carry out multiple design iterations. Thus, the designs may be *inherited* by a next generation or cohort of leaders, in or outside of the doctoral programs. This next generation can make adjustments and bring the original ideas to the point at which expected improvement and actual improvement are sufficiently close. On the other hand, in a more expanded design circle that includes district and university partners, it becomes feasible to carry out multiple iterations.

Integrated Co-design Partnerships

The integrated CDP is an extension of the mediated one. It comes into existence when university-based leadership programs partner with local school districts to train sizable numbers of employees for leadership positions in a given district. In this case, a critical number of district co-designers are trained in design-based thinking. When the district forms a design partnership with researchers around a focal problem of practice, these trained designers from the district play a constitutive role in the co-design team. In an integrated CDP, more people are aware of the benefits of this approach to innovation and are also more tolerant of the trials associated with it. The work can be distributed among many knowledgeable actors who act locally, but who are well connected to the university design network. A sizable group of people in the partnership speak the same language and have a common reference in design-based thinking. In an integrated CDP, university-based researchers are full members of the district-based co-design team.

As authors of this book, we have experimented with one such integrated partnership in a local district. The district formed a co-design team around a focal design challenge: how to enable teachers to participate in professional learning with a focus on students' academic engagement. In some sense, this design challenge is not unlike the one we have described for Eric in this book, though Eric is not involved in an integrated CDP. The cross-functional district co-design team consists of thirteen members: three district administrators, three instructional coaches, four principals, and three university-based researchers. Six of these thirteen people, being familiar with design development and trained in the leadership program, form a strong base.

During the first year, the integrated partnership had undergone its "fuzzy front-end" as some authors call this phase. The co-design responsibilities were widely distributed. The university folks were largely responsible for communicating the knowledge base to practitioners and for organizing data collection. The district actors were involved in all other aspects of the design. Perhaps not surprisingly, given the logic of design development, the team wrestled with three main challenges in this first year:

- *How to frame and define the problem*: For example, the work began with a drawn-out exploration, with the help of videos, of what student academic engagement with content looks like and how typical district teachers teach. We then examined how the learning challenge for the district should be framed. For some members of the team, student academic engagement was about participation strategies that teachers could implement in their lessons with little attention paid to content.

- *How to make explicit the group's intuitive theory action*: Participants put on the table various assumptions about how teachers learn. Some participants believed that teachers learn by being trained in a new approach supplied by a consultant; others thought that teachers learn through unobtrusive encouragement to follow their own leads and trains of thought. Some participants assumed that teachers' professional thinking was already there and simply needed to be awakened, while others asserted that a heavy dose of training in basic competencies was in order.

- *How to make a transition from one mode of innovation to another*: The team began its work within a tradition of buy and buy-in innovation and ended up with the realization that in a co-design process, innovation draws from an exchange between internal and external expertise. This meant that the team needed to assess how a designed model would fit with existing practices and expand on those practices. The team wrestled with who owned the innovation process: the researchers, who always seemed to be sure where they wanted to go without stating their aims clearly, or the practitioners, who knew what worked and, more important, what did not.

Co-design work creates uncertainty, involves unusual and sometimes intimidating intellectual work, and asks participants to give each other equal voice and judge a member's contribution to the process regardless of the bureaucratic or scientific authority of the speaker. When a co-design partnership works well, it is an immensely stimulating and rewarding experience for both researchers and practitioners.

CHAPTER SUMMARY

In this chapter, we introduced the concept of intellectual leadership. We made the following observations:

- Intellectual leaders are a cornerstone of design development. They have acquired the relevant expertise and play a critical role in communicating it to members of the co-design team who may be more peripheral to the research side of the design process.

- Co-design teams distribute the multiple responsibilities inherent in the design process across many organizational roles.

- Co-design partnerships distribute intellectual leadership, allowing multiple actors to contribute perspectives and expertise to the design, the implementation, and the study of innovative interventions.

- Co-design partnerships between universities or other knowledge-creating organizations and school districts or other similar administrative units can vary in the degree of integration. In fully integrated partnerships, researchers work directly inside district-based co-design teams. A critical number of intellectual leaders, trained in design-based thinking, are members of the team.

Understanding
the Problem

with Elizabeth Zumpe

As most people walk around with intuitive theories of action, they also have an intuitive understanding of problems. Most of us initially perceive a problem in a sort of fuzzy urgency. We just know something hurts, but we do not know specifically what it is. A sharper diagnosis goes a step further. It takes this fuzziness apart by asking specific questions:

→ Which symptoms of the problem are noticeable?

→ Across these symptoms, what patterns of behavior are apparent?

→ What underlying or root causes of this problem can be inferred from these patterns?

→ How does the literature help make sense of these inferences?

→ What theories can help explain this problem?

Education is not unlike the medical profession: a remedy is only as good as the diagnosis. This is why the process of diagnosis described here is meant to help designers think past their initial hunches. To put in place a remedy that is likely to make a difference, designers must do what they can to make sure they understand the problem accurately.

When people go to the doctor, they describe an ache or a pain. Of course, the doctor's mind starts generating assumptions about the malady the moment the person starts talking. But the doctor suspends judgment and proceeds with a diagnosis, beginning from the focal source of the person's pain, his or her symptoms, and branching out to other body functions that may be involved. Further tests are conducted, and the data are read. Finally, all the evidence is pulled together. But how does the doctor organize the evidence? The doctor uses his or her grasp of theoretical knowledge accumulated by medical research and contained in diagnostic manuals. This theoretical knowledge allows a physician to look beyond symptoms and infer root causes that he or she cannot directly observe. Without theoretically inferred diagnostic patterns, there would be no diagnosis or treatment. Thus, diagnosis consists of various layers that differ according to the extent to which one makes inferences and uses theory. In a similar vein, problem diagnosis begins with an exploratory needs assessment and continues from there, becoming ever more informed by theory. After looking at Christine in more detail in chapter 6, we trace these steps by looking at how Michelle and Nora work to better understand their problem of practice. We will follow up with Eric's story in chapter 9.

MICHELLE'S UNDERSTANDING OF THE PROBLEM

In addressing the question of culturally relevant instruction, Michelle has decided to observe classrooms to check her assumptions that the teachers at her school have low expectations of students of color because of deficit thinking: the belief that it is the students and their families that are lacking and that their habits justify low expectations. She begins by noticing surface behavior: *symptoms*. They are beliefs, attitudes, or practices that can be seen or heard immediately; in other words, they are readily observable behaviors. For example, she notices a teacher sitting at his desk reading the newspaper during instructional time. She further notices that the classroom is untidy. Something troubles her about this situation. It is something to look into further.

She fills in the symptoms by inferring a *pattern of behavior*. To do so, she makes sense of a set of perceptions or observable behaviors by grouping them together in a pattern that she names. Going back to the teacher mentioned above, she sees him sitting at his desk reading the newspaper, and she sees the untidy classroom. She notices further that his students are sullenly working on work-sheets in individual seatwork. When she talks to the teacher, he tells her that students are completing their homework in class. Getting homework back from students, he explains, is virtually impossible and he has given up even assigning it outside of class. Now, these three or four symptoms add up to a pattern that Michelle names: low levels of teacher effort. "Low effort" is an inference. One cannot directly observe it. One needs to construct it or interpret it. Effort, per se, is an abstraction; it is invisible. But Michelle has seen these symptoms before, and to her, they indicate low teacher effort.

Michelle wants to do something about the observed behavior. But to do so, she needs to know the reasons for the behavior pattern. The reasons are inferred. They are imputed to the observed patterns of behavior, but are removed from direct observations. These inferences often draw on common sense, but when designers need to see them in a broader context and explicitly name this context, they need social theory.

Michelle remembers reading in some articles that low effort is a common result of certain teachers' low expectations of their students. This finding seems to be a good fit with the pattern she has observed. She infers that the teacher has low expectations of himself and his students. But then there are other causal inferences that she could make: the teacher is burned out; the teacher is angry about having been involuntarily assigned to this class. So she can't be sure about her inference without gathering further information and testing her assumptions. When she asks the teacher how he feels about teaching at this school, she discovers that he hates being there. He gives two reasons: he believes that the community does not care about the children's educational success and that the faculty is resigned to this lack of interest and no longer cares either.

Note that the diagnosis of the problem should not be the absence of Michelle's preferred solution, as in "I just know that the low effort the teacher puts into his work is due to low expectations that he has for his disadvantaged students. So I need an intervention that addresses low expectations and deficit thinking, and I happen to have a solution to which I had been committed all along." If educational leaders diagnose problems this way, they will never know what thoughts or actions by the teachers are problematic, and the leaders' ideas of change will revolve around filling an empty vessel. But learners are not empty vessels. They have established patterns of thinking and feeling that somehow have worked for them. Leaders need to change these patterns. But to do that, leaders need to know what these patterns are.

ROOT CAUSES OF BEHAVIORAL PATTERNS

Underlying, or root, causes are factors that explain what contributes to the recurrence of a behavioral pattern or what holds it in place. Understanding these factors requires domain knowledge, that is, knowledge that helps structure the complexity in a field of work. In professional work, this domain knowledge is often theoretical. Underlying factors may be located in the macro-, meso-, or micro-spheres in which all actions are carried out.

We will explain some of these terms. The term *macro* refers to larger societal or institutional influences. In social theory, the term *institution* most often means the interplay of values, obligations, norms, laws, and organizational structures that make up, for example, school, family, or government in general. Institutions are not the same as organizations. George Washington High School is both an organization (a unique conglomerate of locally based actors) and an institution (a living example of all that is common to "school" in American society). Institutional factors are therefore macro. *Meso* refers to factors at the organizational level, and *micro* to factors influenced by individuals and their relationships with one another.

In Michelle's case, the teacher has pointed to macro- and meso-characteristics as reasons for his behavior. The macro-factor is the lack of caring by the communities of socioeconomically disadvantaged families, and the meso-factor is the faculty's lack of caring. It is quite possible that despite the teacher's own ideas about the reasons for his behavior, micro-factors are more strongly indicated: the teacher may be unable to control his classroom and to reach his students in a way that is personally meaningful to them or him, but he deflects this inability by blaming external macro- or meso-factors that remove him as a responsible actor in the micro-space.

Let's look more closely at how the teacher's behavior could be analyzed looking at macro-, meso-, and micro-factors. As we said, macro-factors are societal or institutional. For example, when the interviewed teacher makes assumptions about the community, he may draw from macro-level differences between various status groups in society, for example, between low- and high-income groups or between white people and people of color. Members of society on the whole attach differential value to these status groups. The teacher may use the devaluing of disadvantaged groups as a way to justify his own actions. Underlying factors could also be organizational, or at the meso-level. For example, faculties or leaders in given schools or districts might collectively hold certain beliefs or tolerate low standards of effort. Or organizational policies might create work situations that produce distress for individuals or groups, and the groups respond to the distress with defensiveness (e.g., blaming students).

Macro- or meso-factors, or both, may contribute to a micro-interaction pattern between the teacher and his class of students that might erode face-to-face communications between the adult and the children: the teacher assumes that the students are unwilling to learn, and the students assume that the teacher does not care. These underlying micro-factors may offer good explanations for the dysfunctionalities of the relationship: both teacher and students are reluctant to express their needs for competence and connection. But micro-level factors are often intricately interwoven with meso- and macro-factors. The problem of practice and its envisioned remedy determine how deeply one must dig to the roots and how macro or micro that digging needs to be. Most educational leaders operate on the micro- or meso-level. But leaders must be aware of macro-factors for meso-changes, and macro- and meso-factors for micro-changes. Conversely, many federal or state policy makers, wielding power at the macro-level, are often oblivious to the force of micro-factors that can doom their most well-designed policies. *Macro*, *meso*, and *micro* are relative terms. There are no clear dividing lines, and the levels are mutually intertwined.

CORE PRACTICES AND CONTEXT

As designers begin to read sources in the knowledge base, they discover that some sources speak to broader contextual conditions and some to the core practices of interest. What is *core* and what is *context* depends on the design focus. If teachers such as the one described above are the focus, then changing their attitudes is the core practice and organizational expectations (e.g., wide acceptance of nonteaching behavior) would be the context. If the organization is the focus, then changing organizational expectations would be the core and, for example, the structure of a school's internal and external accountability system would be the context. Or, for a different problem of practice, leaders like Eric may want to understand why instructional supervision in their district is poor. So they read about instructional leadership and discover that organizational demands on principals are many, often preempting principals from involvement in instruction (the context). The literature on instructional supervision describes specific competencies that are needed for good feedback (core practice). Sometimes, leaders may find it useful to define their core practices on multiple levels: for example, the organization's pattern of prioritizing and the principals' habit of giving superficial feedback.

DEEPENING OF NEEDS ASSESSMENTS

Local needs assessments become increasingly guided by theory after the designers have read the various knowledge bases relevant for understanding their problem of practice. With the help of the literature (and keeping their own intuitive understanding of the problem in mind), designers should be able to ascertain that the observed behaviors speak to some broader patterns that may be caused by a variety of factors that they can address in the intervention. Designers need theory and examples from empirical research and practical design knowledge to recognize high-inference patterns, to operationalize unobservable constructs in real life, and to capture causal explanations. Thus, this round of collecting evidence is not about mere concrete description, but about more high-inference explanations. But high inferences need to remain verifiable; designers cannot rely on their intuition, but need evidence, and the literature will show how to collect that evidence in a local situation. Let's see how Christine, Michelle, and Nora approach this task. We will return to Eric in subsequent chapters.

EXCURSION INTO THEORY

Inferences and Theoretical Understanding

Inferences

Inference is at the heart of the human ability to reason.[1] It allows people to know more than what can be literally seen or heard.[2] For example, people use inference when they draw a generalization from a set of particular details.[3] But the same ability to infer that humans need to reason is also a source of human subjectivity. Not all inferences are valid, of course. Inferring is an uncertain mental operation, yet we do it all the time. Indeed, much of how the human mind thinks could be described as "jumping to conclusions."[4] Inference permeates everyday human communication.[5] Without effort, when people try to explain something they have seen, heard, or understood, they typically use high-inference language: the teacher does not care, the student is lazy, the student is smart, the teacher is so motivated, and so forth.

High-inference language can be quite useful for everyday communication. But when it comes to gathering evidence, too much inference leads to bias that may render collected data invalid or unreliable. Even though we speak of high or low inference, inference is not dichotomous but a matter of degree. We already mentioned the metaphor of a ladder.[6] Low-inference descriptions are at the lowest rung on the ladder; these are stated in terms that are the closest to the observed phenomenon, without imposing interpretations on the observations. As descriptions ascend the ladder of inference, the language relies more on analysis or judgment of meaning.[7]

In research, both low- and high-inference descriptions are involved. While low-inference data increase the quality of evidence by allowing for exact descriptions, these descriptions do not speak for themselves.[8] Descriptive data need to be interpreted in reference to unseen or unobservable constructs or concepts that order the world in more abstract ways. Thus, interpreting data involves moving higher on the ladder of inferences.[9] The highest inferences rest on the abstract concepts of theory.

Understanding Problem Diagnosis

Using low-inference observations to generate high-inference accounts that rest on theory is another way to describe what happens when a problem is diagnosed.[10] We already mentioned the case of medical diagnosis. Here we recapitulate its description in more accurate terms: a doctor examines a set of low-inference data—a patient's symptoms, medical history, and test results—and from this evidence taps into his or her existing domain knowledge, case-based knowledge, heuristics, and statistical analysis skills to infer a diagnosis.[11] In the domain of organizational development, a leader or consultant engages in a similar process of diagnosis by gathering low-inference information about an inefficiency in the organization and inferring the causes of, and conditions that contribute to, the problem.[12]

Another take on problem diagnosis in organizations exists in the tradition of Total Quality Management. In this tradition, managers or consultants wanting to initiate improvements in the organization typically conduct a root-cause analysis. In this analysis, they look at a problematic behavior and try to figure out what in the organization might cause this behavior in terms of time management, personnel, skills, equipment, material, procedures, decision making, and so forth. The word *root* is a relative term. In root-cause analysis, *root* tends to connote the factors that the organization controls and that managers can manipulate. This is not the connotation of *root cause* that is often entertained in educational analysis. For example, Michael Rebell and Jessica Wolff employ a different kind of root-cause analysis in their discussion of the achievement gap: "America does not have a general education crisis; we have a poverty crisis."[13] Their root-cause analysis aims at the factors that substantially explain educational attainment, the well-being of young people, and the commitment of teachers. Education is a line of work whose success is fundamentally linked with factors outside the control of managers of educational organizations, for example, economic macro-structures that produce a rampant poverty problem for many children in the United States.

Equity-relevant design development, by its nature, concentrates on factors under the control of leaders, but at the same time, educational leaders would underestimate the problems they are facing if they were to ignore broader societal and institutional root causes. One cannot understand how to reduce racial and homophobic slurs without understanding racism and homophobia as root causes.

Theory and Domain Knowledge

As described in chapter 2, the problems facing educators tend to be ill structured. Addressing such problems more often relies on domain-specific knowledge than does addressing other types of problems.[14] Just as a doctor infers a diagnosis by tapping into domain knowledge about the human body and disease and his or her experience that has generated heuristics, statistical analysis skills, and knowledge of prior cases, so must an education leader tap into domain knowledge to infer a diagnosis—and design an intervention—for a problem of practice.

But what constitutes domain knowledge for an education leader, and in what knowledge bases does the leader need to be expert to be equipped to design an effective solution for an ill-structured problem? Presumably, educators should have domain knowledge on student learning, child development, pedagogy, special needs, and subject-specific content.[15] When an educator is a leader, another set of domain knowledge is needed—resource management, instructional leadership, along with context-specific knowledge related to policies, resources, job design, and the like.[16] When an education leader is also acting as a change agent, domain knowledge in areas such as adult learning, inquiry- or evidence-based decision making, social psychology, and organizational change and development is likely to be needed.[17]

In other words, to make strong inferences that will enable education leaders to understand and address ill-structured problems, the leaders need knowledge about human behavior in social environments like education—and for this, social theory plays a strong role. Explanations of why problems of educational inequity exist and persist, and how educators might diminish this inequality in schools, are steeped in concepts developed in social theory. For example, a diagnosis of the problem of performance pressure encountered by African American students in Advanced Placement classes will be more informed if a leader has some familiarity with the concept of stereotype threat, and a leader might not fully understand stereotype threat without having some knowledge of the macro-level structures of institutionalized racism.[18] At the same time, knowledge of macro-level structures is insufficient for action within a particular school context—for this, knowledge of micro-level behaviors is also needed. Or, more to the point, understanding what makes social problems in educational contexts exist and persist relates to understanding the connection between the macro- and micro-levels of human behavior.[19]

MICHELLE'S DEEPENING UNDERSTANDING OF THE PROBLEM

In light of her initial observations about culturally relevant instruction in her racially balanced school district, Michelle returns to her district committee members. She proposes that they think about their problem of practice more deeply before they proceed to implementing a solution. They are open to listening to what Michelle has to say, but this does not mean that she has their agreement or support.

Michelle strives to become an intellectual leader in her committee, and with the help of resources drawn from her doctoral program, she decides to read up on some literature that can help her understand the problem. She consults several topics in the literature: instruction that fosters student academic engagement; cultural relevance; implementing prescriptive programs; teacher expectations and defensiveness, especially around class and ethnicity; and organizational culture of schools. First she finds that academic engagement involves not only teachers' subject-matter knowledge, cultural competence, and ability to activate student voice, but also instructional complexity, instructional flexibility, and classroom management issues. Prescriptive programs, she concludes, are perhaps useful as scaffolds for less-experienced teachers, but in the long run, the programs do not facilitate student engagement. She realizes that cultural relevance is not just about culturally relevant content, but also about developing a curious, open, and positive attitude on the part of teachers toward the life experiences of students. Moreover, cultural relevance is also about the teachers' own work lives as educational professionals.

Even though societal influences are strong, teacher expectations and explanations of success and failure seem to be influenced by organizational expectations, routines, norms, and discourses at local schools. So, Michelle concludes, the organizational routines (i.e., prescriptive programs) and organizational expectations (especially around teacher performance) are essential in shaping how teachers teach and relate to students. Organizational cultures develop collective justifications that people use in order to feel good about themselves when they face challenging problems in their environments.

Michelle senses that the district equity committee is hesitant to follow her in her analysis. So she finds two other principals who are interested in looking at this issue more deeply. She suggests that they look for evidence of what she has now identified as important causes of disengagement in students of color: limited teacher knowledge and instructional competence, obstructive organizational routines and expectations (including her own as a leader), teachers' defensive responses to failure, teachers' negative assumptions about students and families, and teachers' limited professional curiosity. The data from the three schools suggest that quite a number of teachers in the district feel that they have low efficacy in teaching the more complex parts of the curricular programs and that they cling to prescriptive programs. The principals—Michelle included—seem not too concerned about program implementation with fidelity, but they do want to see high performance on the six-week benchmarks attached to the curricular programs. And the principals' supervisors insist on careful monitoring. Feeling pressure to deliver the numbers, the teachers therefore seem to stick to the script. When they fall short of delivering on the benchmark tests, they deflect criticism by pointing to students' and families' deficits and clamor for more district support. Michelle concludes that teachers' feelings of low efficacy in teaching outside the prescriptive programs and the pressure to perform on tests aligned to the programs has created a prescription and coverage mind-set in teachers that desensitizes them to their students' needs.

After their extended needs assessment, Michelle's group of three has a different idea about their problem, and their search for solutions has moved in a different direction. Initially, Michelle perceived the problem intuitively as one of white teachers who lacked cultural sensitivity and a willingness to engage with equity goals. And as a solution, she was thinking about two measures: workshops in which culturally relevant curricula would be introduced and charismatic speakers who could create an awareness of the problem. After the second round of needs assessment, this perception of the problem has not disappeared, but it has expanded. Work organization, pressures and sanctions, teachers' self-defense mechanisms, and a solid prescription and coverage mind-set now play a larger role. The search for solutions has moved outward toward organizational mechanisms and inward towards fine-grained instructional competence. Michelle and her two principal colleagues conclude that culturally relevant pedagogy needs to be folded into a new adult learning culture around instruction. Administrators need to relax narrow curricular pressures. Teachers need to be encouraged to keenly observe student learning, to approach their work with curiosity, and to tailor their instruction to student learning needs encountered in their daily lessons.

NORA'S UNDERSTANDING OF THE PROBLEM

Through their exploratory data collection, Nora and her leadership team diagnose the following symptoms: racial and homophobic slurs are rampant in their school, and despite the frequency of slurs, the situation is often ignored. As the intellectual leader of the team, Nora reads up on the literature and shares a few key articles with her colleagues. Her knowledge base consists of various overlapping areas: homophobia and racism, the function of slurs and bullying, organizational culture and leadership generically, professional development, facilitation of courageous conversations, and changing school culture for educational equity. From the literature, Nora recognizes four main causes for rampant slurs: (1) society produces racist and homophobic dispositions that are concealed but find an outlet in slurs; (2) people, personally, fear to say the wrong thing around issues of racism and homophobia; (3) organizational cultures maintain patterns of silence around race or sexual orientation, and these patterns make people afraid of stepping on other people's toes; and (4) people lack strategies of intervening. This literature refines the leadership team's needs assessment. The team decides to involve colleagues in informal conversations about slurs. These colleagues report back to the team a variety of opinions. Some teachers simply do not believe that there is a problem with slurs. Other teachers are certain that they have the situation under control. Still others fearfully avoid talking about the topic. Teachers report simply not knowing what to do when a student uses a slur against another student; they fear backtalk from the student. A number of teachers recognize the problem and want to do something about it. But because nobody talks about it at the organizational level and addresses the issue straight on, even people who feel uncomfortable with the status quo feel powerless to do something about it.

Nora and her team have a sense of the underlying causes of their problem of practice. But that does not mean that they know what disrupts this behavior. For this, they need a better understanding of the change process relevant to their problem.

CHAPTER SUMMARY

Nora and Michelle understand their problems of practice more deeply by looking at evidence. Some of that evidence comes from within their organizations, through needs assessments. With this evidence, they note various aspects of the problem:

- *Symptoms*: observable behaviors, beliefs, attitudes, or practices

- *Patterns of behavior*: groups of symptoms that relate to each other

- *Possible causes*: explanations for what makes a pattern occur and recur

Usually the evidence designers gather from within the organization will not answer all their questions. As for Nora and her team, it may not be immediately clear what's at the root of the problem. Or, as was the case for Michelle, designers may find that there are other, overlooked explanations for the problem at hand. To have a better understanding of the problem, therefore, designers need to consult the literature to challenge their assumptions, find out what is known about this problem, and consider the theories that might help them to explain what causes it. In this exploration of the literature, they seek to understand *underlying or root causes*, including these factors:

- *Macro-*, *meso-*, and *micro*-level factors

- Factors related to the *core practices*

- Factors related to the *contextual conditions* of the problem

- *Theoretical understanding* that weaves together macro-, meso-, and micro-factors

8

Understanding the
Change Process

Design development studies are action oriented. Having a clear idea about the problem of practice and knowing its causes is a first step, but it is not sufficient. Knowing, for example, that GLT (Grade-level team) development will have to deal with distressed teachers who are challenged in central aspects of their competence does not mean that Christine's team knows what to do about it. And although Michelle's group knows that habitual compliance with prescriptive instructional programs has prevented teachers from finding deeper connections with their poor students of color, the group does not know how to lessen and overcome this problem. They cannot simply walk up to their teachers and tell them, "Today is a new day. Stop what you are doing, and listen to what we want you to do *now*."

Adults do not learn this way, though in alienated work environments that bank on control rather than self-determination, employees are often treated this way. For example, Eric, as a district administrator, knows that busy principals focused on administrative procedure may dispense with their instructional supervision duty by looking for simple lesson structures that they can easily observe and tally. But this insight does not tell him how to bring home to his principals the concept of student academic engagement. He can't just give his principals a workshop during which he says to them, "The state has adopted new standards that require us to up our game. We need to pay attention to the way students learn more complex subject matter content. You will be evaluated on these new standards in short order. Now listen to me carefully . . ."

Finally, knowing that her faculty's silence about rampant slurs has something to do with the fears surrounding racism and homophobia does not mean that Nora's team has learned how to lessen the effect of these institutional forces. The team surely cannot confront their colleagues by announcing, "We are a social-justice school. And yet we hear slurs all the time. Shame on you for not doing more about it. You need to acknowledge your racism and homophobia."

The relationship between the causes of problems and the dynamics of the change that will lessen the power of these causes is rarely straightforward. But sometimes, educational leaders treat this relationship as more straightforward than it is. They use directive and control as their "motivation" strategy and fill colleagues or subordinates with interminable professional development as a "learning" strategy. But leaders cannot expect to advance on equitable schools this way. Equitable schooling comes about when adults use their scarce resources wisely and efficiently to equalize learning opportunities; consider students complex human beings, capable of cognitively and morally complex reasoning; and treat them with respect, dignity, and fairness. Equity-minded designs need to enable change processes that follow the same principles for *adults*. Overly controlled, disrespected, and de-intellectualized teachers are not likely to be receptive to the message of equity.

The observation that educational change is complex is almost a self-evident banality, given the sheer human complexity of educational settings experienced in an especially acute way by those closest to the core of the work. Yet, when educators act as change agents, they need to reduce this complexity and decide on the forces, or drivers, they believe will cut through this complex web of human relationships and move it in the desired direction. We have used the term *drivers* before. In the change management literature, this term has a special meaning: it encapsulates the main forces that managers or leaders believe will be of high leverage to effect intended changes.

Equity-relevant designs pivot on results, but this does not mean that *any* change process that produces results on whatever indicator we may have chosen is acceptable. The ends do not justify the means. In the United States, for over a decade, we in the field of education have had the benefit of experiencing one pervasive macro-design for school improvement: high-stakes accountability as spelled out in the No Child Left Behind (NCLB) Act of 2001. NCLB advanced a specific adult "learning" model that was heavy on measurement, sanctions, control, and corrective intervention as its main drivers. These drivers seem to have largely been successful in raising test scores on state assessments, but they encouraged an adult learning model that by all indications led teachers to narrow and fragment the curriculum and make instruction more teacher-centered and controlling.[1] Designs can go wrong, and the authoritativeness of government is surely no guarantee for having found the best-practice solution.

In this chapter, we discuss the change process in more detail. We address the following questions:

→ Why is it so difficult to improve and change education organizations?
→ What main organizational dimensions are implicated in educational change?
→ What assets can educational leaders use to address problems of practice?
→ What do actors within the organization need to learn or unlearn?
→ What are the main drivers that foster or elicit this learning?

To answer these questions, we begin by looking at the political and organizational context of change within education organizations. Next we introduce *asset maps* as a way to highlight the strengths that a change in an organization may take advantage of. We look into the idea of change drivers and apply it to Nora's design challenge. We show how identifying promising drivers helps her understand the complexity of her change process.

CHANGE AND STABILITY

On the surface, educational organizations can look as if they are in a constant flux. They seem to engage in continuous improvement, but below the surface, these organizations are hard to change.[2] Students, parents, teachers, and communities expect schooling to be conducted in established ways. Courses, diplomas, grades, curricula, norms of behavior, classrooms, and so on, are rooted in traditional beliefs of what a "real school" ought to look like.[3] Bolstered by most people's first-hand experiences in the system, these beliefs are communicated from one generation to the next. Dramatic changes in schooling are often not the schools' own making, but occur in association with dramatic changes in norms, values, expectations, and demands in the wider society.[4]

Often, changes emanate from top-down policies pushed by powerful interest groups and elite actors or by bottom-up social movements. An example from history may be the dramatic struggle to end legal racial segregation in the United States and the slow, cultural reorientation regarding corporal punishment. Thus, in schools, educators, parents, students, and local communities interact with each other within relatively fixed formal organizational structures, and shared meanings cannot easily be dislodged or changed. To those who spend time in these organizations or interact with them, inequities in schooling often appear as the natural way things ought to be or at least ought to be coped with as fact.

Changing the behavior of those who provide services in educational organizations involves organizational structures and resources that distribute learning opportunities. Changing behavior involves knowledge and skill, attention, motivation, and setting priorities and goals. But most of all, it involves shared meanings, interpretations, expectations, norms, values, rituals, and routines that are largely tacit and subconscious. Shared meanings hold together schooling as an institution, an enterprise that is at its core full of ambiguity and contradiction. Educational organizations have developed specific cultures as a way of coping with this ambiguity. Organizational cultures—summarized by Edgar Schein as "the ways we do things around here"—have a seemingly proven track record of getting things done and maintaining people's sense of self-worth, or doing an acceptable job.[5] People, therefore, can get defensive when this culture seems under attack.

Because of this defensiveness, leaders can't simply change people by telling them what they think is wrong with them or what they believe are the root causes of their behavior. Leaders can't change people's attitudes by simply scolding them, confronting them with their "failures," or telling them that they are self-serving, defensive, compliant, or conformist in the face of injustice. Effective leaders need ways to reduce defensiveness and strengthen courage. They need to strategize a process of change that unfolds in the zone of the next level of work, within people's capacity to stretch. That capacity is significantly boosted when one starts from people's assets and strengths. Challenges and pressures are part of the picture of change, but change is easier when those aiming to change others uncover people's positive desires for autonomy, competence, belonging, and justice.

SHIFTING TOWARD ASSET-BASED CHANGE

As there are many ways to define an ill-structured problem of practice, there are many ways one could go about solutions, or processes of change, that may improve on the problem. When thinking about these possible ways, designers should consider the relevance of multiple individual and organizational dimensions of human action, if they are going to move people:

- Knowledge, skills, and competence
- Values and aspirations
- Rules and regulations
- Routines, habits, and norms
- Tools, instruments, and artifacts in use
- Goals and goal setting
- Motivation, commitment, and energy
- Autonomy and freedom
- Desire to connect and belong to a community
- Authority of demands, expectations, and priorities
- Micro-politics of who wins or loses status

These dimensions can be put in a matrix called an asset map. This map guides the assessment of assets and main dimensions of change. Some envisioned changes may be knowledge- or skill-intensive. Some may involve work on new values or the rekindling of old commitments. Others are about new goals and the unleashing of new energy. Change processes that upset the autonomy, power, or status of some people in the organization and favor others may have to reckon with the micro-politics of authority, hierarchy, status, and autonomy. Table 8.1 shows how Christine, Michelle, and Eric use an asset map to sketch the assets and main dimensions of change for their change projects. The asset map lists the assets that are present, not those that are lacking.[6]

At the core of change is *learning*, that is, the unlearning of unwanted beliefs, attitudes or practices and the learning of new ones. Even when leaders change a rule, use a new instrument, create a new organizational structure, or allocate new resources, at the core, people need to learn what to do with these new conditions. From their understanding of the problem, leaders already know what the unwanted behaviors are or where existing behaviors set limits. But they do not know how to dislodge these behaviors, what to replace them with, and what learning processes need to unfold in people. Note that we are not yet talking about activities. When educational leaders become designers, they first need to know what people need to learn or unlearn.

EXCURSION INTO THEORY

Drivers of Change

In complex organizations, the unfolding of change processes is full of contingencies and unforeseeable events, and change is often the result of what Bernard Burnes calls an "untidy cocktail" of rational planning, political struggle, movement-like evangelizing, contradictory beliefs and worldviews, structural impediments, and so on.[7] Some have used complexity and chaos theory to explain change in educational organizations.[8] But organizational change is not random. Beginning with Kurt Lewin's early work on planned organizational change, researchers have aimed to identify organizational levers or drivers that can foment particular change dynamics and produce intended outcome.[9] Market pressures and new technologies are the main drivers of change in a dynamic of firms competing with each other for profit, often resulting in higher productivity. Scholars of high-stakes accountability in schools have found that sanctions, for example, the

TABLE 8.1   Map of assets that support the change process: three design projects as examples

DIMENSION OF CHANGE	INDIVIDUAL OR ORGANIZATIONAL ASSETS		
	Christine	*Michelle*	*Eric*
Knowledge	Senior teachers and administrators are on hand to spread their experience and expertise to novices.	Teachers implement a solid curriculum that is adopted by the district and that can be tweaked toward teaching for understanding.	Principals are knowledgeable about standard evaluations.
Values	All participants value a safe and orderly school.	Participants desire to reach all students.	Principals value good instruction.
Rules	All schools have clearly spelled-out behavioral rules that can be used as a point of departure.		Instructional supervision is a mandatory part of the principal's job.
Routines	Participants understand that over-referring will not solve the problem.	Teachers are practiced in teaching reading and comprehension skills.	The existing instructional supervision practices are a good point of departure.
Tools and materials	The positive behavior intervention and support (PBIS) model is available.	Culturally responsive materials and strategies are available.	Observation tools and videos are available.
Goals	Middle schools embrace reduction in referred students and better problem solving for individual students.	District aims toward better cognitive outcomes, higher student participation.	District aims toward high academic achievement for its schools.
Competence	Senior teachers are on hand to share expertise.	Teachers are solid in implementing a literacy program.	Principals for the most part are competent administrators.
Motivation	Novices are eager to learn how to manage classroom and want to be humane teachers.	Teachers are positively inclined toward students and worried that the prescribed material and pacing may not reach all students.	Most principals are eager to improve their supervision skills.
Autonomy		Teachers are appreciating more autonomy in reaching students.	
Community	Teachers suffer and want to connect.		
Authority	The district and administrators are behind the change effort.	The adoption of the new core curriculum is moving the district away from narrow monitoring of fidelity to the script.	The district is behind the change effort.
Status	All stakeholders share a common urgent problem regardless of status.		New competence enhances principals' status with teachers and affords better feedback.

threat of school closure, can be powerful drivers of change, though the change dynamic they trigger can vary.[10] Some schools anxiously freeze up while others begin an earnest search for solutions. Market pressures, new technologies, or accountability sanctions are external drivers that push an organization to change, but how they link to internal processes is often tenuous and unpredictable. Internal drivers are those that the organization itself manipulates to achieve its goals.[11]

W. Warner Burke and George Litwin have introduced a model of organizational change and performance that locates some of these drivers in the organization (though they themselves do not use the term *driver*).[12] The model makes a distinction between transformational and transactional dynamics of change. In transactional dynamics, behavior is changed through a negotiated give-and-take. In transformational dynamics, new behavior emerges when leaders appeal to, and mobilize, employees' values or commitments. Leadership, organizational mission, or organizational culture drive transformational change. Formal organizational structure, policies, procedures, tasks, management practices, incentives, and so on, drive transactional change.

Another model of change, suggested by Quy Nguyen Huy, consists of four main drivers and their attendant change dynamics: commanding, engineering, teaching, and socializing.[13] He links these broad driving forces to the content of intended changes and the envisioned time horizons. For example, a commanding dynamic is indicated when organizations need rapid change due to market urgencies. Engineering applies when workplace processes are to be changed over an extended period. A teaching dynamic is indicated when organizations are trying to make episodic or intermittent changes in people's beliefs, and longer-term socialization comes into play when social relationships need to be transformed. Within each of these broad forces, commanding, engineering, learning, and socializing, there are more specific drivers that aim at concrete behavior change. For example, in a socialization dynamic, collegial groups, continuous communication by authoritative leaders, and episodic check-ins are suitable drivers of change, while work process reengineering may be driven by short cycles of data-driven trial and error organized in cross-functional learning teams or inquiry groups.

Depending on the intended change, some drivers may be more important than others. Determining which drivers will have the most leverage in addressing a particular intent is key in developing a sound understanding of the change process given a specific problem. As we will explain in detail later in this chapter, driver diagrams are illustrative maps that outline the main drivers in play to move a group of people from a problematic behavior to a desired one.[14] Such diagrams help show which drivers are likely to have the greatest influence on the learning or unlearning that needs to take place.[15] Moreover, driver diagrams facilitate collaborative work; they become a shared reference point for problem solvers or designers to brainstorm possible interventions.[16]

Organizational Change as Learning

The core of change, especially in educational organizations, is learning.[17] Organizational learning can occur at various levels of depth. The terms *single-loop* and *double-loop learning* have been widely used to describe these various levels.[18] In single-loop learning, learners address routine organizational problems that can be remedied without examining deeper values and assumptions that govern decision making. In double-loop learning, more deeply entrenched problems are addressed. At this level of learning, governing values and assumptions that are ordinarily tacit or taken for granted become part of the learning process. Double-loop learning especially considers people's unacknowledged defenses against threats to their competence, self-worth, and status in the organizational hierarchy. Many equity-relevant problems require double-loop learning. Designers concerned about these problems need to understand how a change process can help people engage in deep learning and overcome defensiveness. Good theories of action rest, for the most part, on plausible theories of deep learning that is fostered by change drivers.

NORA'S UNDERSTANDING OF THE CHANGE PROCESS

What must people learn—and unlearn—to disrupt an organization, so that silence, fear of talking about race and sexual orientation, and helplessness can be addressed? In looking at the problem of racial and homophobic slurs in high schools, Nora's team uncovers interesting literature on courageous conversations, but the team members are not sure what the content of these courageous conversations should be. They find in their local district a consultant organization that specializes in facilitating courageous conversations, and they plan to contact the consultant. Nora and her colleagues also read about how silences can be disrupted through cognitive dissonance between what people feel they ought to do (normative commitments) and what people are actually doing. When people become aware of these sorts of dissonances, conversations may ensue. The literature also tells them that any kind of deeper cultural change requires a delicate balance between dissonance and psychological safety.[19] Helplessness, the team learns, can be overcome with open communication and an incipient willingness to take risks in a safe environment. Also useful are concrete strategies that guide people on how to act when they face someone who is using slurs. These new strategies need to be practiced regularly so that people become comfortable with them and effective in using them. Now Nora's team has a set of concepts that help the team understand what they need to learn or unlearn.

Drivers

But how should Nora and her leadership team get the desired change off the ground? Complex organizations, such as their school, are not places in which managers announce changes and workers implement them as planned. Rather, Nora's team needs to find change drivers that may sway faculty members to engage with the desired change, in the process creating a self-reinforcing dynamic that hopefully is strong enough to withstand distractions, competing demands, or inertia. Leaders could engineer a change by moving people into different jobs. They could also reorganize roles, tasks, or procedures; allocate resources differently; exploit new incentives, or use new technologies. They could teach by spreading new knowledge and skills and by communicating new ideas or values. They could employ training, collegial reflection, and inquiry. Or leaders could socialize by continuously reminding employees of the organization's mission or by modeling the behavior that they want their employees to exhibit. They could engage in debates on value conflicts or goal ambiguities. Finally, they could use straightforward command and control.

What are suitable drivers in Nora's case? The team recognizes that the desired change is not about getting the work done more efficiently. So manipulating tasks and procedures, for example, is not an appropriate driver of change. Goals and incentives are not good drivers, for the same reasons. Nor is technology involved. The team cannot simply command teachers to intervene whenever they hear a slur, since they subconsciously ignore the high frequency of slurs; nor can leaders simply confront the teachers, since this would reinforce the teachers' defensiveness. Working on a shared vision, modeling behavior, faculty-wide debate about values; follow-up reflection in smaller, more informal, collegial formats; and training in new competencies are the drivers that the team selects to facilitate voluntary participation of teachers in changing the culture of their school. These generic drivers need to be made more concrete with respect to slurs: an awareness of value dissonance ("we are a social-justice-themed school, and yet, we ignore slurs), guilt, and discomfort; the psychological safety to acknowledge these difficulties; and an appeal to shared values are elements of courageous conversations. Two additional drivers reinforce the commitment to act: a deeper understanding of, and reflection about, how slurs function and hurt and, finally, competence and a sense of efficacy in knowing what to do when teachers hear slurs. Figure 8.1 outlines all these more specific drivers of change.

Activities

Once the problem is diagnosed and suitable drivers of change are selected, activities are planned accordingly. These activities work in specific contexts and rely on local knowledge and ideas. More about this in the following chapter.

FIGURE 8.1   Nora's driver diagram

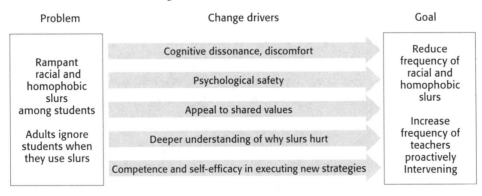

Contexts

In Nora's case, the literature makes it clear that the wider political and normative environment and the values of local communities are essential in moving equity-focused designs forward. In this case, Nora is lucky: her context bestows her with a strong set of assets. Her district's policies and leaders are thoroughly in favor of creating a positive climate of cultural diversity. She can also bank on a cadre of social-justice-oriented teacher-leaders. The literature also indicates that courageous conversations require time, resources, and energy. Here, Nora sees constraints: her district is characterized by resource scarcities, organizational turbulence, low programmatic coherence, high turnover, and very little extra time for professional development. How can the team make its intervention stick under these circumstances?

In sum, designers' understanding of the change process spells out how they think people will change their beliefs, attitudes, or practices in the desired direction. Designers should keep in mind the following specifics of the change process:

- The learning that needs to take place and the motivation that needs to be instilled
- The main, relevant dimensions of change
- The drivers believed to motivate the intended change dynamic and the problem-specific activities in broad strokes
- The context-specific conditions that may either benefit or hurt implementation

Design-based thinking benefits from intuition and innovation, but a theory of action that logically conceptualizes the connection between both the problem and the change process is key. Beyond using common sense, leaders draw from the established professional knowledge base: research, theory, and professional design knowledge.

In sum, Nora and her team want to do something about the rampant racial and homophobic slurs in their school. Their knowledge base, accumulated through Nora's intellectual leadership, consists of various overlapping areas: homophobia and racism, the function of slurs and bullying, organizational culture and leadership generically, professional development, facilitation of courageous conversations, and changing a culture for educational equity. Each body of literature helps the team formulate a deeper understanding of the problem and its causal factors and better envision an intervention likely to succeed. The literature on slurs (e.g., on the effects of slurs and their embeddedness in societal structures of economic inequity and cultural oppression) helps the team members understand their problem and the obstacles in reducing slurs. The literature on organizational change processes gives them a general idea of how organizations change their deep culture. The literature on professional development for equity describes the effectiveness or ineffectiveness of various cultural-change projects in educational settings. And sources discussing courageous conversations go to a practice at the heart of an equity-centered change process. Finally, the literature on social justice leadership gives the design team the needed emphasis on normative commitments, moral energy, and the forces needed to marshal against obstacles and odds.

After consulting a wide swath of sources in the knowledge base, Nora is ready to conceptualize the complex ecology within which design-based change unfolds.[20] Through Nora's initiative, the group has come to understand the societal, institutional, and organizational context (e.g., homophobia, racism) of the core practice they are trying to change. They zero in on this core practice (e.g., the slippery nature of slurs, willful ignorance and silences) and have a theory about what learning is needed (e.g., cognitive and normative dissonance, safe space, value conflict, competence, and efficacy) and what formats of change are appropriate to get the learning going against obstacles (e.g., schoolwide debate, courageous conversations, transformative leadership). Now that the change is broadly conceptualized, Nora's team is ready to specify its goals, aims, or desired state and plan activities accordingly.

CHAPTER SUMMARY

This chapter described how designers gain a deeper understanding of the change process related to a focal problem of practice. We have described the following about organizational change:

- Designers must understand the environment in which they are attempting to make improvements; educational organizations are governed by meanings and traditions shared among many stakeholders and by work routines that structure what people do on a daily basis in taken-for-granted ways.

- To disrupt these taken-for-granted beliefs, attitudes, or practices, one cannot simply tell people what is wrong with them.

- Designers need to search for assets that they can use to their benefit as launching pads for change. Building on assets stretches people's capacity to change.

- Identifying drivers concentrates the change process on those learning dynamics that designers believe will have the largest impact on moving people toward the intended changes. Drivers reinforce assets and diminish the power of inertia. They add more knowledge and skill, more motivational energy, higher aspirations and expectations, a higher sense of efficacy, and a keen sense of hope and optimism.

PART II SUMMARY

Design development combines disciplined inquiry about improving on focal problems of practice with action. In part I of the book, we discussed what focal problems of practice might be suitable and how they might be defined and framed. We showed that designers use the full benefit of their practitioner intuition to get a start on their theory of action. Needs assessments and consulting the professional knowledge base put this theory of action on an increasingly analytical footing.

In part II, we fleshed out the theory of action more fully. A deeper understanding of the problem and the change process has complemented the theory. Designers gain an understanding of the problem by studying symptoms, patterns of behavior, and possible causes. Gathering evidence, from low-inference descriptions to increasingly higher-inference interpretations, is linked to social theory. Theory helps designers see the connection between micro-, meso-, and macro-factors. These factors are the root causes that produce and reproduce problematic practices. Some of these root causes are under the direct control of educational administrators. But others, especially those producing inequity and injustice, are deeply interwoven into the very fabric of society shaping macro-structures of institutions, meso-structures of organizational procedures, and micro-structures of educators interacting with students on a daily basis.

There are many ways to imagine change processes for a given problem of practice. Designers need to make choices. These choices are not arbitrary. Equity-relevant change processes are multidimensional, often transformational, and assets-based. Identifying change drivers reduces the complexity of the change process in the minds of the designers and thereby makes the process more manageable. The change drivers highlight, and help designers focus their attention on, learning dynamics that will—hopefully—have the largest impact on moving people toward the desired changes.

Depending on the robustness of the professional knowledge base, theories of action predict behavior changes with varying degrees of certainty and conjecture. Typically, design development should occur in co-design teams that distribute design responsibilities among different members, who fulfill various roles or functions related to the chosen problem of practice. Within co-design teams, some members must be the source of intellectual leadership while others are legitimately more peripheral to that function. Partnerships with universities or other knowledge-generating organizations that value intellectual work facilitate this type of leadership. After compiling their theory of action, designers are now ready to get close to action when they translate theory into an actual set of activities that make up their intervention.

Preparing to Intervene

9

Designing Interventions

An intervention design consists of a sequence of activities that together or in combination intervene in existing knowledge, beliefs, dispositions, or routines in order to prompt new learning that leads to new practices. The activities could revolve around new inquiries, materials, tools, rules, procedures, or financial resources that foster opportunities for new practices to take hold. Interventions are *designed* and *pivot on outcomes.* That is, interventions are formal activities planned for a defined period, with a precise goal or desired change in mind, for a specific organizational setting. But this does not mean that designers should expect to reach the full scope of outcomes in the first few iterations. Intervention designs are artifacts or concrete expressions of underlying theories of action. They are not unlike a teacher's lesson plan that lists instructional activities, but implies the teacher's underlying idea of how students learn the new content.

In this chapter, we address the following questions:

→ How can designers move from ideas to activities—that is, turn their ideas about how adults develop new beliefs, attitudes, and practices into activities that will foster adult learning?

→ How do designers make sure that the activities they choose actually move adult learners to the envisioned desired state?

→ How do designers deal with the tension between the need to predict the outcomes of their design and the need to be flexible?

→ What role do small-scale interventions play in the big picture of making schools more effective and more just?

Two sides of designing interventions are in tension with each other. On one hand, designs bank on firm predictions. On the other hand, they are imbued with the fluidity of human action. Design development marries the real-life challenges of organizations, with all their human complexity, contingency, and unpredictability, with the controlled and systematic approaches of researched interventions.

A good design is compelling, sometimes even enthralling. When we feel that an object is useful, comforting, and aesthetically pleasing in a certain economy and simplicity of design, we consider it well designed. A well-designed object serves our needs well because designers have expended special effort to come up with shapes and functions that meet these needs. Behold the design of a beautiful lesson: from beginning to end, students and teachers are engrossed in the new content, participation is high, the lesson artfully moves from phase to phase, student learning seems to flow effortlessly, and the lesson ends with a dazzling synthesis of what has been learned. Behind this beautiful lesson is a designer who has a keen understanding of the students' learning needs, who knows what stimulates and comforts them, who knows how to create access to new and challenging content with effective scaffolds, and who finally has a deep professional appreciation for the aesthetic of learning that "flows."[1] But even the most effective teachers know that the best lesson plan can go awry when the kids have a bad day.

In the design of an intervention, all members of the co-design team, and even those peripheral to the co-design effort, have a stake, and all can contribute with good ideas. Thinking like a designer, therefore, means being willing to transform one's own learning. According to Argyris and Schön, there are two patterns of learning, which they termed model 1 and model 2.[2] In model 1, actors want to be in control and win, but do not acknowledge that these values govern their actions. In the organization, they advocate for their position in ways that discourage inquiry into, or testing of, the effectiveness or appropriateness of their approaches. Since they know better, they encourage limited learning that leads to defensiveness and "self-sealing" among people involved in the learning.[3]

In model 2, actors value informed choice and are open to questioning their preferred approach's effectiveness or rightfulness. They encourage inquiry and critique that allow learners in the organization to overcome defensiveness and tap into the deeper governing values and assumptions that hold existing beliefs and practices in place. Equity-relevant designs are not done *to* people but are developed *with* people in a co-design dynamic. Therefore, interaction in a co-design team means deliberately creating a culture of dialogue that enables all members, regardless of status and role in the organization, to engage in model 2 learning.

The aim is not to plan fixed and comprehensive interventions that are implemented with fidelity, but to distill some prototypical elements (activities, tools, learning principles) that are iteratively tried out, analyzed, and revised until an acceptable balance between ideals and reality has been achieved. Most often, the final form and impact of the intervention cannot be anticipated with clarity. Thus, designers operate with uncertainty, but they aim at bounding this uncertainty by being crystal clear about their intended outcomes and the role each piece of an intervention plays in the unfolding of the theorized learning process.

Three qualities make design development *research-based* (more about this in chapter 10):

- Interventions consist of carefully planned tools, activities, or organizational formats that are hypothesized to elicit or foster the kind of adult learning needed to achieve intended outcomes.
- Trial and error in accomplishing outcomes is deliberate; it is undergirded by a theory of action drawn from the professional knowledge base. The theory's validity can be assessed by evidence that intervention activities generate.
- Data are collected according to reliable procedures that document and evaluate the design implementation process and impact.

Most continuous quality improvement approaches are similar in principle: they engage in evidence-based inquiry to test assumptions about change to verify a theory of action. But the approaches may differ in how much they stress pragmatism over theory. Some approaches privilege practical, intuitive wisdom and short trial-and-error cycles. The approach chosen here stresses the role of intellectual leaders as scholarly practitioners. They thoroughly consult the research and professional knowledge base around a focal problem of practice, and they think carefully about their problem and their change process. Their goal is to plan interventions that are research-based. But quick tryouts or mini-experiments may precede the implementation of their full intervention.

CHRISTINE'S INTERVENTION DESIGN

We described earlier how Christine's district task force brainstormed an intuitive understanding of its focal problem (i.e., behavior management in middle schools staffed with large numbers of novice teachers), conducted exploratory and more systematic needs assessments, and ended up narrowing and redefining their problem of practice as one of developing grade level teams under distressing conditions. Through Christine's leadership, they found the professional and research knowledge base on PLCs useful for spelling out the basic steps of developing PLCs. These steps included aiming at a shared vision, clarifying a common mission, setting goals, and creating a collective focus on student learning. But the task force also found that PLCs are not easy to implement and that, under even normal circumstances, teacher learning communities can gravitate toward contrivance, superficiality, or conflict as they run up against established norms of privacy and isolation in the face of performance anxiety. In searching for ways to shore up PLCs under conditions of distress, they discovered a different knowledge base on group and work-team development, group conflict, and work-team diversity. This knowledge base gave them ideas for their theory of change. They realized that novice teachers needed to learn how to seek help and to support one another, how to better address behavioral problems of students they shared, and how to navigate the treacherous waters of conflict, distress, and disagreement that may occur when people experience adversity.

The task force identified three main dimensions of work-team development: ways for groups to self-organize under difficult circumstances, ways for groups to manage productive conflict and abate interpersonal tensions when disagreements or stressful situations make consensus difficult, and ways to increase competence and problem-solving capacity in the focal task of the GLTs (Grade-level teams). This was a difficult problem of practice, but there were strong assets as well: the stakeholders clearly shared with one another the problems of safety, orderliness, behavior management, and students' emotional needs. The task force assumed that the teachers—especially the many young teachers, given their sense of suffering, need for support, and eagerness to learn new ways—would want to connect with one another. And all the district schools had senior expert teachers who could be drafted into leadership roles. Thus, the task force settled on five main drivers of change:

1. Establishing a shared understanding of the GLTs' purpose
2. Creating a basic structure of group functioning, protocols of interaction, and rules for accountability
3. Leading by senior teachers, who socialize novices and gradually share responsibility with them
4. Managing productive conflict
5. Using behavioral management approaches that emphasize positive behavior intervention and support to counteract teachers' defensive behavior toward their students

The task force is now ready for the actual design of an intervention that translates the five drivers into a set of meeting formats, tools, and sequenced activities. As every teacher who translates an understanding of how students learn new subject matter into a set of lessons knows, designing an intervention that fosters adult learning according to the designers' intent is a creative act, guided by clear-eyed analytics and fuzzy intuition.

While Christine, up to this point, has played a leading role in accessing the knowledge base and guiding the data collection for the needs assessments, all members of her task force are deeply involved in designing activities. Collectively, they come up with ideas that one person alone would have been unable to generate. Given the resources and assets that the district has at its disposal, the task force cannot directly influence all GLTs with their intervention, but they can influence the leadership of the teams. They decide that, whenever possible, the leadership team, convened at the district and drawn from each middle school, should consist of three senior teachers who will be spread over each grade level (6 through 8), at least one grade-level counselor, and at least one volunteer novice teacher from each school. Members of the task force are especially proud of the way they intend to creatively combine GLT facilitation with a socializing function for the senior teachers. This approach is not something that they found anywhere in the literature, and yet it seems essential for their situation and potentially very useful for many districts in a similar predicament.

The task force recognizes that, given the urgency of the problem, training these leaders will have to occur concurrently with their new role in the school-level GLTs. Therefore, the whole design will consist of inquiry cycles in which team leader training and immediate tryouts of this training will alternate. The intervention is envisioned to last for four months with five discrete training sessions immediately followed by reflection on implementing these sessions in the school-level GLTs. The design team envisions the work to continue for a whole year and for elements of the intervention to be repeated on an ongoing basis. A sketch of the intervention design appears in table 9.1.

Table 9.1 omits the details of the content, materials, learning tasks, inquiry prompts, and so on, that will be at the heart of the design's effectiveness. But it gives an idea of what the task force is planning to do. Note that some activities will be carefully planned, such as the training, and some will be more open. During the more open inquiries, protocols for group self-organizing will be practiced while issues may emerge as problems in the GLTs. Christine and other members of the task force are convinced that they will be able to rely on a solid foundation of preplanned activities to deal with unexpected events without losing sight of the adult learning that their intervention aims at. This assumption, of course, can only be tested through empirical data.

Christine and the rest of the task force aim high. As described earlier, their deep thinking moved them away from triage. Instead, they came to face the stark organizational reality of their situation through needs assessments. And they appreciated the necessity of continuous and sustainable improvement, given their district's constraints and assets. Though the task force feels fortified by a solid

TABLE 9.1   Christine's intervention design

WEEK	FORMAT	CONTENT
1	Discussion and training in grade-level team (GLT) leaders, chaired by task force	▪ Establishing common purpose and goals; instilling new hope ▪ Discussing why functioning GLTs are essential
2	Reports from GLTs, inquiry into topic, problem-solving, chaired by grade-level counselor	Same as week 1
3	Training for GLT leaders, chaired by task force	Getting organized: discussing rules, protocols, mutual support, accountability
4	Reports from GLTs, inquiry into topic, problem solving, chaired by senior teacher	Same as week 3
5	▪ Training, centrally conducted by external consultant for all GLTs ▪ District professional-development day	Training in the positive behavior intervention and support (PBIS) approach
6	GLT session, cochaired by senior and novice teachers	Applying the PBIS approach
7	Training, conducted by Christine	When disagreements undermine the team: managing productive conflict in GLTs and GLT leadership
8	Reports from GLTs, inquiry into topic, problem solving, cochaired by senior and novice teachers	Same as week 7
9	▪ Split session: novice and senior teachers meet separately ▪ Training and inquiry, conducted by members of district task force	Exploring the socializing role of senior teachers: competencies and expectations, formal and informal communication
10	Joint inquiry	▪ Creating awareness on sharing advice ▪ Informally observing self and others: Who supports me? Whom do I support? What advice is exchanged?
11	Self-organizing of GLT leadership group, plan for the year, occasional visits by task force	Looking to the future: sustainability of productive GLT work

theory of action that is based on the professional knowledge base, they assume that in the first time around, their attempts may not work out. So they are building into their design plenty of opportunities, most notably during the inquiry sessions, to observe where their assumptions may not hold. They know that their problem of practice is one that will endure, requiring consistent intervention. Consequently, learning from this first iteration will help them make adjustments and solidify their design for future use.

MICHELLE'S INTERVENTION DESIGN

Michelle's team of three principals brainstorms about the intervention design by building on their theory of action. In their understanding of the problem, culturally relevant instructional practices are not only a matter of materials and instructional formats, but also about an entrenched "mind-set of prescription and coverage," as they have come to call it. This mind-set discourages teachers from keenly observing their students' needs and paying attention to their students' lives and sense of curiosity. The team has framed the problem as one of adult motivation, experience, and cultural sensitivity; instructional competence; and organizational culture, with a critical perspective on their own leadership practices. The district equity committee's focus is on introducing culturally relevant content and material into the literacy program. Although Michelle's smaller team of three principals wants to create a design that is embedded in that agenda, her group is convinced that simply introducing new reading material in workshops for faculty will not work.

After consulting the various areas of professional knowledge applicable to their focal problem, the team asks a number of key questions that ultimately lead them to their drivers of change:

- How can we lessen the prescription and coverage mind-set?
- How can we lessen the climate of control that makes teachers fearful, and how can we open up new spaces for learning?
- How can we build on assets and create positive experiences for teachers in relating to, and interpreting, literary text?
- How can these experiences become the springboard for new instructional formats?
- How can we make sure that we still cover the literacy and reading skills that the benchmarks demand?
- How can we have richer conversations around the benchmark tests that model to teachers the kind of pedagogy we want them to pursue with their students?

- How do we help teachers plan lessons that foster students' deep interpretation of rich and culturally meaningful text?
- How do we make sure that teachers solicit their students' experiences and become more sensitive and responsive to them?

The team recognizes that these questions hint at a huge undertaking, and at first Michelle and the three principals are a little intimidated by their own ambitions. But they want to show their district colleagues that cultural responsiveness requires a more comprehensive approach if it is to be successful in their district. Identifying the main change drivers makes their whole project more wieldy. They settle on five change drivers (figure 9.1).

The first driver is *pedagogical benchmark conversations*. Among all the features that make up the schools' organizational culture, the team selects the principal-teacher conferences about the benchmarks as the most powerful practice that shape the prescription and coverage mind-set. These conferences are thus the main driver for changing expectations. During these conferences, teachers and instructional supervisors engage in what Michelle's team calls pedagogical benchmark conversations—discussions that go beyond the usual accounting and expedient strategizing (as in, "What items do we need to reteach to which students?") to address pedagogy.[4]

FIGURE 9.1   Michelle's driver diagram

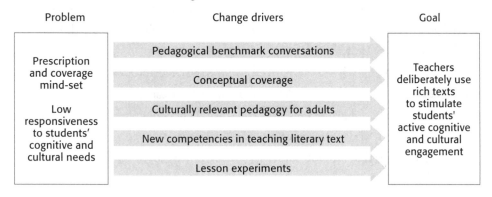

The second driver is *conceptual coverage*. The literacy program and the district benchmarks are a reality that no principal and no teacher can ignore. "Coverage" of material will be necessary for "cover," so to speak. But coverage also ensures that certain reading skills are actually learned by students, and the principals do not want to lose the benchmarks as tools to ensure this. But if teachers learned how to cover the program conceptually as opposed to procedurally, they could change out texts and become more independent from the prescriptive program. For conceptual coverage, teachers would need to know how to identify the reading skills of a specific piece of the program and transpose them to texts of their choosing. Conceptual coverage would also create security and allay teachers' fears that if they veered too far from the program, their benchmark tests would decline.

The third driver of change is *culturally relevant pedagogy, or CRP, for adults*. If teachers are to be responsive to students' thinking and feeling when the teachers expose them to culturally relevant material, the adults need to have their own responsiveness rekindled—thus the need for CRP for the adults. The team believes that when adults recognize how powerful literary text can be for their own deep understanding of life, they will be more likely to create these kinds of learning experiences for children.

Fourth, teachers develop *new competencies in teaching* their students how to interpret text in personally rich and meaningful ways. At present, teachers mainly teach simple comprehension of text and relatively superficial text features that the benchmark tests emphasize.

Finally, in *lesson experiments*, teachers try out the richer texts and ways of interpreting them in lessons that they collectively plan and debrief. This will facilitate the integration of new knowledge into practice.

These five change drivers now need to be translated into a sequence of activities that foster the kind of learning the team believes is needed. The goal is to increase the number of lessons during which teachers deliberately use rich texts to stimulate students' active cognitive and cultural engagement.

The team members divide their intervention into three blocks: anticipation, new skills for teachers, and application. The first block, anticipation, is two-pronged. At the organizational level, they decide that they will kick off the new conversation with several focus groups for teachers. Michelle and her team are excited about this idea. They plan to have each principal run one or two focus groups in another principal's school, with prompts that invite teachers to be frank and to brainstorm on how to improve the benchmark conversations. In parallel, the CRP group will come together, and the participants will begin with their first activity: reading a dramatically rich text that encourages them to interpret and share their own life experiences around cultural identity. The second block, new skills for teachers, concentrates on teaching interpretation skills for students reading rich texts and transposing the program's reading skills to the new texts (conceptual coverage). The last block, application, consists of two main activities. In the CRP volunteer group, lessons are planned and experimented with. For the school as a whole, new protocols, derived from the focus groups and ideas gleaned from sources in the knowledge base on conversations about tests, are tried out to initiate pedagogical benchmark conversations. The design team plans these three blocks, planning twelve sessions over a period of three months.

ERIC'S INTERVENTION DESIGN

To recap, Eric's intervention design, aimed at improving instructional supervision among the principals in his district, is actually his second iteration. In the first iteration, Eric quickly moved from his intuition to action. Being disappointed by his results, he began to reflect more deeply. His reasoning, coupled with keen observation of his principals, helped him understand his problem in its multidimensionality: surface or symptomatic behaviors, motivations or dispositions to act, competencies and deep understanding, and organizational context. First, he noted that principals do not visit classrooms (surface behavior). His explanations of why the problem occurs and recurs were the following:

- Principals are under enormous time constraints and are pressed to find the time (organizational context).
- They say they feel uncomfortable so they avoid instructional conversations with teachers (disposition: motivation, efficacy).

- Principals use vague and superficial language that does not seem to help teachers analyze their own instruction (competence).
- Principals rarely comment on the academic side of instruction when they observe instructional sequences, relegating academic engagement and disengagement of students in subject-matter content to a minor point (deep understanding).

Eric's goal or desired state at the end of the intervention is to have principals understand the concept of academic engagement. He wants to make it a central concern during instructional conferences conducted by principals with teachers so that they would pick up on this important concern for their instruction.

He consulted the professional knowledge base on instructional leadership and instructional supervision, as well as readings on student academic engagement, adult learning theory, professional development, and coaching. The knowledge base supports his understanding of the problem and helps him narrow his change process down to five drivers (figure 9.2). These drivers pick up on the identified root causes of the problem and guide him toward the kinds of activities that may elicit or foster the required learning to produce the intended effect.

His first driver is the *principals' desire or motivation to improve student learning*. He will use evidence from research to demonstrate that academic engagement is an effective way to increase measurable student achievement.

FIGURE 9.2   Eric's driver diagram

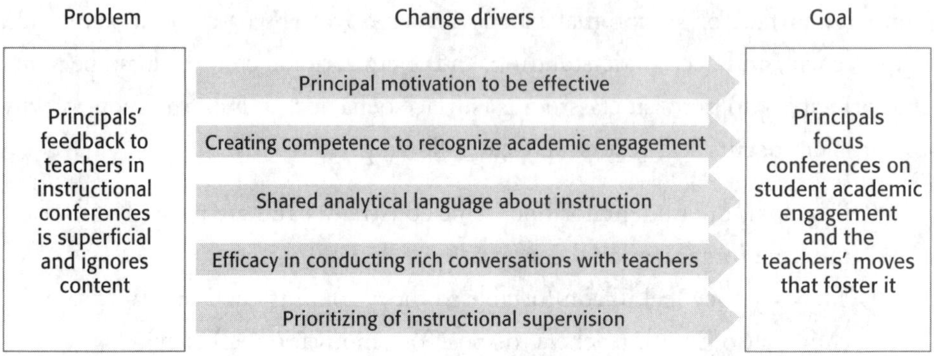

His second driver is the *creation of new competencies*. He will show the principals what academic engagement looks like and how it can be recognized in student behavioral cues (e.g., class participation, substantive peer conversations, motivation to seek help, an embrace of learning from error, questions and feedback that flesh out misconceptions, students' ability to reflect on their thinking during the lesson). Literature on effective lessons for academic engagement taught him that.

His third driver, amplifying the second, is the fostering of an *instructional framework and analytical language shared* by principals in the district and, in a step further, shared with teachers. He will facilitate this through lesson design and observation tools.

His fourth driver is the *principals' sense of efficacy*. Adult learning theory suggests to him that as principals gain new understanding and confidence, they will be more inclined to try out the new competencies in practice. The literature on professional development and coaching makes it clear to him that a combination of learning new skills and trying them out in consultant and peer coaching interactions would be effective formats of learning. The instructional supervision literature yields an observation tool that seems simple enough for the principals to use, but sophisticated enough to spot students' engagement with academic content.

His fifth driver is *prioritizing*. The desire to have an effect on student learning, the new competence in making a difference in a key variable of student success, and the new sense of efficacy in having conversations about all this with teachers will make principals more willing to prioritize classroom visits and instructional conversations, even when these leaders face a high work overload. From the literature on organizational culture change and normative incentives, however, Eric learned that principals need clear expectations from the relevant district leader (Eric himself); ongoing encouragement through peer check-ins, which Eric intends to organize in the monthly principal meetings; and feedback from teachers as the recipients or beneficiaries of the new practice.

Eric's theory of action results in a twelve-session intervention design for his district's principals (table 9.2). He believes that he has found a high-leverage intervention design that follows directly from his theory of action and the change

TABLE 9.2   Eric's intervention design

WEEK	FORMAT	CONTENT
1	Workshop	Introducing the concept: ■ What is academic engagement? ■ How effective is it? ■ How can we see it in classrooms?
2	Workshop	Analyzing instructional sequences on video: ■ What is the academic content of a given sequence?
3	Workshop	Analyzing instructional sequences on video: ■ Reading student cues ■ Using an observation tool
4	Workshop	Analyzing instructional sequences on video: ■ Observing teacher instructional moves ■ Using an observation tool
5	Coaching and inquiry	Conducting instructional rounds focused on student academic engagement in schools to diagnose teaching patterns in vivo
6	Inquiry	Debriefing observed patterns from the rounds
7	Coaching	■ Observing and analyzing lessons ■ Practicing teacher conferences with peers
8	Workshop	Preparing principals to conduct professional development sessions for their faculties: ■ Creating observation criteria and sharing observation tools
9/10	Coaching	■ Principal–teacher conferencing and subsequent tryouts ■ Using a conferencing tool
11	Peer observation	Observing one another having conferences with teachers through videos
12	Inquiry	Sharing feedback from teachers about principals' conferences

drivers he has identified. He decides to run his intervention repeatedly with various groups of principals until the district's instructional leaders have immersed themselves in the concept of student academic engagement, the competence to discern it in the classrooms, and the willingness to lead their teachers in this direction. And importantly, he will make room for the design in the district's schedule for principal professional development.

Compare his original intuitive design to the full-fledged intervention design he has now put together. Originally he thought his drivers of change were the use of an observation tool, watching videos, and professional conversations. He later recognized that these were *activities*. These activities still play a key role in his design, but they are attached to the *learning* in terms of motivation, knowledge, attitudes, and specific practices that principals require to more deeply influence instruction.

NORA'S INTERVENTION DESIGN

We have already presented in more detail the theory of action that guided Nora's leadership team as it addressed the problem of teachers not intervening when they hear slurs uttered by the high school students. In the emotional dimension, the members knew they had to deal with silence, discomfort, fear, denial, and defensiveness that surround racism and homophobia in American society. These macro-societal factors would nevertheless impinge on the faculty's micro-interactions, even though their school was declared a zone in which social justice was to prevail. In the cognitive dimension, the team members knew they had to find ways to collectively communicate information about the difficult topic and train the faculty in practical ways of intervening. They settled on a change process that consisted of these elements: cognitive dissonance between what is and what ought to be, shared commitment to social justice values, the creation of a safe space to talk, a deeper understanding of the functioning of slurs, the learning of new practices that may increase motivation to act in an uncertain situation, and a sense of efficacy. These elements match the change drivers discussed in chapter 8.

As they brainstorm how their theory of action might be channeled into an intervention, they conclude that the cultural change they envision will not occur in formal venues alone, such as whole-faculty professional development. Instead, they realize that informal communication between members of the leadership team and other faculty is needed. They consider these informal interactions an integral component of their design and plan to alternate informal and formal venues. The sketch of their intervention appears in table 9.3.

Nora and her leadership team hypothesize that a series of ten discrete activities, some formal, some informal, may create in the faculty the motivation to act,

TABLE 9.3   Nora's intervention design

SESSION	FORMAT	ACTIVITIES

1	Whole faculty, groups	■ Recapping antibullying campaign
		■ Stimulating cognitive dissonance:
		  □ Confrontation with observation tallies (frequent slurs, little intervention by adults)
		  □ Interpretation of the data
		  □ Discussion of veracity, meaning of the data
		■ Naming the problem

2	Informal conversations, follow-up, feedback	Same focus as session 1. Individually, leadership team members reach out to the faculty members they normally talk to and engage them in informal conversations about session 1 content.

3	Whole faculty, groups	■ Establishing a safe space:
		  □ Discussing norms of courageous conversations
		  □ Assuming good intentions when people speak
		  □ Recognizing delicate nature of topic
		  □ Acknowledging that people can misspeak
		■ Clarifying the role of facilitators and leadership team

4	Informal conversations, follow-up, feedback	Same focus as in session 3. Individually, leadership team members reach out to the faculty members they normally talk to and engage them in informal conversations about session 3 content.
5	Whole faculty, groups	Appealing to shared values: ■ What it means to teach in a social justice school ■ What it means for our school if we tolerate slurs
6	Whole faculty, groups	Understanding the multiple functions of slurs more deeply: ■ What slurs signify ■ What emotions they trigger ■ How they express racism and homophobia ■ How students use them
7	Informal conversations, follow-up, feedback	Anticipating actions: ■ Mobilizing readiness to act ■ Sharing ideas about next steps

8	Small groups	■ Developing intervention strategies:
		  □ Phrases to be used when teachers hear a slur
		  □ Prompts to be used when students brush off or talk back
		■ Trying out scenarios

9	Individual	Experimenting with intervening: ■ Making notes about experiences ■ Reflecting on the effectiveness of one's response ■ Tinkering with one's response or strategy ■ Recording one's feelings
10	Whole faculty	■ Reporting on experiences ■ Sharing one's feelings ■ Assessing one's effectiveness ■ Refining strategies

the competence to intervene, a sense of efficacy, and, as they hope, a new routine of dealing with slurs. Moreover, they hope that these qualities will be sustained beyond the period of intervention. Regular leadership team meetings, during which the team plans to reflect on the proceedings of their design, are wedged between the informal conversations and formal professional development sessions.

QUICK TRIALS OR MINI-EXPERIMENTS

Before designers implement the fully designed interventions, it makes sense to try out parts of the design. People who will not be full participants or informants for data collection are good candidates for mini-experiments. Intervention activities about which the design team feels insecure are particularly primed for quick trials. Christine's team feels especially unsure about the organizational socialization aspect of the design. Since the district has several schools with similarly high numbers of novice teachers, the task force assembles a group of five senior teachers from elementary schools and high schools and tries out the activity. The group planned to communicate the new socializing role with short narratives or vignettes in which informal, but continuous advice giving and support by senior teachers are exemplified. The mini-experimental group relates well to the vignettes. So the vignettes are now included as activities in the design. Nevertheless, because the mini-experiment is conducted out of context, the five teachers seem a little puzzled about how to apply the vignettes in their own work. The design team decides that in the full intervention, the activity will become embedded in a larger project. In this way, things will be clearer.

Before the full intervention, Michelle's group conducts three quick trials on culturally relevant instruction in the district's middle schools. The principals that form the design team try out the focus-group prompts in one school where the principal is willing to rethink benchmark conversations but is not interested in running a CRP group. They also read a few adult stories with volunteer teachers from non-participating schools. And they vet with the district equity committee some alternative student texts as replacements for pieces in the literacy program. After the quick trials, they feel confident that the prompts and materials they have chosen will work for their full intervention.

The first few sessions of Eric's intervention depend on suitable videos of lessons that can demonstrate student academic engagement to the principals—with Eric's help or that of the coach. He tries out a whole collection of videos with a few teachers on special assignment for the district. He finds that many of the videos place the teacher in the center and neglect footage of student voice. These videos will not do the job, and he is glad that he has tried them out. He does find a small collection of suitable videos, but they tend to show lessons delivered to students who do not look like students in his district in terms of demographics. He ends up asking a few strong teachers in his district to teach some effective lessons, and during these lessons, he has a video camera face the students, not the teacher. He ends up with a decent collection of videos that he again runs by his mini-experimental group. When these videos seem to do the job, Eric is confident that the first sessions of his intervention will be solid.

Though Nora and her team feel insecure about the change process, they find it hard to imagine mini-experiments with discrete activities taken out of the context of the whole process. They can, however, try out what to say to students when teachers hear them utter slurs. And Nora's team does that in several mini-experiments with students. They find that the statement "Ladies/Gentlemen, this is not the kind of language we use at our school" puts students on notice but keeps the statement matter-of-fact. A number of follow-up phrases related to racist or homophobic slurs are suggested by various websites.[5]

CHAPTER SUMMARY

In this chapter, we explained that designing an intervention involves the following steps:

- translating ideas about how adults learn new beliefs, form new attitudes, or try out new practices into activities that designers believe will foster the envisioned adult learning;

- applying identified drivers of change to real-life settings;

- sequencing activities that will move participants from point A, the baseline, to point B, the desired state reached when the intervention ends, in accordance with a theory of action;

- creating imaginative solutions out of unique needs and circumstances, although the solutions may nevertheless have usefulness beyond these contexts;

- piloting activities in quick trials or mini-experiments.

Making Design Development Research-Based

Our ambition in this book is high: we want to develop research-based interventions. What does this mean? To base an intervention on research, designers must ground their thinking in science and conduct research on the intervention as it unfolds. Up to this point, we have addressed the first part of these requirements: how to base one's thinking on science. We have shown that design-based thinking holds intuition, creativity, and flexibility in tension with theory, prediction, and firm plans. We have also described how designers facilitate the scientific basis of interventions through careful definition of the problematic practices and desirable states, evidence-based assumptions about needs and assets, relevant research and professional knowledge, a testable theory of action, and a deliberate translation of an adult learning process into a set of sequenced activities. Now we turn to the second challenge: how to make sure that the implementation of the intervention is studied with scientific principles. In this chapter, we use Eric's story to illustrate how this second challenge can be met with success. To this end, we address several questions in this chapter:

→ What is a methodology?
→ What procedures should be used to make sure that the implementation of the design generates good evidence?

→ Why do designers need to make outcome and process of the intervention visible and verifiable through data?

DESIGNING WITHOUT METHOD: ERIC'S FIRST ITERATION

In the design space, designers want to make robust connections between their intentions and actions. They want to be certain that it was actually the intervention that led to the intended outcomes. They make these connections more robust with logic and procedure. We have already shown how a well-founded theory of action provides the logic for a specific intervention design. This logic connects point A (the problematic state or behavior) to point B (the desired state or behavior) *conceptually*. We now look at ways that connect points A and B *procedurally* through the methods of research.

Why do educational leaders need procedures? Why can't they just design an intervention, see how it is working, then redesign and see again, and so forth, until they get to a place where the intervention seems to change the behaviors the leaders want to change? In Eric's case, he has his multistep program for helping district principals with instructional supervision, and with each iteration, he could check how many principals have made the changes he has in mind. He could then adjust accordingly until he is satisfied with the effects. Why would he need bothersome methods? This is Eric's thinking.

Eric begins his intervention with the principals of ten schools in his district. He invites them to participate, and all ten decide to attend. But, given his position in the district, it's unlikely anyone would have turned him down.

When he conducts the first workshop, everybody is excited by the new emphasis on academic engagement. The principals seem especially persuaded by the effectiveness ratings of academic engagement practices documented in the research literature that promise student achievement gains. Eric is satisfied and thinks that the first session went well.

The second and third sessions are a little more difficult. He decides to focus instructional videos on English language arts (ELA). The participants compare high-engagement and low-engagement lesson sequences. The observation tool seems pretty straightforward. Among other things, the principals are to judge class participation. That seems fairly easy. As the camera zeros in on peer conversations in student groups, the principals are supposed to judge the substance of conversations. That seems much harder. It requires some understanding of the knowledge domain (ELA) and grade level being observed, and there is wide disagreement among the participants. They are next asked to look for interactions around learning from error. They find few such interactions in the low-engagement lessons and rich conversations around student error in some of the high-engagement lessons. They look at teacher feedback and note that in the low-engagement lessons, most feedback comes in the form of teachers giving correct answers and then asking students how many "got it right," or the teacher asks around until one student has the correct answer. In the high-engagement lessons, the teacher goes from group to group and gives the students brief check-in questions that prompt some students to explain what they have been doing. And so on. After the comparative analysis, the principals voice how useful the video analyses have been for them. Eric is satisfied again.

For the fourth session, Eric has invited an experienced instructional coach to lead instructional rounds. In groups of five, principals visit real classrooms. After discussing their low-inference observations, the principals analyze the live lesson sequences they observed with the observation tool they used for the videos. As in the previous sessions, some dimensions of instruction are easier to analyze than others. Eric notes that the coach, in the end, gives a lot of analytical summaries of what the principals should have seen. There is a good deal of agreement with the coach. This is the first round, Eric thinks, and the principals are practicing their analytical language. Three sessions later, Eric sees that with some help from the coach, the principals have begun to use the analytical language of the tool with more independence.

Eric is quite excited that the principals remain highly motivated in the subsequent sessions. The conversations are lively, and all the participants consider the coaching sessions very valuable. By the end, the final session in which Eric can observe what has been learned, the principals seem familiar with the observation tool and use the language derived from it. On some dimensions of the tool, most principals seem pretty firm (i.e., the dimensions come up in the conferences and there is peer agreement in follow-up conversations); on others, there is no clear pattern. Eric notices that almost all the principals skip one dimension: the substance of student conversations. But somehow, he glides over this omission. In the follow-up focus groups, teachers who have been observed are very positive. They welcome the classroom visits, and they are happy to be receiving richer feedback in a timely manner. Eric concludes that the design has worked.

But has it? Eric's criteria of success, implied in his thinking, are the following observations:

- Principals support the intervention and are highly motivated. They progress from session to session and become better at handling the instrument. Principals express that they are learning a lot.
- Principals talk about academic engagement and use the analytical language associated with the tool when they observe teachers. Observed teachers find that instructional conferences have become much richer and more useful to them.

No question, there is evidence of a worthy process and desirable outcomes. But do these outcomes indicate that the principals have reached the desired state that Eric had initially envisioned and that the intervention has contributed to the learning? Let's compare Eric's concern at the beginning with his criteria of effectiveness at the end. Initially he wanted the principals to understand the concept of academic engagement and make it a central concern for instructional conferences with teachers so that teachers could pick up on this important concern. But now he uses two criteria for impact that are only tangentially related to student academic engagement: richer conferences (as reported by the observed teachers) and the principals' use of analytical language (Eric's own observation). And the quality of the designed activities is now judged by these criteria: the principals' buy-in, motivation, report of usefulness, and observation of continuous progress in using the tool.

What has happened? Apparently, the criteria have shifted sometime between the beginning and the end of the intervention. As described earlier, Eric, after the first spontaneous tryout of his professional development session, was not satisfied with the principals merely learning new vocabulary. He had noticed that the principals were using the new vocabulary without recognizing patterns of academic engagement. Hence, the use of analytical language was a criterion that Eric had originally rejected as insufficient to indicate the principals' competence in flagging the students' academic engagement. But now, at the end of a full intervention, he is using it as the main indicator of success. In his understanding of the change process, Eric was mindful of the principals' motivation and efficacy, and the participants' positive responses indicate to him that the intervention has done the job. But do their positive responses to the professional development sessions indicate that the process also improves the *principals'* academic engagement, that is, their engagement with the most difficult cognitive or subject-matter dimensions of *students'* academic engagement? It's hard to tell.

Yet Eric is convinced that the design has worked, and everybody around him seems to confirm this with their enthusiasm—until he has a conversation with the coach he had brought in for the various sessions. She puts it to him this way: "No question, your workshops did something for the principals that was better than what they had experienced previously, but it didn't work. It's very simple. Most everybody could identify surface instructional moves by the teachers. But of the ten principals, eight could not read the student behavioral cues of academic engagement, even at the end. And the other two could already do it in the second session, which means they didn't need your workshop."

Eric's first reaction is to dispute the coach. Because there are no data, it is his impression against hers. The design was successful, he believes. He painstakingly consulted the professional knowledge base, developed a theory of action, and put the intervention together. That was a lot of work, he thinks. Who among the other administrators in his district would go through all that trouble? He wants to believe that what he designed actually worked.

But the coach's challenge provokes him. He can't completely dismiss her, because he remembers now that he himself had observed that the participants, for the most part, could not judge the quality of student conversations. Why had he forgotten about that when he declared his design a success? Also, the coach is the only one in the picture who is not under his supervisory authority. What if everybody else felt subconscious pressure to please their supervisor, or pretended? Why did he ignore this possibility until now? He is finally swayed when he realizes that the coach has many reasons to talk up the design since her work is on the line as well. When she disputes the effect, she is being reflective and self-critical. Eric concludes that the coach is obviously better at keeping a check on her personal biases than he himself is. "Well," he thinks, "she can afford it; she lives off critical inquiry, whereas I am an administrator who needs to look efficient no matter what." But he is no longer certain that his design worked.

As a district administrator, Eric likes the clarity of procedure and dislikes nagging uncertainties. Wondering what he could have done differently to be more certain about his design, he concludes that he would have to make sure to do the following:

- Focus his attention on the right things, those that are most indicative of the core learning he wants to see.
- Fix his measures of success or impact so that they would not drift up or down, depending on what he was perceiving to be happening or what he wanted to see.
- Become aware of his tendencies to see what he wants to see.
- Reflect on his position of power when judging the responses of subordinates.
- Make his findings defensible with data to other people who may find his problem of practice compelling, but who doubt the strength of his design.

In other words, he has recognized the need for method.

MOVING INTO THE METHOD SPACE

There are many ways to perceive reality. When we read a good novel, we know that the characters in the novel are fictitious, yet they teach us something about ourselves. They reveal a deeper reality that fascinates us, yet they are fiction. How can fiction reveal reality? A good writer uses techniques that make us identify with characters in a story. We identify because the characters and situations are recognizable to us, even when the scenery is making the familiar strange. The narration resonates with us at a deeper intuitive and emotional level. It is perceived as trustworthy, and its trustworthiness opens us up to the deeper insights that the narrator's characters reveal: catharsis, the cleansing of emotions through higher discernments. Narrative techniques are the appropriate method for a novel.

This is not what we are after in design research. At the core, we as researchers are cool and detached. We really want to know what works; the beauty of robust findings makes us quiver. Narration and trustworthiness are part of the picture, but our "plot" revolves around a dispassionate connecting of logical and procedural dots. Our goals are not identification with heroes and catharsis, and we want to avoid fiction at all cost.

Rather, we intend to make our design development projects research-based. Christine, Michelle, Eric, and Nora have done a lot of thinking already. Their thinking has supplied important elements of the research base for their project. They have taken the following steps:

- Defined and framed a problem of practice
- Conducted assessments of needs and assets
- Stated a design challenge
- Consulted the professional and research knowledge base that helped challenge their intuitive thinking
- Developed a theory of action
- Derived from this theory of action an intervention design

But now the four educational leaders need to take the next important step: making sure that their interventions yield robust findings that can stand up to scientific standards according to their chosen methodology, design development research. The two most important steps in this endeavor are to make the process of their intervention visible and to make verifiable their claims that the design worked (or didn't). Both visibility and verifiability are grounded in data. But data need to be collected in a specific way depending on designers' research purpose and the context within which they carry out this research.

EXCURSION INTO THEORY

Research Methodology

Broadly speaking, scholars call an activity *research* when they systematically explore phenomena in the natural and human world and try to understand how facts or events come about. Doing this systematically means using clear logic and meticulous procedures. When little is known about a phenomenon, it needs to be described so that researchers may discover patterns and typical behaviors. Researchers attach names to these patterns or types—defined categories that abstract the details from the wide variability of concrete life. These categories help researchers create mental order where, previously, randomness prevailed. For example, researchers might observe a classroom in which students walk around, talk to each other, walk over to the teacher, sit down at their desks, all seemingly at random until the teacher mentions the term *learning stations*. Now the commotion makes sense. Once a phenomenon is described in this categorical way, researchers can explore how it may come about or what causes it. In the beginning, the search is exploratory. Broad questions cast the net widely. The search narrows as causes become better understood. Firmer hypotheses emerge and can be tested and confirmed or disproved. When the purpose shifts from contemplating the world to changing it, investigators may want to know in a systematic way what interventions might bring about intended changes and how and why these interventions do so. Each purpose requires a different approach to the way the research is carried out.

Methodologies

Two conditions challenge research in the world of human action: it is often impossible or undesirable to control the environment in which research subjects or participants act. When this is the case, cause and effect claims become tenuous. And the researchers themselves are always part of the study, introducing subjectivity and bias into the research design. Researchers have developed specific ways, called methodologies, to mitigate these two problems. The term *methodology* calls attention to a set of truth claims (e.g., positivist, interpretivist), procedures, methods of data collection and sampling (e.g., interview, observation, survey, random samples, stratified samples), and types of data (e.g., qualitative, quantitative) that together undergird a particular approach to research.[1]

Each methodology serves a particular research purpose. Depending on the research intent, the state of the knowledge base, and the type of research environment, one methodology may be appropriate over another. When firm hypotheses can be formed and action can be tightly constrained in the research environment, experiments may be indicated. When control of the research environment is impossible, exploration of people acting in their naturalistic context is desirable, and there exists a natural boundary around the phenomenon of interest (e.g., teachers' beliefs about student ability in some high- and low-performing schools, the use of categorical funds in a particular district, the attitude toward immigrants in one particular city)—that is, when the context can be bounded, case studies may be appropriate.[2] If researchers are seeking to generalize from a decontextualized sample to a larger population, then they may choose to conduct a statistical analysis of large-scale survey data. When researchers want to undertake and research an intervention in a real-life setting that nevertheless may be transferable to other settings, design research or design development methodology is a good choice. The terminology used in the literature varies. The term *design development study*, used here, indicates a type of design research that is ongoing and evolving, rather than resulting in fixed products.

Design Research Methodology

In discussing design development methodology, we largely follow the work by Tjeerd Plomp, Nienke Nieveen, Jan van den Akker, and others from the Netherlands Institute for Curriculum Development.[3] They define *educational design research* as "the systematic study of designing, developing and evaluating educational interventions (such as programs, teaching-learning strategies and materials, products and systems) as solutions for complex problems in educational practice."[4] Design studies are collaborative; they involve practitioners and researchers and are best carried out in teams.

When educators and researchers face complex problems of practice for which there are few definite or confirmed solutions, guidelines, known remedies, how-to guides, or "validated principles," design research is a suitable approach.[5] Design research methodology has been developed for the uniqueness of a research environment that calls for complex problem solving in real-life settings. Two conditions apply in this environment: context matters, but varies widely, so it cannot be predicted, and the development of solutions is uncertain work that, even though it builds on what is known, requires innovation, creativity, and repeated trials in the design space.[6] Design research methodology gives researchers the structure to conduct systematic inquiry in the midst of this uncertainty. The inquiry is simultaneously tight and loose. Designers use a structured process for planning, implementing, and evaluating interventions to predetermine and specify intervention elements, but they also leave room for false starts, an adjust-as-you-go approach, and repeated trials.

At the core, design development methodology is cyclical. Plomp explains that "analysis, design, evaluation and revision activities are iterated until a satisfying balance" between the desired state and the realized outcomes of an intervention has been achieved.[7] Reeves depicts the design research approach as an iterative process (figure 10.1).[8]

All design research begins with a preliminary phase. We have already discussed this preliminary phase in previous chapters. Suffice it say here that the preliminary phase results in a theoretical conceptualization of the change. Various terms are used for this conceptualization: conceptual framework, theoretical model, or theory of action. Here, we prefer *theory of action*. A theory of action is formulated in if-then statements that are conjectural but plausible in social scientific terms, reflecting the open-ended nature of change in complex environments. In the subsequent phase, prototypical interventions are planned and implemented.[9] They are prototypical because they represent an early stage in which designs still need testing and adjusting in practice. Finally, in the assessment phase, the effect of an intervention is evaluated.

Two types of data are collected: formative and summative data. Formative data are collected while the implementation of the intervention is under way. These data help

FIGURE 10.1   Design research as an iterative process

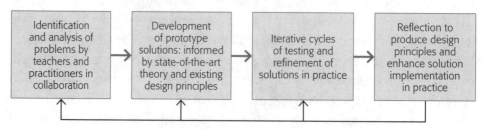

Source: Adapted from Thomas Reeves, "Design Research from a Technology Perspective," *Educational Design Research* 1, no. 3 (2006): 52–56.

researchers understand events, critical incidents, or discrete activities through which learning and change unfolds. Summative data ascertain the effects of the intervention. One useful approach to measuring effect is a baseline-to-outcome comparison.[10] In fact, since participants in design studies usually start from multiple baselines, the effects may be captured through the assessment of differential growth. The interplay between formative and summative assessment and between multiple baselines and differential growth is familiar to many educators. For example, teachers introducing a new concept in a curricular unit may assess the spectrum of understanding of the concept across a group of students when they begin the unit and the differential learning outcomes at the end of the unit. Success is not measured by the fact that all students received an A at the end, but that all students grew substantially on a summative test that is administered to them all. But they grew differentially, depending on where they started, and formative data help teachers ascertain what activities helped the faster and the slower learners.

In design studies, formative and summative data are not always strictly separated. Plomp uses the term "semi-summative" for the assessment of outcomes to indicate that formative and summative data can be interwoven. An example of this overlap would occur when participants in a professional development intervention are asked to perform a similar task or are asked similar questions at the beginning of the intervention and at the end (summative). To enhance this information, designers may ask participants to also reflect on their growth, or lack thereof, in various dimensions of the intervention (formative).[11] Summative and formative elements merge.

An intervention design is researchable when it consists of a set of planned formal activities around which an accurate and efficient search for evidence of change and effect can be organized. The search for evidence proceeds with established or prescribed methods of collecting, analyzing, and interpreting data that connect baseline, process, and outcome. Thus, one characteristic of design development methodology is that it requires researchers to be mindful of the precision of both the intervention design (a stream of change activities) and the research design (a stream of data collection activities) that may run parallel. Precision, however, does not mean inflexibility. Planning cannot preclude the necessity of last-minute changes. When activities planned for step 1 did not have the envisioned effect, activities for step 2 may need to be rearranged. But with good planning of the overall intervention, haphazard changes are avoided. Deliberate changes do not disrupt the flow of good data.

The purpose of design development studies is to ascertain that the design has had the intended effect and what activities, tools, formal organizational structures, resources, and so on, contributed to the intended effect. Two types of data are useful toward this end: impact data and process data.

CHAPTER SUMMARY

In this chapter, we have made several points about how to ensure that design development is research-based:

- Visibility and verifiability are two main principles that undergird research and that are accomplished by collecting data.

- Research follows agreed-upon rules of what counts as evidence; these rules are called methodologies.

- Research also follows agreed-upon conventions and procedures of data collection, called methods.

- Design development studies consist of an intervention design (a stream of change activities) and a research design (a stream of data collection activities).

11

Collecting Impact and Process Data

Design development studies pivot on outcomes. As designers, we intend to make a difference and accomplish an effect. It can be tempting, in the face of the urgent needs we have identified, to just get on with it—to put the intervention on the ground and worry later about whether it worked or not. Unfortunately, such an approach is likely to leave us without any way of knowing whether the intervention actually worked and, if it did, how. And only if we know whether an intervention performed as predicted, and why, can we know whether we've really figured out how to address our important problem.

This is why the research design that accompanies the intervention consists of both impact and process data. Impact data pick up on outcomes; process data document the fluid change process.

To plan for collecting impact data, design developers need to ask several questions:

→ Whose behavior are we primarily trying to shift?
→ What part of their behavior might show with high probability that the intended change has occurred?
→ Who might give a fairly unbiased account of these changes in the environment of those whose behavior we are trying to change?

➜ What indicators and metrics are suitable for this purpose?

To plan for collecting process data, design developers need to ask these questions:

➜ What parts of the change process do we need to document in order to know why or how a change occurred?
➜ During implementation, what key behaviors or critical events do we need to observe or capture?
➜ What indicators might pick up on the effect of certain activities?
➜ How can we fold data collection procedures into the implementation of the intervention?

UNIT OF ANALYSIS, UNIT OF "TREATMENT"

One of the most important steps in all research studies is to determine the *unit of analysis*—a decision that precedes the decision on which data to collect. The unit of analysis of a study may be individuals, groups of individuals, an interplay of procedures, whole organizations, and so on. Or the study may aim at multiple units. When teachers reflect on their lessons or classrooms, they intuitively select units of analysis. Sometimes they look at one student and compare that student with another. The unit in this case is individuals. Sometimes they compare their first period with their sixth-period class. The unit then becomes a group. Or teachers may want to understand how the design of the lesson reached various groups of students. The lesson becomes the unit of analysis. Each time the unit of analysis shifts, the evidence under consideration shifts, too.

Design development studies not only study people, but also "treat" them, or influence them with an intervention. The term *treatment* is borrowed from experimental research. Given that in our version of design studies, educational leaders co-design with participants rather than experiment on them, the leaders really do not treat the participants in a strict sense, but instead try to influence them, with fairly circumscribed sets of activities nevertheless. A number of actors may be influenced directly or indirectly by a design. But which set of actors will need to enact the intervention for the project to succeed? Which set of actors is directly targeted? Which set of actors may participate, but may not be the primary learners? The set of actors directly targeted as primary learners is the unit of "treatment." (Despite the dubious connotation, we do not have a better word for it.)

In Christine's case, the intervention aims at newly minted leaders of grade-level teams, but the GLTs (Grade-level teams) in the various schools ought to be influenced by the intervention as well, and, ultimately, student discipline ought to improve. Yet, a ten-session intervention cannot do all of this at once. It can be the trigger of something that may be sustained over time. The task force determines that the unit of treatment for its intervention is the leaders of GLTs. These leaders need to attain new skills in facilitating work teams and in processing approaches to positive behavior interventions and support. Teachers in GLTs are fairly unbiased observers of whether the leaders have accomplished their tasks and therefore whether the intervention has been successful. But the teachers are not the unit of treatment.

In Michelle's case, the unit of treatment for the CRP intervention in her elementary schools seems to shift. First, she and her district equity committee concentrate on teachers. Teachers are seen as lacking new culturally sensitive inspiration and instructional material. But when it becomes clear that the way teachers teach in the constrained environment of monitored pacing and audited benchmark performances is part of the problem, administrators become part of the treatment. The project on culturally relevant pedagogy comes to be reconceptualized as extending to organizational expectations and culture. In the end, Michelle envisions an intervention for a group on culturally relevant pedagogy and a whole-school shifting of the discourse among teachers and administrators away from prescription to sensitivity toward students' cognitive and cultural needs.

In Eric's case, the principals may influence teachers through instructional supervision or the culture of their school, so his unit of treatment for his intervention, data collection, and impact metrics is the principals. In Nora's case, the focus is on teachers and their behavior when they encounter students using slurs, but students may be fairly unbiased judges of teacher behavior changes compared with teachers' self-reports, which are mostly unreliable when it comes to racism or homophobia. The unit of treatment for Nora's design is teachers, but students may be an important source of data on teachers. One could also describe this relationship in a different way. For the purpose of Nora's design, teachers are proximal actors—the direct targets of learning and change—whereas the students are more distal actors. They may learn and change once teachers have changed their behavior, but the students do so only indirectly.

Focusing on proximal actors, that is, those the most affected by the design, as focal units of analysis or units of treatment does not mean that researchers cannot extract data from others. Sometimes, more distal actors (those more indirectly affected by the design, but still peripherally involved) can give unbiased perceptions of changes in proximal actors. As described above, teachers can be a less biased source of information on principals than the principals' own testimony, or students can play this role for teachers. Consequently, distal actors' perceptions are useful ways to ascertain impact.

IMPACT DATA

Impact data compare the relevant beliefs, attitudes, or practices among study participants at the beginning and end of the study on a common metric. All implementations should begin with a baseline assessment. This initial assessment is a standardized metric so that similar observations, surveys, structured interviews, document analyses, or task analyses can be conducted at the beginning and the end of the intervention. Designers should focus on low-inference or operationalized behaviors that indicate the state of affairs on the main components of the design before and after the intervention. The baseline assessment also succinctly corroborates whether the designers' previous needs assessments and thinking were correct.

Baseline data enable designers to assess growth when they collect the same or similar data at the end of the intervention. Impact is established when the data show growth in at least some dimensions. To develop impact metrics, researchers need to clearly define relevant beliefs, knowledge, skill, competencies, attitudes, practices, or performances and use good assessment instruments so that the parameters don't change in character because of faulty memory or vacillating expectations. We described how easy it was for Eric to downgrade his outcome expectations and adjust them to his observations and effectiveness biases.

How do our four leaders create baseline-versus-outcome data to make their project's impact visible and to avoid biases like those encountered by Eric? They do so in two ways. First, they focus on direct and indirect outcomes. Through previous needs assessments and careful thinking (see chapters 4–9), they already have a good idea of their problematic and desired behaviors. Now they need to determine the most important beliefs, skills, practices, and so on, that indicate the project's most important direct learning, change, or performance goals, and perhaps some indirect ones as well.

Second, the leaders develop indicators, or instruments. Key beliefs, skills, competencies, attitudes, practices, or performances need to be captured with indicators or instruments that allow for a standardized metric. Standardization means that the instruments generate a score, rating, or rubric. An effect of the design is most likely to be detected on metrics that capture changes directly prompted or fostered by a given design.

Leaders cannot fudge on impact data. As was stressed before, design development studies pivot on outcomes or, better, on an accurate idea about what kinds of outcomes, if any, were reached. By their very nature, iterative designs will not reach their full desired effects on the first try. While deep learning and reflection gained through the projects are valuable, leaders of educational organizations, who are ultimately called to produce results for students, need to discipline themselves to aim at effects. So designers need to keep a personal distance from the chosen impact metrics by reducing the need for high-inference interpretations. Hence, impact data should aim at low-inference, relatively transparent behaviors that designers can standardize with instruments that lead to evaluative rubrics, quantifiable ratings, or low-inference observations that can be standardized.

CHRISTINE'S IMPACT DATA

Christine and her district task force debate what the main direct outcomes of their intervention should be. As a reminder, their intervention aims at developing leadership in GLTs to enable these teams to successfully handle less severe discipline problems. They discuss a variety of options for which they list arguments in favor or against:

- *Better student discipline*: They find this option too hard to assess and too removed from the intervention, even though this outcome is what ultimately needs to be accomplished, but probably not yet as a direct result of a ten-session intervention.
- *Self-reported usefulness of the professional development intervention by participating GLT leaders*: The group finds that this indicator has a direct relationship to the design focus, but it does not pick up on the new skills or performances that the GLT leaders are supposed to have learned.
- *GLT leaders' performance*: Performance would be an interesting way to capture growth, but there are two problems with using this outcome. First, a baseline would be hard to define, since most GLT leaders are totally new to their roles. And second, visiting the various GLTs in the schools would be too time-consuming.

After considering all these outcomes, the task force finally settles on three outcomes. The first is growth in the GLT leaders' effectiveness. This parameter seems important and directly related to the design's learning goals, but how does the design team collect relatively low-inference, unbiased data on this? Responses that participants give right after having been exposed to new content in professional development workshops seem to ask for bias. Christine's group settles on a structured interview conducted with each GLT leader at the beginning and at the end of the intervention. The interviews are tightly structured: the team leaders are given statements about self-assessed skills related to the focus of the intervention (group self-organizing, interpersonal facilitation, productive conflict, positive behavior support). They rate these self-assessments on a five-point scale and subsequently explain their ratings with follow-up prompts. A rubric picking up on the main development steps in each dimension allows for a relatively low-inference interpretation of the interview responses. Scale ratings and rubric scores together indicate differences between time 1 (baseline) and time 2 (outcome). Structured interviews promise to be very informative and can be conducted under the direct control of the designers.

The second indicator the task force settles on is a brief, anonymous survey given to teachers in GLTs. The survey asks them to rate the effectiveness of work in GLTs at time 1 and time 2. The survey is administered by the team leaders.

The task force uses the number of students referred to the counseling office at time 1 and time 2 as its third indicator. Because the GLT leaders are supposed to collect and be aware of these data during the entire intervention, the team considers the data a feasible indicator. But student referrals are a more indirect outcome of the design.

MICHELLE'S IMPACT DATA

Thinking about what kind of data to collect to show an impact simplified matters for Michelle's team. The intervention was envisioned as a rather complex, multidimensional effort involving motivational, instructional, and organizational aspects to help her district improve the cultural relevance of instruction. But as the team members think through their design in terms of data, they realize that at the core, their unit of "treatment" and analysis is really the culturally relevant pedagogy group and that changing the conversation about benchmarks should actually be regarded as changing an important context variable for the CRP group participants. And if this is so, the team reasons, the activities related to the benchmark conversations should be captured as process data. This also means that the CRP group participants will have their own focus groups so that process data can be collected on them.

As impact, the team members decide that ultimately their intervention is about a performance, the performance of teaching a rich text to a class of elementary school students. They therefore decide to give teachers two texts at the beginning and ask them to create a lesson plan. One text comes directly out of the literacy program; the other is a rich CRP-like text. At the end of the intervention, they will ask teachers to repeat the exercise with only the rich text. After each performance task, they will ask teachers a set of questions in a structured interview format. With these two data points—the completion of the actual task and the teachers' thinking about the task—the team develops a rubric to rate the quality of the lesson sketches and the teachers' depth of understanding of the task.

ERIC'S IMPACT DATA

Eric identified the focal behavior for his design as the principals' ability to analyze lessons and communicate to teachers how their instructional moves encouraged or discouraged student academic engagement. Of the many indicators and approaches he could use, he decides to focus on a performance-based assessment: the principals will analyze an instructional sequence on a video at the beginning of the intervention and then a similar one at the end. Afterward, he will prompt them with specific questions that will indicate how well they understand the essential principles of academic engagement. He has developed a rubric around this depth of understanding. In a second step, he has planned a role-play activity in which he will play the teacher and will have a conversation with each principal. In this conversation, the principals give the "teacher" feedback, and Eric asks prepared questions. Again, he has developed rubrics for each of these questions; the rubrics asses the quality of the principals' responses.

NORA'S IMPACT DATA

Nora's leadership team begins designing its impact metric by identifying the key behavior she and her team want to change: the tendency of teachers at her school to ignore racial and homophobic slurs when the teachers are within earshot of students exchanging these words. The team members first think they might explore whether teachers' attitudes toward slurs might have changed during the intervention. They think of some questions that they might ask at the beginning and the end of the professional development sequence. But Nora is not certain they would ever get uncensored responses from the teachers. So instead, she and her co-designer team now plan to spread out in the school, observe the hallways and cafeteria unobtrusively, compile a tally of occurrences of slurs uttered near teachers, and note whether the teachers intervene. A similar procedure is to be carried out several weeks after the end of the intervention. If the frequency of slurs has gone down, and teachers intervene more frequently, the design will have had an impact.

Impact data speak directly to the main dimensions of behavior that are targeted by the intervention. Outcome expectations, represented in rubrics, ratings, and the like, should be gauged so that real baseline behavior and expected growth for the period in which the intervention is planned to be implemented can be captured. In this way, the instruments are sensitive to actual growth and pegged to the participants' stretch capacity. In Eric's case, the principals will not all learn to give high-quality feedback on student academic engagement. But they may grow toward it. The instrument needs to pick up on these developmental steps. As a baseline assessment, the metrics need to realistically represent existing knowledge, beliefs, practices, and so forth, at the time when the intervention begins. If the instrument does this, it is also geared toward the participants' next level of work. As shown in Nora's case, designers need to be aware of participants' biases. They cannot expect a participant to give an unbiased response, particularly if they are dealing with attitudes and beliefs that are affected by strong social desirability, for example, attitudes toward race, inequity, or morality.

PROCESS DATA

Process data capture the implementation of the intervention. Implementation is a naturalistic process so the data collected are more open-ended and adjustable to the situation. Qualitative data, such as interviews, informal conversations, and observations, accommodate the fluidity of the process. But there are limits to capturing this fluidity. Design development studies are not in-depth case studies or thick ethnographic descriptions. Process data are collected for one specific purpose, to explain impact. Thus, the collection of process data is tightly circumscribed and must be economical. This means that when it comes to process, the design researchers need to make choices. When the intervention is implemented, the whole process with all its complexity will unfold before the researchers' eyes and ears, but it cannot be entirely captured with data. Only what is captured with data will be subject to subsequent analysis. All else will enter into the researchers' intuitive understanding of the proceedings they behold and may congeal into holistic impressions that are useful for data analysis, but cannot constitute the evidence for research-based findings.

There are various ways in which design researchers identify and select the pieces of process data they need:

- *Chunking*: The structure of the intervention design breaks down the organic learning process into chunks. The main chunks are the activities that make up the intervention and the learning goals that are attached to them. But other ways of chunking are possible, too. For example, researchers could decide that a sequence of activities over a certain duration will produce a particularly salient behavior pattern that should be captured. Or they could focus on critical incidents that will demonstrate that a shift may have happened.
- *Focusing on key behaviors*: There is so much to look at in these chunks, researchers need to choose which salient behavior they need to see. They could focus on how a new tool is used, how a new procedure is implemented, how a particular concept is used, how a particular belief is uttered, how a particular disposition is displayed, how a particular practice is implemented, and so forth.
- *Developing indicators*: Once salient behaviors are chosen, indicators that make the quality of these behaviors visible are useful. To capture inner states that are not visible—for example, learning, motivation, joy, or resentment—the designers create observable indicators from which they infer inner states. But even overt behavior needs to be categorized, and a focus needs to be established.
- *Creating instruments*: These are devices that help designers get organized. An interview protocol, an observation protocol, or a questionnaire helps in the main task of collecting data.
- *Generating data*: Indicators and instruments will generate a stream of data. What sort of data will be generated? For example, do the indicators allow for quantification or some sort of standardization that results in a metric or rubric, or are they pointing to patterns that are captured in a more narrative

way? Do the designers observe the participants, talk to them, or analyze artifacts that the participants create?

ERIC'S PROCESS DATA

We described how Eric's theory of action resulted in a twelve-session intervention design for his district's principals. He now needs to decide which data to collect on this process, and when to collect them. To decide what kind of data is needed for each activity in his intervention, he thinks about the purpose of each activity across the multiple sessions. For example, he plans for the first session to be an introduction to the concept that he wants principals to learn and focus on: academic engagement. So for process data, he wants to note whether the principals actually seem to engage with and understand this central concept by the end of the session. He decides that he can do this with a kind of exit-ticket formative assessment in which principals write about what they have learned. Similarly, in sessions 2 through 4, in which principals will be practicing their analysis of lessons, Eric plans to design worksheets on which the principals can record their answers—answers that can provide process data.

However, he also notes that the principals' discussions during the sessions might lend additional insight into the progress of the intervention, but that the participants might omit these discussions from their writing. Thus, Eric also decides to write a short memo after each session to keep track of any insights about how the intervention is working. He also realizes that some sessions might be particularly important in understanding the outcome of his intervention—especially when principals will be debriefing their instructional rounds and observing each other's teacher conferencing. For these sessions, Eric thinks that an audio recording would be helpful because having an exact recording of what is said will enable him to do a more in-depth analysis later on. An outline of how he organizes his process-data collection is presented in table 11.1.

Eric does not collect data on the whole implementation process. He believes that the selective stream of data that he creates will be sufficient to understand and document the essentials of the change process. The short self-reflections after each

TABLE 11.1 Eric's process data

SESSION	ACTIVITIES WITH PRINCIPALS	COLLECTION OF PROCESS DATA
1	Introducing the concept: ■ What is academic engagement? ■ How effective is it? ■ How can we see it in classrooms?	■ Post-session summary reflection: □ What have you learned from this session? □ What was new? □ Where are you still fuzzy in your understanding? ■ Short reflections and feedback to be repeated for all sessions
2	Analyzing instructional sequences on video: ■ What is the academic content of a given sequence?	Collecting worksheets on which the principals note what they think is the focal content of given sequences
3	Analyzing instructional sequences on video: ■ Reading student cues ■ Using an observation tool	■ Collecting worksheets on which the principals describe student cues ■ Brief summary memo by Eric on what he observed
4	Analyzing instructional sequences on video: ■ Observing teacher instructional moves ■ Using an observation tool	■ Collecting worksheets on which the principals describe teacher moves ■ Brief summary memo by Eric on what he observed
4a	Reviewing sessions 2, 3, and 4 if needed	No data collection planned; data collected on ad hoc basis
5	Conducting instructional rounds focused on student academic engagement in schools to diagnose teaching patterns in vivo	No data collection planned
6	Debriefing observed patterns from the rounds	■ Audio recording of this session, to be analyzed according to depth of understanding and principals' skill in correctly identifying student academic engagement
7	■ Observing and analyzing lessons ■ Practicing teacher conferences with peers	No data collection planned
8	Preparing principals to conduct professional development sessions for their faculties: ■ Creating observation criteria and sharing observation tools	No data collection planned
9/10	■ Principal–teacher conferencing and subsequent tryouts ■ Using a conferencing tool	Observation: ■ Which dimensions of the tool are easy, and which are difficult?
11	Observing one another having conferences with teachers through videos	Audio recording of this session: ■ Principals' comments on their colleagues (i.e., their meta-understanding of the process) is analyzed
12	Sharing feedback from teachers about principals' conferences	Written memo of principals' responses to the feedback

session and the worksheets will give him a sense of the continuity of the learning process. His two key performances for the process are sessions 6 and 11. They will tell him if the principals were able to apply the content from the previous sessions in an independent analysis of a lesson or, finally, in an independent performance as instructional supervisors. He will need these two data points if he wants to claim in the end that the learning process fostered by the intervention produced, or at least plausibly contributed to, his outcomes.

NORA'S PROCESS DATA

As described earlier, Nora's theory of action resulted in a ten-session intervention design for her school. The leadership team now needs to decide what sorts of data to collect on this process, and when to collect them. Given the delicacy of the topic, the team members believe that audio records are out of the question, except during the last session, when, they believe, teachers will have sufficient comfort with the topic. Otherwise, data can only be collected unobtrusively and anonymously, though teachers must be made fully aware of what is being recorded in writing.

Since the first two sessions are about creating cognitive dissonance through the slur tallies, the team wants to note whether the planned activities actually accomplish this goal. The team decides that two of its group members take notes independently during the discussions on how teachers respond to the data and where moments of agreement and disagreement come up. Session 3 is about creating a safe space. To note whether teachers seem to perceive that a safe space was indeed created, Nora's team decides to ask for teacher reflections about the session, in the form of a free write. For session 5, two team members record the main points of the discussion. For session 6, the intervention is designed to prompt teachers to reflect on the emotional impact of slurs. The team decides that the process data needs to gauge how deep this reflection is—do the teachers stay on the surface, or do they demonstrate a willingness to dig deeper into their own personal experiences of, and feelings about, slurs? The team will carefully observe and note what their colleagues say during this session. They devise a plan for its process-data collection (table 11-2).

TABLE 11.2   Nora's process data

SESSION	ACTIVITIES	COLLECTION OF PROCESS DATA
1	■ Recapping antibullying campaign ■ Stimulating cognitive dissonance: □ Confrontation with observation tallies (frequent slurs, little intervention by adults) □ Interpretation of the data □ Discussion of veracity, meaning of the data □ Naming the problem	Given that Nora is in the background, she takes charge of the note-taking with these tasks: ■ Recording the teachers' responses to the slur data ■ Noting who embraces the data, who rejects them, and what main arguments are communicated ■ Capturing critical moments and noting her low-inference observations at these moments ■ Summarizing her findings and reflecting on the session in reference to the goals of the session ■ Writing up her analysis in a research memo
2	Same focus as session 1. Individually, leadership team members reach out to the faculty members they normally talk to and engage them in informal conversations about Session 1 content.	■ All informal conversations and feedback from session 2 are discussed in the leadership team, which comes to consensus on what next step to take. ■ Nora writes a research memo on the main content of discussion and main decisions.
3	■ Establishing a safe space: □ Discussing norms of courageous conversations □ Assuming good intentions when people speak □ Recognizing delicate nature of topic □ Acknowledging that people can misspeak ■ Clarifying the role of facilitators and leadership team	■ Teachers free-write at the end of the session to the prompt: How do I feel about the slur project at this moment? ■ Volunteers share their writing with the leadership team. ■ Two leadership team members take observational notes with the help of an observation instrument tailored to session 3.
4	Same focus as in session 3. Individually, leadership team members reach out to the faculty members they normally talk to and engage them in informal conversations about session 3 content.	Same data collection process as in session 2
5	Appealing to shared values: ■ What it means to teach in a social justice school ■ What it means for our school if we tolerate slurs	■ Teachers provide anonymous feedback following writing prompts: □ Can we tolerate slurs? □ Can we make a difference, or are we over our heads? □ Can I make a difference, or is this too much for me to deal with? ■ Two leadership team members take observational notes with the help of an observation instrument tailored to session 5.

(continued)

TABLE 11.2 Nora's process data *(continued)*

SESSION	ACTIVITIES	COLLECTION OF PROCESS DATA
6	Understanding the multiple functions of slurs more deeply: ■ What slurs signify ■ What emotions they trigger ■ How they express racism and homophobia ■ How students use them	■ As teachers share personal experience with slurs, note takers briefly summarize narratives. ■ Two note takers record critical or noteworthy incidents with respect to the learning goals of the session. ■ Teachers write a short summary of their understanding of slurs; summaries are collected and later analyzed with a rubric on depth of understanding.
7	Anticipating actions: ■ Mobilizing readiness to act ■ Sharing ideas about next steps	Same data collection process as in sessions 2 and 4
8	■ Developing intervention strategies: □ Phrases to be used when teachers hear a slur □ Prompts to be used when students brush off or talk back ■ Trying out scenarios	■ Team audio-records session. ■ In an observation protocol, two team members record the phrases, prompts, and strategies that are being discussed and selected to be tried out with students in the next week or two.
9	Experimenting with intervening: ■ Making notes about experiences ■ Reflecting on the effectiveness of one's response ■ Tinkering with one's response or strategy ■ Recording one's feelings	No data collection planned for these individual activities
10	■ Reporting on experiences ■ Sharing one's feelings ■ Assessing one's effectiveness ■ Refining strategies	Team audio-records session as teachers share positive or negative experiences.

The team does not collect data on the whole implementation process of their intervention. Data collection for this design is not easy, because of issues of privacy and potential controversy. However, the team members believe that the selective stream of data they generate will be sufficient to understand and document the essentials of the change process. Given that it is difficult for them to produce records of low-inference behaviors, they rely on relatively high-inference memos and reflections (for example, the free-writes or Nora's memos from leadership team meetings). They nevertheless believe that all of these data, together, will give them sufficient evidence of the kind of learning that takes place.

CHAPTER SUMMARY

In this chapter, we described the importance of impact and process data and the distinction between them. Impact data ideally are standardized metrics that pick up on the difference between baseline and outcome. Process data select out of the flow of implemented activities the qualitative descriptions of adult-learning incidents that must be documented.

We followed the four leaders as they planned how to collect their impact and process data. We showed that impact data require several features:

- A specified *unit of analysis* or *unit of "treatment"*—the particular people whose behavior the educational leaders want to shift

- A determination of the *direct goals* of the intervention—the most immediate beliefs, practices, or attitudes that designers predict their intervention will change

- A set of *indicators* that allow those behaviors or attitudes to be observed or detected

- A *metric* that can measure those indicators before the intervention (as a baseline) and after it (to look for growth)

We described the following steps required to obtain process data:

- Determining the main *chunks* of the change process that need to be documented

- Considering the key behaviors to observe or capture, and deciding on the signs that indicate them

- Identifying the specific types of data that can and will be collected during implementation

- Planning specific procedures for collecting each type of data

12

Making Design Development
Studies Rigorous

Novelists are similar to researchers in that both make behavior visible, the novelist with narrative techniques, the researcher with research methods. But the novelist does not need to verify. The expressiveness of the narration is proof enough. Researchers, however, need to prove that their claims about human behavior are confirmable by evidence. In design development studies, we make one central claim, namely, that our intervention, carried out under certain circumstances, will produce the desired change for those who participated in the process. In this chapter, we specifically look at criteria that ensure the rigor of data collection and analysis.

We address two key questions:

→ How do designers ensure reliability of data collection?
→ How do they ensure the validity of their claim that X (the intervention) plausibly influenced Y (outcome or growth)?

Many people, even if they are not involved in law or law enforcement, have some sense of how a court of law functions, even if their knowledge mainly stems from television. Far less is known about how research works. But research functions not unlike courts of law. "Courts of research," that is, the community of researchers who decide whether they accept a study as robust and its findings as worthy of their attention, and courts of law share the principle that only certain evidence is admissible to establish culpability (in law) or causality (in research).

The rules of evidence between the two arenas differ, to be sure, but in both fields, only certain select evidence counts. An experienced police investigator follows his or her instincts or intuition about crime, but the officer knows that only certain evidence will be admissible in court to make the case. A practitioner with ample practical experience is not unlike a police investigator. He or she understands educational change much as an experienced police officer may understand crime, but only certain evidence will play in the court of research. Police investigators are trained in court procedures so that law enforcement can credibly represent a case to the judge on the witness stand. Researcher-practitioners are trained in research procedures so that they can credibly present the fruits of their design development work to a skeptical public, a court of researchers, and other practitioners. The standards of admissible evidence in the research court are higher than fuzzy impressions or intuition. No matter what methodology a study uses, the study must have high reliability and validity to sway the judges.

RELIABILITY AND VALIDITY OF RESEARCH

On television, court proceedings resemble human drama in fiction more than an actual account of reality. In fiction, we are spared the tedium of technical detail that in reality plays such an important role. Design development research, like all research, is as much about technical detail as it is about lively drama. We do not want to be tedious, and equity-relevant design development is rarely tedious. But the sheer expressiveness of a narrative, or an implementation story, will not do the trick of persuading a critical audience that the design is worth its consideration unless drama is coupled with rigor. There are several things researchers can do to ensure rigor:

- Collect and analyze data with consistent procedures that other design researchers could repeat in their own study.
- Ascertain that narrow outcome metrics actually speak to the broader learning they are designed to capture.

- Establish that growth occurred by comparing baseline and outcome using the same metrics.
- Provide evidence that at least some of the intervention activities were effective when they occurred and that these activities, in combination, could have produced the change according to the theory of action.
- Check researcher biases with self-reflection techniques or by involving critical friends or participants in the researchers' thinking.

In other words, to create a rigorous study, we as designers need to consider the data collection procedures we put in place, and the indicators, instruments, or metrics we use to generate the data. We must also understand the relationship between the impact data and the process data and the relationship between the artificiality of research and the real-world situation. And finally, we need to worry about ourselves as researchers. (See also next chapters.)

First, to develop effective data collection procedures, researchers take these important steps:

- Design tight and low-inference instruments to collect impact data.
- Plan intervention activities with precision.
- Make deliberate changes when needed.
- Develop interview protocols, conversational prompts, or observation criteria that are targeted to critical incidents or learning goals of chosen activity chunks.

In chapter 11, we showed how Eric and Nora create a systematic and reliable data flow parallel to the intervention activities. This systematic data flow makes the data collection procedures transparent so that the next researcher who wants to inherit their designs and try out a next iteration will be able to repeat what they did with reliability.

Second, we pay attention to instruments and metrics. Naturally, these tools can only capture a sliver of the core behaviors researchers want to grasp. These instruments and metrics do not naturally occur in the real world unless researchers construct them. Thus the tools are constructs of human imagination. But what these constructs capture must be representative of the broader knowledge, skills, beliefs, attitudes, or practices targeted for change in the first place. When the constructs do so, we say that they have construct validity. Educational systems in many countries commonly evaluate school performance through centrally administered state assessments. From the vantage point of the state government, the state tests represent broader school performance. But when the tests are a bad fit with the learning needs of students in a given school, say, because the majority of students are nonnative speakers and the state test is in the national language, the state tests can be said to have low construct validity.

Let's take Christine's impact metrics: a scale and a rubric score on a structured interview with professional development participants (i.e., GLT [Grade-level team] leaders in training); mean effectiveness ratings by teachers in GLTs; and a change in the number of referrals to the counseling office over time. The interview scores are directly tied to the work in the intervention and will give much information on the learning process of the participants, but Christine needs to deal with bias (the participants want to please the researchers) and with her subjective interpretations of the interview narratives.

The ratings from the teachers in the GLTs are more objective, that is, potentially less biased, than the interviews may be, but they contain far less information. One does not know specifically what a teacher's rating of "satisfactory" or "unsatisfactory" may stand for. Nor does Christine's task force know for sure that a score difference from time 1 to time 2 can be attributed to the work the group did in the professional development intervention for leaders. But Christine's task force can construct a plausible connection, since the professional development directly trains team leaders on aspects of grade-level teamwork that Christine will survey teachers on.

The number of referred cases to the counseling office does not have such an immediate connection to the leaders' professional development, the core of Christine's intervention. If anything, that number may go up or down because of the work in the GLTs, but a host of other factors may also be at play, for example, reorganizations in the counseling office or changed administrative policies. So by itself, this last indicator may not be as valid an impact metric as the group wished.

That is, Christine may have a harder time justifying that referrals directly connect to the change targeted by the intervention. At the same time, referrals are the one indicator that encapsulates the effectiveness of Christine's design, because the work of GLTs must ultimately result in better management of student behavior at the grade level, and a reduction of referrals may be a good indicator of success. Depending on how hard it is for the group to make a plausible connection between its constructed instruments and the actual human behaviors they stand for, the instruments, metrics, and so forth, can be said to have high or low construct validity.

Third, an important concern is making plausible connections between intervention and outcomes or between process data and impact data. With the help of the data collected for both the impact and the process, designers need to plausibly show that the intervention—and not something else—produced the results. They should be able to show that there is, indeed, a difference between baseline and outcome and that this difference can be credibly linked to the process or, more specifically, to data about the process. These data must demonstrate the effectiveness of at least some key activities related to the theory of action.

In Nora's case, if, at the end of her design, she finds that teachers intervene more often when they hear slurs, she will also have to show that some key activities in her design worked according to plan. For example, the participants may have uncovered some clear cognitive dissonance in the first session, shown a strong willingness to interrogate the seriousness of why slurs hurt so much, and felt a clear sense of efficacy around new strategies of the intervention. Consequently, Nora's impact data reasonably connect with her process data; her theory of action corroborates her claims. In the court of research, her study would be found to have high internal validity.

Fourth, designers consider the relationship between their design and the real world of schools, districts, or other educational settings. Designers want their interventions and research designs to work in the real world. The good news is that the interventions are usually deeply embedded in the reality of educational organizations. In this respect, design development studies have high external validity. Designers are not conducting some far-fetched experiment with some undergraduate economics students in the basement laboratory of the business school, though sometimes, when researchers are in positions of authority, they need to be vigilant and create safeguards that permit participants to "act real." But extending findings beyond the context in which the design is implemented is a different challenge altogether. This will be discussed in chapter 15.

EXCURSION INTO THEORY

Testing Theories of Action with Rigor

Data from the implementation process in combination with assessment of impact, together, guide systematic reflection on the theory of action that underpins the intervention. The researchers ask, Can the learning that occurred during implementation be plausibly linked to the outcomes? If strong learning occurred and outcome data indicate growth, then the researchers can conclude that the theory of action is supported by the evidence. If very little or no learning occurred during the intervention, then any impact could be spurious and related to factors outside the intervention. If learning was strong during the intervention along intended dimensions, but it did not lead to growth, then the researchers may conclude that the theory of action or the metrics need revising.

Methods and Data

Design research is primed for mixed-methods studies in which quantitative and qualitative data are collected.[1] If impact, for example, is established via a baseline-growth-outcome assessment, the metrics should allow for standardization over the time span of the intervention. These metrics could be quantitative measures or qualitative rubrics that allow for quantifiable ratings. Standardized quantifications enable researchers to reliably draw conclusions about the changes that occurred as a result of implementing the intervention. To improve on a design prototype, researchers need to have sufficient information about the process.[2] Process data are geared to capture the emergent nature of a change process and be open to course corrections during implementation. Qualitative data are suited to accommodate these needs. But quantitative data (e.g., questionnaires with Likert scales) could indicate gains produced by specific intervention activities.

Capturing the implementation process with qualitative data, however, does not aim at richly textured ethnography or thick description of actors, their context, and researchers interacting with both.[3] Rather, data are bounded by the objectives and activity chunks that mark the intervention design and implementation process. Data collection is guided and constrained by the categories that make up the theory of action.[4] Eschewing open-ended, grounded approaches to qualitative data collection, designers should, as much as possible, specify and plan data collection and analysis procedures for process data ahead of time.[5]

Rigor

The rigor of any study rests on the study's reliability and validity and the degree to which researcher bias is held in check. We call a study design *reliable* when metrics or procedures used in the study are transparent to independent observers and could potentially be replicated in a similar study that yields similar results. Standards of reliability are most easily met in controlled research environments, such as those that apply to experiments. Some aspects of design research enhance reliability: the predetermined and prespecified nature of the intervention, the standardized metrics for impact, and the theory-guided collection of process data during implementation. Other aspects threaten it: the flexibility, creativity, and innovation needed in a design space that has as its "material" a complex set of social interactions with relatively few technical constraints—the situation typical of educational settings.[6] Careful documentation of course corrections, a redesign of data collection instruments, and an awareness of the reasons for adjustments may alleviate these threats.

A study has high validity when theoretical concepts, constructs, and conclusions drawn from empirical patterns about descriptive characteristics and causal relationships are well founded and when these conclusions accurately match the real world. For design development studies, internal validity, construct validity, and external validity are of main concern.

As explained above, a study has high internal validity when the study design justifies claims about causal relationships between a treatment and an outcome. In experiments, internal validity is established under highly controlled conditions. In design development studies, internal validity depends on evidentiary connections between process and outcome and whether these connections can be bolstered with sound arguments. When researchers can show that the intervention unfolded according to plan, that the strength of the process in prespecified dimensions is reflected in growth on these dimensions, and that the process was informed by a scientifically framed theory of action, internal validity can be said to be high. But even when plans must be adapted and new elements planned, internal validity could still be maintained if researchers can definitively show how the new or adapted elements influence the process of change.

Construct validity seeks agreement between a theoretical concept and a specific measure or metric. The most sensitive part of a design study is the establishment of direct impact with observations, performance tasks, structured interviews, survey questionnaires, and so on, evaluated with metrics that can be standardized. Researchers need to ensure that these metrics are indeed adequate expressions of the authentic belief, attitude, or practice that the intervention targets in real life. In design development studies, tests of construct validity can be think-aloud sessions with nonparticipants in similar roles, the application of impact metrics on nonparticipants who seem to already exhibit the desired behaviors in real life, and reflections on impact metrics and culminating activities in light of exhibited learning during the implementation.

The external validity of a study is high when the results (assuming high internal validity) can be assumed to occur in real life and the findings extend beyond the study's participants and their situation. Experiments may have low external validity when they force people to act in contrived ways that seldom or never occur in real life. In educational design development studies, low external validity is rare, since the design is carried out in the natural life of organizations and rarely do researchers exert control in these settings. Although contrived features of designs are conceivable, participants' "talking back" can be expected or encouraged.[7] On the other hand, context specificity of all design research limits the claims of external validity beyond the specific context studied.

Researcher bias is a problem in all studies, irrespective of the methodology used. Bias occurs when researchers slant the research toward the results that they expect or want to show. In design research, the most important biases are observer-expectancy and observer-advocacy biases. These biases nudge researchers toward the desirability of showing impact and effect. A strong commitment to certain solutions may skew the researchers' views of the problem. Careful initial conceptualization and constant revisiting of problem definition and framing may guard against this bias. A strong commitment to effects may encourage researchers to omit data from the interpretation, search for effect in the data, and fail to entertain alternative explanations. An easy check on this kind of bias is the strict separation of design and implementation functions from evaluation functions and to assign these functions to different researchers. When, as is often the case, design research is carried out by researchers who combine the roles of designers, interveners, and evaluators, biases may develop for which action research methodology has developed appropriate safeguards. We will discuss action research in chapter 13.

CONTEXT SENSITIVITY

Interventions are usually sensitive to context. Education is a business that is relatively simple in technical terms, but highly complex in human terms.[8] So interventions are subject to the unpredictability of many human beings interacting with each other. There is, however, regularity in the midst of this unpredictability; otherwise, teachers could not teach class every day and administrators could not guarantee that school takes place predictably for a whole school year. Yet, designers cannot fully control or standardize the environment in which they implement an intervention. So they need to specify the organizational context in which the design is supposed to work and in which it is feasible. Relevant contextual preconditions for implementation include the following:

- knowledge, skill, and competence of participants and project directors or change agents;
- adequate time, money, and energy for the implementation;
- motivation of participants to follow through to the end of the intervention;
- political or moral support, or both, from leaders to keep the intervention a priority;

- fit with an overall strategic orientation of the district or other organization.

Many of us are familiar with programs and interventions that come into districts and schools with great promise. Educators pick them up with initial enthusiasm. Extraordinary money, effort, training, leadership support, and so on, are poured into the new initiative. When the extra attention moves elsewhere, the initiative fades away. Often, it cannot be sustained in the ordinary flow of work. Feasibility of a design is enhanced when it does not make extraordinary claims on people's time, energy, or skill and when it can coexist with shifting priorities and organizational turbulence, both of which are not uncommon in schools and districts. If change is fundamentally about learning, it has to take place in the zone of people's next level of work, that is, within their capacity to stretch. A good local needs assessment should provide information ahead of time on what kind of change is feasible. But data collected during the implementation should spot when design activities are overloading participants.

CHAPTER SUMMARY

In this chapter, we looked closely at what it means to conduct a rigorous study. We explained that rigorous design development studies meet the following criteria:

- Ensure reliability of data collection procedures.
- Make sure that validity is high, that is, that both impact data and process data speak to each other in a way that plausible connections between intervention and outcome can be made.
- Create data that can be interpreted to guide the next iterations.
- Check for bias.
- Specify the contextual conditions under which the design is practical.

13

Integrating Action Research into Design Development

When leaders use design development to address the urgent needs facing their organizations, they benefit from their insider knowledge, authority, and influence, yet these same benefits can also be daunting impediments. This is because people will inevitably run up against their own biases—their ingrained assumptions about "the way we do things around here." Leaders' desire for objectivity will conflict both with their strong hopes that they have indeed made some progress in addressing a troubling problem and with their passionate beliefs about what is morally and ethically the right thing to do. But if people are not careful, these beliefs will thwart their best intentions and inhibit measurable progress.

Biases are an inherent problem in all research, but when the change agents act as design developers at the same time, biases become an even more daunting challenge. Action research methodology addresses this situation. The methodology was developed to enable researchers to act in their organizations and study an action while still maintaining a distance from the action—a distance that is typical for researchers. Action research comes into play when designers wear multiple hats. In this chapter, we answer several questions about reducing bias:

→ What sorts of blind spots or biases might change agents encounter when they conduct research at the same time?

→ What techniques can change agents use to keep these unpleasant side effects of an otherwise privileged insider perspective in check?

→ What self-reflection capacity do these change agents need to sustain a research stance in the midst of their commitments to the improvement of their organizations?

In fiction, the novelist is the author of his or her characters. The writer knows them intimately; in fact, they are created from the imagination of the author, who manipulates them to his or her liking. In experimental research, the researcher is nowhere to be seen when research subjects act. For example, in an experiment on students' extrinsic or intrinsic learning motivation, subjects are selected randomly and two groups are given the same motivating task. The treatment group is told that an extrinsic reward or an evaluation of the quality of the task is awaiting them at the end, while the control group is told nothing of the sort. The researchers observe from afar to determine whether one group voluntarily continues the task longer during a free period than does the other group.

In design development studies, researchers cannot control the participants. After all, the researchers are conducting the design "experiment" in the real environment of educational organizations, though they assess baselines and outcomes with robust instruments and conduct intervention activities with a precise plan. The distance between participants and researchers, however, is highly problematic. In small design studies, researchers may play multiple roles: they plan, implement, and evaluate the design. In large-scale design studies, where these roles are usually played by multiple people, evaluators are more likely to remain objective and unbiased by their desire to demonstrate the success of the design to which they may have committed as planners or implementers. How do we make sure that the conflation of all these roles does not end up turning researchers into novelists who have intimate insider knowledge of their participants, but also have no distance from them?

When the functions of planning, implementing, and evaluating belong to one individual or one team, the rigor of the study is threatened. The threats have to do with the various biases that come from being a transformative leader and action researcher at the same time. Administrators and leaders may face several challenges to the rigor of their studies:

- They may have authority over the participants in the study, which may distort how both parties communicate with each other.
- They may be passionate about moral and ethical issues, which may cloud detached, critical thinking.
- They may feel compelled to fulfill role expectations of being effective no matter what.
- They may develop an advocacy stance for their designs.

To think through these challenges, designers need to augment design development methodology with the methodology of action research. Action research embraces transformative leaders and places them in the center of the research endeavor. It draws its strength from the researchers' insider knowledge of the organization that engages in change. Action research methodology has developed some procedural safeguards so that the research conducted by transformative leaders does not turn into fiction. As we explained, in experiments, control and distance are externally imposed. In action research, control and distance move inward. Control and distance become internal through critical self-reflection and reflection with others. So, for example, action researchers keep self-reflective journals, engage in communication with critical friends, or make the study participants co-designers who provide ongoing critical feedback. Action researchers reflect on their own positions of authority and their own desirability biases up front.

EXCURSION INTO THEORY

Action Research Versus Design Development

When organizations face problems that leaders feel compelled to address, research in action, rather than research about action, is indicated.[1] In action research, realities facing individuals within the organization—the contextual details and the practical concerns—are an integral part of understanding change.

Action research unfolds in real time through a cycle of diagnosing, planning, acting, and evaluating.[2] As data are systematically collected for these various steps, a narrative emerges and explains what happened and why, documented with evidence. Because the action researcher is "not neutral but an active intervener making and helping things happen," the researcher creates distance from participants through reflection.[3]

The strength of action research, namely, insider knowledge and an understanding of change through the direct experience of it, is also the weakness of action research. When researchers are also change agents, they play multiple roles as initiators, implementers, and evaluators all at the same time. Thus, it is critical for those engaging in this type of research to explore their tacit assumptions, make them conscious, and check biases.[4] In particular, they need to guard against the emergence of advocacy bias. As introduced earlier, advocacy bias occurs when the researcher's wish to see an effect influences how he or she interprets data. It is especially important to search for competing explanations for observed patterns and to strive to rule them out with contravening evidence.[5]

Because action research and design development share some important features, they are complementary methodologies. Both center on addressing real-world problems in real-world contexts. Both use iterative processes of inquiry. However, the two methodologies are not interchangeable. In design development, formative and summative evaluation could be a separate function from designing and implementing the interventions. Since design development hinges on ascertaining results, the separation of functions in design teams would make the research more robust. In action research, these various roles and functions usually conflate, but the research also does not aim per se at verifying results or measurable effects. Compared with action research, design development methodology banks on more structured action sequences for which reliable data collection protocols can be developed up front.[6] Likewise, given that process and impact data are collected with careful attention paid to reliability, the internal validity of explanations can be more easily established in design development than it can with action research, which leaves data collection procedures relatively open and unstructured.

In action research, change processes come into view in a more organic flow of individuals interacting with each other. However, the researchers' intimate involvement with the participants can jeopardize research validity and rigor. To bolster validity, cycles of meta-reflection run parallel to data collection in action. In meta-reflections, action researchers continually examine their position and decisions self-critically and make them transparent to others. Journaling, checking assumptions with participants, and collaborating with impartial third parties are ways to facilitate this reflection. Data analysis may be ongoing and may involve checking with participants about emerging hunches. Competing explanations are actively sought and investigated. Findings may be tested when shared with co-designers, key participants, and critical friends who have more distance from the project.

The way we combine action research with design development here is obviously not the only conceivable one. One interesting version of integrating action research with design methods is the *social design experiment,* an approach developed by Kris Gutiérrez and others.[7] A social design experiment is a way for "imagining and designing robust learning ecologies" that enable learners to imagine a more just world and to create spaces for equitable pedagogy.[8] Learning opportunities are deliberately co-designed with learners to create consciousness about, and deliberate use of, contradictions to push the boundaries of existing or established practices within institutions. In education, contradictions between theory and practice are focal nodes of learning and activity. Social design experiments aim at creating learning opportunities mediated through materials, artifacts, or conversations that enable learners to look at the present through the perspective of the future.

Our approach to design development is similar to that of Gutiérrez and colleagues in that we want participants in the designs to aspire to imagine a more equitable world. We take aim at the contradictory complexity of inequitable practices, and the core of our equity-oriented design development focuses on empowering co-designed learning. But our approach differs on key points. Design development of the kind we envision should be a form of critical pedagogy for co-designing participants, the way Gutiérrez and her team describe it.[9] But we have ambitions that go beyond that. We want to create practical design knowledge that is informed by theory and that can travel from one context to another. Toward this end, design development of the kind we are advocating must pay careful attention to the impact and process of the intervention. The development follows robust data-collection procedures that abide by the criteria of reliability and validity and, at the same time, incorporates the transformative potential of action research.

PASSION AND DISPASSION

Equity-minded leaders accomplish little without passion. The work is hard and often goes against the grain of the normal functioning of their organizations. As stated earlier, equity-oriented change creates value dissonance with those who accept the status quo and involves political conflict with those who have benefited from or defended inequities. Equity-relevant improvements involve innovation, morality, politics, motivation, risk taking, and courage. They also require fortitude and passion. Yet, research requires dispassion, the ability of the researcher to suspend judgment, to challenge his or her own assumptions, and to let evidence be the guide. Action researchers compose studies dispassionately, so that the evidence has a chance to refute the researcher's cherished beliefs. Research is about trying to disconfirm what one feels passionate about, not about designing facile ways to confirm it. If assumptions and findings hold up despite being challenged with dispassion, they become credible.

Being passionate and dispassionate at the same time can be hard, yet action research conducted by those who are change agents in their own organization seems to call for it. The four leaders whose projects we have been narrating approach this paradoxical demand of action research in different ways. Common to all four is personal reflection on their beliefs, assumptions, strengths, weaknesses, functional roles, and commitments at the time of designing the research and during its implementation. The four leaders also share a collective approach to designing and implementing interventions in the context of functional groups whose members become co-designers or critical friends. Moreover, all the leaders show intellectual leadership that is supported by knowledge-creating institutions, such as universities. Christine works with her district task force, Michelle is a member of a district equity committee that is interested in her initiative, Eric develops a strong relationship with a coach in his district, and Nora from the start convenes a leadership group to get the work done at her school.

In all instances, however, the four leaders are really leading the change projects. They are the ones who actively engage their colleagues in defining and framing the focal problem of practice and the ones who provide the research knowledge that undergirds the theories of action. They are also the ones with the training to think through the challenges of rigorous data collection and analysis. Given their centrality, the leaders' assumptions and biases hold great sway over the shape, outcome, and interpretation of the designs and interventions.

For Christine, being passionate and dispassionate comes relatively easy. She undertakes her project from the start with a cool problem-solving attitude. She herself is a middle school principal, and when it comes to a safe and orderly environment at her school, she just wants to know what works. She must find a new way to deal with this issue since for the near future, she will have to cope with large numbers of novice teachers unless she manages to hold on to some of them for longer. Moreover, members of her district task force face the same basic problem. While her problem is essential for the functioning of schools, Christine sees that her design development is just a first step in addressing the full complexity of the issue, and she is determined to remain open to unexpected turns of events.

For Michelle, passion for equity and commitment to a view of society as deeply divided by ethnic divisions and racism generates her emotions and frames her problem. She stays true to these commitments throughout the duration of her design, but she accepts the possibility that other ways of seeing the problem might improve the quality of her thinking. Being willing to listen to others, most notably her vice principal, helps Michelle temper her passions. When she begins to look at her problem in organizational terms, her own contribution to the problematic behavior becomes evident. Michelle builds into her design some components that challenge her as a leader to create an organizational culture that is conducive to cognitively and culturally sensitive instruction. She resolves to look at her intervention through the eyes of her assistant principal, whom Michelle wins as her critical friend.

Eric acts as a self-assured manager, and he believes in himself, his intellectual competence, and his ability to run his organization. Once he has decided on a course of action, he charges forward with the confidence that he is doing the right thing. He likes to think of himself as methodical and exact, and he prizes these attributes as virtues in his administrative role. Eric is confident, and he does not like to overlook loose ends. The latter attitude helps him keenly observe where his thinking goes wrong and where his assumptions are not confirmed by his observations. Confidence and exactitude struggle with each other, but in the end, he keeps sight of what it takes for principals to do what he thinks must be done: help teachers see how they foster or inhibit student academic engagement. To slow himself down, he elects to write regular journal entries and analytical memos about the unfolding of the project, and he shares these memos with the collaborating coach.

Nora is a fearless administrator who runs a tight ship at her high school, but she is also a moralist deeply attracted to being the leader of a social-justice school. She takes this idea seriously and strongly believes that her teachers should do so as well. She is actually quite astonished and a little outraged when she discovers that the faculty ignores rampant slurs by students in her school. She is convinced that something must change. More than any of the four leaders, Nora trusts in the collective leadership and wisdom of her team, and as part of her design, she has the team make regular reflections about the intervention.

In the end, all four leaders balance their passion for equity with a passion for truth. That is, they desire to know what works, given what they value.

CHAPTER SUMMARY

In this chapter, we explained that transformative and passionate leaders can use design development to address the urgent needs of their organizations, but that doing so according to the standards of rigorous research means learning how to follow passion with the dispassionate stance of a researcher. We look to action research methods to learn how to guard against the bias that comes along with wearing many hats at once. Action research methodology requires that leaders undertake the following approaches:

- Commit to making their tacit assumptions explicit.

- Be willing to question those assumptions, even the beliefs they hold dearest.

- Expand on their self-reflection capacities.

- Check for bias, especially advocacy bias, every step of the way.

- Search for refuting evidence.

- Involve many critical voices in interpreting findings.

PART III SUMMARY

Rigor in design development studies primarily rests on good theory that has some value in predicting behavior. The type of theories we are after for design development are *theories of action* that stress actionability, pragmatism, and conjecture.

In parts I and II of this book, we showed how designers, through a variety of steps, come to formulate a theory of action for their design. When theories of action are matched with concrete activities, designs become implementable interventions (chapter 9). Designs become research based when distinct methodologies are followed and systematic data collection methods enable visibility and verifiability of focal behaviors (chapter 10). Interventions need to be accompanied by procedures for collecting process and impact data (chapter 11) on which various plausible means-ends explanations can be based. The rigor of these explanations depends on appropriate reliability and validity standards that apply to the research methodology chosen (chapter 12). When designers wear multiple hats as planners, implementers, and evaluators, design development benefits from the inclusion of action research methodology (chapter 13). Part IV will look at issues related to implementing the intervention and deriving lessons or design principles from the data collected.

Implementing and Iterating Interventions

14

Implementing Interventions

with John Hall

Implementing interventions as part of a design development study involves a lot of moving pieces. As discussed in previous chapters, equity-relevant problems of practice are not simple, making learning processes unpredictable. Whether interventions foster new beliefs, attitudes, or practices through professional development; aim at developing new tools; or try out new organizational structures, they require leaders to coordinate an intricate interplay of materials, activities, and people. Implementation takes place in organizational contexts that, more often than not, may be in flux. Priorities may shift, distractions may sap participants' energy initially committed to the intervention, and resources may disappear. As a result, interventions can rarely be implemented with *fidelity* to the design. While flexibility and adaptation are needed, there are limits. Activities must be accompanied by a reliable stream of impact and process data, and adaptations must stop short of mutating the original design to a point where testing the design's theory of action becomes impossible.

Though designers encounter many challenges, four main categories stand out:

→ Complexities of the learning or change process within the design
→ Instabilities of the context external to the design

→ Logistics and coordination of running the intervention and collecting data

→ Leadership challenges

When the four designers we have followed throughout the book implement their projects, they encounter a variety of challenges related to these four categories. In the narratives that follow, we exemplify one of these four categories for each designer.

CHRISTINE:
Unforeseen Complexities of Adult Learning

As described, Christine and her district task force put together a design that they believe will address a unique need in their middle schools: how to strengthen behavioral management in schools staffed by large numbers of novice teachers. The intervention concentrates on developing leadership for middle school grade-level teams (GLTs). In their theory of action, the co-design team members believed that their approach needed to integrate three main elements that they considered a creative answer to their district's needs. First, the approach should make work teams functioning so that they would process novice teachers' vulnerabilities, agree on policy, follow up with accountability, and lend mutual support. Second the approach should create new collective and individual competencies in behavior management. And finally, the design should build on an explicit socializing role of senior teachers related to both work-team development and behavior management. The co-design team imagined that learning could unfold in two alternating formats: (1) workshops during which the leaders (senior teachers and select novices) would receive direct information and (2) follow-up sessions, which would be dedicated to reports from the schools, troubleshooting, and inquiry. GLT leadership meetings would take place on Mondays after school, the hours being paid for by the district. School GLT meetings would take place on Wednesdays during early-release days. So Monday learning could be applied to Wednesday sessions and reported back to the leadership group the following Monday.

Toward this end, the co-design team planned an intervention of ten sessions lasting for ten weeks. As was shown in chapter 9, the sequence of activities is envisioned to begin with an overall statement of the purpose for the GLTs, move to issues of team self-organizing, then introduce a promising program that would afford the GLTs leaders and their school teams new technical competence, and, finally, address the socializing role of senior teachers in an explicit way. The design team is aware that the GLT work is going to be, or at least should be, a whole year's focus for the middle schools. So the ten sessions of GLT leadership development are seen as the introduction of this work, though because of resource constraints, the GLT leaders will be largely on their own after the ten sessions, except for occasional follow-up meetings. So the learning during these focal sessions of the intervention will count heavily.

As implementation of the design unfolds, it becomes clear that responsibility for the intervention and the data collection rests on many shoulders, so logistical problems are rare. Also, the task force has established a conducive context for the intervention. Despite a history of instability and project overload in the district, the stakeholders recognize the focal problem of practice as a burning issue, especially in the district's middle schools. For this reason, the ten-week intervention is fully supported by top district decision makers and the middle school principals. Realistically, it is less clear what might happen after the ten weeks, but for now the context for design implementation seems promising.

The first two of the ten sessions unfold as planned. The senior teachers who were asked to participate in this project and the select novice teachers who volunteered understand the purpose of the undertaking. They are glad that the district is finally doing something about this problem, and they hope that, with support from the district, an advance can be made. They concur with the district task force that functioning GLTs are one important vehicle of change. When the GLT leaders come back for the second follow-up session, they report that the teachers in the school-site GLTs were hopeful and expressed a clear desire to connect on this issue. But the school-site teachers also voiced concern that this design might be yet another half-baked initiative pushed by the district and destined to "go nowhere." Christine and her task force feel the weight of responsibility when they hear these comments. In their short debriefing after the design's second follow-up session, a member of the group—a teacher on special assignment in the district—voices what the group thinks: they cannot afford for this design to fail and to frustrate these teachers' expectations—not on this issue. They are hopeful that their thoughtfulness may pay off in the end.

The third session comes off without a hitch. GLT leaders agree that rules and protocols are needed to set the teams on a course of effective interaction and problem solving, and the leaders are eager to learn these technique and apply them to their school GLTs. In the fourth session, however, the picture becomes complicated. The leaders were asked in the previous session to communicate the importance of punctuality and GLT members' accountability for assigned tasks. A comment from a senior teacher generates a heated discussion: who will enforce this? She does not want to be some sort of supervisor for her younger colleagues. Even though she has much more experience than many of the others do, she is a teacher of adolescents and does not want to be a manager of adults. If she wanted that, she would have become an administrator.

Others have a different take on this issue. They feel that their seniority and expertise give them natural authority in the GLTs. But even they feel already overburdened by their many responsibilities as senior teachers. The issue is laid to rest for this session in two ways: First, the task force and the GLT leaders jointly agree that the senior team leaders' authority is informal, that the senior teachers are not enforcers, and that the GLTs could create multiple roles that spread the responsibility for rules and self-organizing procedures among many team members. Second, the facilitator points out that a separate session is planned for later on this topic. In the task force debrief, the designers feel they are put on notice that their idea of socialization may be more complicated than they have imagined.

The break, however, comes with the fifth and sixth sessions. In the fifth session, the designers planned a central district-level training session in positive behavior intervention and support (PBIS) conducted by a well-known external consultant.[1] They had reasoned that gripe sessions within GLT meetings should be avoided and that the novices needed new technical skills. During the training, the participants follow the consultant's directions and assignments. But in the next session, although novice teachers in many GLTs acknowledge that PBIS could be useful, they also voice strong disappointment. They were initially told by their GLT leaders that this project was going to be different and their problems would be taken seriously. But being asked to follow rules and procedures and being trained in a program does not bear out these promises. The teachers want to be heard as promised. GLT leaders in most instances immediately retreat and invite people to share. There ensues a landslide of frustrations, helplessness, pleas for advice, and a repeat of what has already been communicated in earlier needs assessments.

All this is reported in the following GLT leadership meeting. Christine responds by suggesting that the whole leadership team immediately needs to take charge and rethink the next steps. The group concludes that the designers have overlooked an important component of the design: the most pressing needs of the many novice teachers and an opportunity to articulate them and process them. In their theory of action, the task force had anticipated the novices' vulnerabilities and distress in their earlier discussions. But somehow, in their eagerness to avoid gripe sessions, they may have underestimated the power of these feelings and the time it would take to process them.

The design team wonders what to do. As the intellectual leader, Christine assembles an ad hoc committee of three people and goes back to the drawing board. This committee comes up with a plan for two sessions on a structured approach to processing what they call "a burning issue for the team." These burning issues can be brought up by any GLT member as long as they affect members of the group because of policy, group procedure, shared students, and so on. The issue is put on the agenda a week before the meeting during which the issue will be processed. It gets processed within a forty-five-minute meeting: team members name and define the problem, deepen their understanding of the problem, decide on a change process or change strategy, and assign responsibilities, ensuring that the airing of concerns results in accountable actions. In the next session, GLT leaders report that this simple protocol has calmed the waters. The teams raised a whole slew of burning issues: lunchtime detention, good-behavior awards, hallways, school uniforms, interfacing with the counseling office, communication with the administration, what to do about certain disruptive students. Interestingly, some PBIS strategies seemed to have been taken up.

The schools' professional development calendars for this intervention are limited to ten sessions. The co-design team decides to ask the district and the schools to add two more sessions to the calendar. This is not an easy political feat, but in the end, the designers succeed.

MICHELLE:
Unstable Organizational Context

As described, Michelle's design aimed at making teachers more responsive to students' cognitive and cultural needs. Coincidental with her work with her two principal colleagues, the state government introduced new standards and assessments for its accountability system. The district invested in a new curriculum for math and English language arts, replete with new materials and benchmark tests. The times of highly prescriptive programs were over, but district administrators made it clear that they wanted the new scope and sequence to be followed, the materials taught, and the benchmarks to be used for regular monitoring in the district's elementary schools. The state had also allocated substantial new monies for English language development, which the district used to purchase a comprehensive program that promised not only to introduce a whole new way of teaching literacy but also to create a whole new dynamic of organizational improvement with a focus on teacher professional learning and parental involvement for grades K–3. At the same time, the district equity committee, Michelle's true passion, fizzled out. Attention shifted to the new core curriculum.

Shortly before implementation of the design is to begin, one of Michelle's two co-designers and fellow principals asks to be released from her commitment when she is told that she will be assigned to a different school next year. Michelle herself is told that her school will be closed at the end of the year and she will be the principal of two combined elementary schools at a new site. The other principal is hesitant: with everything that the district asks them to do at this point, he feels that teachers will not be inclined to deal with one more thing. He will continue to be part of the design, but he suggests that they only work with a CRP volunteer group and they drop the benchmark component. Michelle reluctantly consents. The intervention is now reduced to nine sessions and only with volunteers, who Michelle assumes are teachers who already have a certain curiosity about CRP.

And this is indeed the case. This is not exactly what Michelle had in mind when she began, but she figures that this will be her first incomplete iteration, and she will be at it again another year, under more auspicious circumstances. The intervention with the after-school group of CRP volunteers, now restricted to issues of curriculum and instruction, plays out largely according to plan. The volunteers are highly motivated by the reading of the adult literary text and the subsequent sharing of relevant life experiences. They are grateful for the opportunity to expand beyond the narrow perspective on coverage. They read the new student texts with an eye to the reading skills demanded by the literacy program, and they try out new instructional approaches to interpreting text with students.

EXCURSION INTO THEORY

Implementation Research

Three lines of research are especially useful for understanding the implementation of interventions: design fidelity, policy implementation, and institutional theory.

Design Fidelity

In the early 2000s, when comprehensive school designs and prescriptive instructional programs were popular approaches to reform, a debate ensued among educational researchers as to whether one should—and could—aim to implement programs with fidelity. As explained earlier, design fidelity means that educators carry out their work according to the scripted stipulations of instructional programs or organizational models.

Back then, these interventions were mostly developed externally by researchers, consultants, or publishing companies. Some argued that it was eminently important for educational reforms to become more rigorously science-based. In this view, careful design development and rigorous evaluations conducted with quasi-experimental methods would yield interventions (e.g., instructional programs, organizational models) with a scientific base of proven effectiveness. But interventions would have to be implemented with procedural fidelity if these effects were to be replicated in real life.[2] Procedural fidelity means that users are expected to follow the surface procedures laid out in the intervention and are not free to veer from scripts, materials, or organizational features that are part of the package.

Those who opposed this view held that the circumstances in an educational environment were just too complex and unpredictable for the fidelity demand to be realistic.[3] They questioned the external validity of the supposedly rigorous design and evaluation studies, meaning they doubted that the controlled nature of these studies could be reproduced in the real life of schools and districts. But if programs would or could not be replicated with fidelity, the programs' effect sizes, identified by controlled studies, could not be replicated, either, in real life. Scientific standards and methodologies, they argued, needed to be suited to the situations of real educators whose actions science was called to illuminate.

The demands for fidelity seem to produce trade-offs. A line of research around three then-popular designs, but now largely forgotten, found that for some programs, implementation with procedural fidelity can lead to significant changes in teachers' instructional practices.[4] But the studies also found that teachers implementing procedurally prescriptive programs tend to emphasize the instructional strategies demanded by the program, to the detriment of other strategies not explicitly demanded.

Policy Implementation

Educators adapt when they implement new policies. Sometimes this adaptation occurs in opposition to directions provided by policy designers.[5] In other cases, designers anticipate adaptation.[6] Meredith Honig and colleagues describe the increasingly complex environment within which implementation occurs: a plethora of data on students and teachers, competition for resources, intensified accountability, and the accretion of federal, state, and local policies.[7] It consequently becomes impossible to ignore local variability when implementing a program. Richard Elmore and Milbrey McLaughlin describe the process as mutual adaptation, wherein practitioners modify an intervention to meet local needs while also responding to the expectations of the intervention designers.[8] In some cases, practitioners may believe that their actions fully align with the intentions of a designer, when in fact they interpret and significantly alter the intervention to the extent that their current practices persist.[9] Policies and program designs can have a significant impact on local practices, but implementers will make modifications that reflect their specific circumstances.[10]

Policy Churn in the Institutional Context of Education

Design and policy implementation research make a good case for expecting interventions or policies to be shaped and adapted by local forces. But some researchers and theorists have gone further, arguing that much of what educational organizations do is not about implementation per se, but about churning out policies that give the appearance of change.[11]

Educational systems must please many constituencies, and given the nature of the task, educational goals are often ambiguous and sometimes mutually exclusive. Most educational leaders of public schools do not operate in a market, but operate in an "institutionalized environment."[12] In an institutionalized environment, leaders are judged by what seems appropriate and legitimate in the eyes of concerned publics (parents, community, politicians, media), rather than what is most effective.[13] When these voices perceive the system in crisis, one of the most legitimacy-enhancing responses is the idea of continuous improvement. To give the appearance of constant change, an unending influx of reforms churns through the system, absent any rational expectation that they could actually be implemented[14] Implementation is not the purpose of constant reform. To keep up the public message of improvement, problems become fuzzy (e.g., "the achievement gap") and the stream of solutions accelerates, delivering legitimate reforms du jour that presumably fit the ill-defined problems. When problems are only loosely connected to solutions, the system can no longer be considered rational. Design development is an attempt to keep the spinning wheels of ill-crafted changes at bay.

ERIC:
Logistics of Data Collection

As we have outlined earlier, Eric, the district assistant superintendent, designed an intervention for his district's principal meetings and professional development workshops to improve on instructional supervision. His emphasis is on the ability of principals to facilitate formative learning processes, not summative evaluation. This is his second iteration if we consider his very first time more of a quick trial. His aim is to introduce into his principals' instructional leadership the idea of student academic engagement. Academic engagement is furthered, he reasoned, when students are given the opportunity, through rich lessons, to engage in ideas, skills, or inquiry methods related to the subject matter. In his theory of action, Eric theorized that this concept of academic engagement is learned when principals have the opportunity to observe real-life lessons on video, are asked to identify the content being taught by the teacher, read student cues of their engagement with ideas, and study the teachers' practices that foster engagement (or not). Subsequently, principals would apply their new insights to classrooms in their school during instructional rounds, a procedure they are familiar with, and translate their new analytical skills into instructional conversations with teachers. Eric's twelve-session intervention follows these main steps (see chapter 9).

As is his usual style, Eric largely works on his own. He feels confident about his ability to design and implement professional development activities, but being a researcher and collecting data is something he is less familiar with. When he planned to collect process data, he anticipated logistical problems since he would have to run most sessions of the intervention himself (four sessions would be run by an instructional coach). He therefore planned to collect very few process data (chapter 11). He mainly collects the worksheets used by the participants and some feedback forms. In addition, he plans to have a couple of key sessions audiotaped for later analysis. Since impact data are being collected before and after the intervention, this data collection schedule largely frees him to manage the intervention.

Eric's intervention comes off without a hitch. He had tried out the videos before, and he had gained experience with video-based learning during the first iteration. His first four sessions play out as Eric expected. He collects data from each session. A cursory glance at the worksheets and feedback forms seems to confirm his overall impression: in this iteration, the principals pick up on the complexities of student academic engagement with the help of the observation instrument. Specifically, the principals seem to focus on content and name student cues and teacher moves. When the principals make their instructional rounds with the observation instrument in hand, Eric is not present. The activity is managed by the coach. But when they come back for the debrief of the rounds, Eric attends the debrief and audio-records the session. He discovers in amazement that his participants were largely unable to apply their analytical skills when they made the rounds. Instead of talking about patterns of the students' engagement with the content, they describe how they saw students participating, raising their hands, being on task, or engaging in group work. In terms of teacher moves, the principals describe how they observed creative projects or strategies that motivated students to participate.

Eric is puzzled. He goes back to the process data and discovers that they are not fine-grained enough. His data are perhaps good enough to confirm or disconfirm that some learning occurred, but cannot show how the principals learned. For this reason, he cannot tell why the participants could not apply the skills from the first four sessions to the instructional rounds. He decides to conduct some interviews with the participants on their experiences during the rounds. One principal's comment echoes what most of the others recount: "You gave us lessons to observe in videos where the content was clear and all we had to do is look at what the kids and the teachers were doing. During the rounds, we were in that classroom for ten minutes. And by the time we had figured out what the lesson was all about, it was time to move on to the next."

Eric is relieved. This is good news despite the bad news. It was the format of the rounds, the short duration in the classroom, that caused the breakdown in the use of observation skills. If this is so, Eric reasons, principals should still be able to apply their new observation skills to the conferences, the topic of the next block of sessions.

But now he takes a closer look at his process data for this block. He realizes that he will have to collect more detailed data to ascertain how the principals execute the new task: applying their new skills to conferences with teachers. Eric decides that he will ask a couple of principals to stay after each session to discuss with him, in a sort of think-aloud, what they thought about communicating the difficult concept of student academic engagement to teachers. He is a little afraid that this is asking too much of these principals, but he feels that at this point, he has no choice. He thinks that, alternatively, he could ask the coach to run some sessions while he observes and collects data. But to do this, he would have to develop an observation instrument, perhaps jointly with the coach, that he could use to focus his attention while she ran the sessions.

Eric's experience exemplifies the difficulty of managing both an intervention and a stream of data collection, especially when the multiple responsibilities of design development cannot be distributed among a group of co-designers, as is the case for Eric, who largely works on his own. Eric tried to address this situation by economizing on data collection. If the design works as intended and impact and process data render a consistent picture, somewhat sparse process data may be serviceable. But when designers want to explain how or why certain processes occurred or did not occur, especially when interventions run off-course, more fine-grained data are necessary.

NORA:
Leadership

Nora's project, as we described, is about reducing racial and homophobic slurs in her social-justice-themed high school. In its theory of action, the design team assumed that adults would increase their inclination to intervene if they were confronted with cognitive dissonance in a safe space where they could have courageous conversations about the meaning of slurs and if they gained a sense of efficacy and confidence about what to do when they heard slurs. To this end, the team put together a five-session whole-faculty professional development interspersed with small-group activities and informal conversations stimulated by members of the design team (chapter 9).

To start the conversation with baseline data, the team fanned out in the hall-ways the week before the first session and tallied the number of times they heard slurs both when no other adults were around and when other adults were within earshot. For the latter situation, the team also counted the number of times the teachers intervened. The team also surveyed students on the frequency of hearing slurs and the frequency of observing teachers intervening. The data were clear and consistent: teachers at the school largely ignored slurs.

Presenting the data at the first meeting generates what the team intended: some teachers agree that the data represent reality, others simply deny that this could be reality, still others question the validity of the data, and some teachers assure the team that the data are not relevant for them personally, since they do not tolerate slurs. A lively conversation ensues during which the various conflict-ing positions generate dissonance, as intended. During the week after the meeting, informal conversations, which the team members expected to occur, reinforce the sentiment that indeed the question of the teachers ignoring the slurs has created powerful ferment for change that the design team is eager to take advantage of.

The second whole-faculty meeting is supposed to reaffirm the faculty's shared values and create psychological safety by spelling out the rules, norms, assump-tions, and expectations for courageous conversations. The meeting unfolds in a wholly unpredicted direction when some teachers name and pronounce the actual slur terms in the discussion. An African American teacher asks that the N-word, fully spelled out or enunciated, should not be used in the conversation. A white teacher insists that to talk about slurs, one has to use the words.

Several other teachers enter the discussion. They reaffirm the African Amer-ican teacher's request and ask that the N-word, as well as other slurs, should not be used in the discussion. Some participants go as far as to say that slurs should *never* be allowed to be used. This comment draws opposition from a white English teacher who asserts that this proscription would infringe on freedom of speech and that Mark Twain and other novelists use the N-word in respectable literature and that she discusses this in her literature classes with the students. And to show her resolve, she uses the N-word in its full form a couple of times. At this point, a whole group of teachers show their disbelief, turning away with indignation. Nora, who is not the facilitator for this meeting, steps in and tries to calm the antagonists. But her efforts are in vain; the meeting ends with each side digging in. The informal conversations after the meeting lay bare a faculty deeply divided over this issue.

In the design team meeting before the next session, team members voice their moral outrage. Insisting on pronouncing the N-word is just plain wrong, they say. There is widespread agreement in the team that some teachers apparently do not belong at a social-justice school and should not be here. Listening to her team, Nora is becoming frightened. The situation seems to call for forceful action on the part of the principal. For Nora, this is no longer about her design, but is about her *school*. She suggests that two things are needed now: a clear policy for using slurs and a period of healing. The team completely agrees. It decides to draft a policy and send it via e-mail to all the faculty for comments, to be voted on at the next faculty meeting. The essence of the policy is spelled out in one key statement: Slurs are not to be used and tolerated under any circumstances at "Social Justice Academy." The period for commentary does not generate any comments other than consent.

The following faculty meeting is planned as a time of healing, with teachers participating in cooperation exercises and sharing their personal stories. When the policy is put up for discussion at the meeting, only muted and vague comments are made. The policy is approved, since no objections are raised. In the following healing segment of the meeting, teachers politely go through the exercises, none of them related to the issue of slurs, but Nora feels that her faculty's spirit is damaged.

What should she do? She talks to a small circle of critical friends in her university program. Listening to the wisdom of colleagues of color, white colleagues, and lesbian and gay colleagues, she discerns the core of her predicament: transformative leadership and courage. She realizes, upon reflection, that she acted like an administrator when the conflict in her faculty scared her. She reached for the safety of policy and rehearsed harmony when she should have found a way to address the conflict about the N-word head-on. She recognizes that she will lose all credibility as a transformative leader in the eyes of her teachers if she misses this opportunity of learning through conflict. She knows that she could safely continue on the "path of contrived consent" as one of her critical friends called it, or she could take the risk and open up the conversation again. She chooses to take the risk.

In the next design team meeting, she announces that the team needs to revisit the slur policy again because she now believes that it is unworkable. On second thought, there are too many legitimate exceptions to a blanket proscription of all speech related to slurs—art being one area—but perhaps also friends bantering with each other under certain circumstances. Yet she is convinced that slurs should not be used in faculty discussions, because as the next session in the intervention design would have made clear, slurs hurt. The design team is hesitant, and none of the members feels confident enough to facilitate any of the following sessions. If Nora wants to go forward, she would be on her own. This is tough. She knows that everything will pivot on the next session, on why slurs hurt.

In preparation for the meeting, Nora sends out an e-mail to her faculty. In the note, she repeats the various points she has made with the design team: First, she says she honestly has had a change of mind; the policy is not workable. Second, there are indeed circumstances in which slurs might be tolerable, and these are circumstances in which slurs are not meant to hurt. Third, the faculty meeting is *not* one of those circumstances, because slurs hurt people. Finally, she invites her faculty to reaffirm their commitment to social justice and to explore with her in the next faculty meeting how the school should handle this difficult issue.

In the next meeting, she begins by writing down a "dictionary" of abbreviations for slurs on the board, spelling them out in full and suggesting that from now on, the faculty only use these abbreviations. She asks the participants, why does it hurt a black person when he or she hears the N-word fully spoken, or why does it hurt a gay person when he hears the F-word directed at him? The ensuing discussion calms Nora. Her faculty displays an immense earnestness and sense of responsibility. She asks another question: why do some people not feel the hurt as strongly? A further prompt asks, why do some people feel very hurt by some slurs but feel free to use other slurs? This is followed by, does Mark Twain use the N-word to hurt people? With each question, Nora grows more confident as she listens to her staff. So she finally asks, why would it be better for us not to fully pronounce the slur words but use the abbreviations in faculty discussions about slurs? In the end, the white English literature teacher speaks up. She thanks the faculty for the discussion and says that she has learned a lot. Clapping. Nora's design is back on track.

CHAPTER SUMMARY

In this chapter, we have examined the trials of implementing interventions while conducting design research. We grouped these challenges into four categories:

- Complexities internal to the design

- Instabilities external to the design

- Logistics

- Awareness of one's role as a transformational leader

Using the experiences of our four composite leaders, we have shown that the expectation of implementation fidelity is unrealistic. Educational leaders need to be prepared for adjustments and unexpected course changes. Note that the design teams were not completely caught off-guard by the turns of events. In its theory of action, Christine's group members had anticipated that they needed to deal with the intensity of distress and vulnerability, but somehow their intervention did not accommodate these needs sufficiently. Michelle was compelled to compromise on the scope of her intervention because of dramatic changes in the organizational context of her design effort. Eric knew that he had to economize on data collection if he wanted to go it alone. He tried, but found it difficult to handle the multiple functions of design development without a team. If there was one theme that cast a shadow of uncertainty over Nora's design work, it was the team's awareness that it was trying to do something difficult. She and her team just were not prepared for how difficult it is to puncture what Carolyn Shields calls the "pathologies of silence" around deep structures of taken-for-granted inequity.[15]

15

Deriving Design Principles

with John Hall

The purpose of design development is to discover an ensemble of tools, materials, tasks, organizational structures, and any other activities that are apt to set in motion a process of learning that improves on a focal problem of practice. This ensemble is the intervention, the final product of a given design development effort. The product may be in various stages of development. In some instances, it may require further study and further iterations. In other instances, the product may be solid enough to be used when a similar problem of practice in a similar context is indicated. But how should this product be represented so that it becomes most useful for the next users?

On the surface, the intervention takes place with activities being laid out in specific segments, with a specific duration, and in a specific sequence. One could describe the procedural activities in a script that tells the user what to do step-by-step. By following the script, the user would replicate the activities and, in doing so, presumably reproduce the intended learning that underlies the script. For reasons discussed throughout the book, replicating surface procedures in detail is not what design development should aim at. We believe that both the learning process within the design and the context in which it unfolds are so complex that users will be likely and compelled to adapt the procedures or activities, regardless of the designers' intent. And this adaptation serves the purpose of making designs fit the teachers' specific circumstances and skill sets. It seems more useful, therefore, to aim at a more enduring core, around which surface procedures may be adapted to the next users' situation and needs.

This core is what Jan van den Akker and Thomas Reeves call "design principles."[1] Design principles combine the *how* with the *why*. They spell out the essential features of procedures and activities, and they connect procedures to the substantive learning these procedures promote. To say this more concretely, the next users of a design will need to know what effects the intervention has had and in what dimensions the effects are strong or weak. Users will need to know which activities within the intervention turned out to be effective or ineffective, which main features of the activities contributed to the effect, and what sort of learning, hypothesized by the theory of action, might have been promoted.

There are a number of analytical steps that need to be taken to derive design principles from the data. Designers assess impact by looking at the indicators or data points they chose for the impact data. They look at the implementation process data and identify activities that were powerful and that weren't. They review the rigor with which they collected and analyzed data. In light of the impact and process data, the designers revisit their theory of action. They reflect on their own roles as co-designers and leaders. Finally, they summarize their findings in a set of recommendations for the next iteration or the next use.

CHRISTINE'S DESIGN PRINCIPLES

Christine's design challenge was to improve teachers' management of student behavior through collaboration in GLTs (Grade-level teams). The design focused on GLT leaders who could facilitate team meetings with efficiency and who could anticipate conflict and instill hope. These leaders were to involve the GLTs in cooperative problem-solving, which would result in policies for the team and strategies to handle individual students. As senior teachers at their schools, the GLT leaders were to assume an informal socializing function for the many novices that staffed the schools in Christine's district. The intervention was designed for a public school district serving populations with a high percentage of disadvantaged students, especially immigrants of color.

Christine and her team of co-designers assess the impact of the intervention with the data collected at the beginning and the end of the intervention. They conduct structured interviews during which the GLT leaders self-rated their effectiveness on multiple dimensions and explained these ratings. Explanations are scored on a rubric. The total number of points that could be obtained is 50. On average, the GLT leaders improved by 15 points, with relatively small differences among individuals. The leaders' explanations indicate that the intervention created a modestly strong initial induction into the new leadership functions.

Gains are strongest in the dimensions of purpose, hope, cooperation, and an understanding of the informal role of senior leadership. The weakest growth is in the dimension of problem solving for behavioral problems. The short survey of mostly novice teachers in GLTs shows a similar pattern: modest growth in most dimensions, but neutral ratings in the task dimension. Support by senior teachers is highlighted as positive in the novices' survey responses. The number of student referrals to the counseling office, Christine's third indicator, shows a decrease by 15 percent on average, not as much as the designers had hoped, but a move in the right direction.

Christine and her team conclude that growth was modest to strong in the group processing and self-organizing dimensions, but weak in the task dimension. The GLTs seem to have made inroads in their collaborative relationships, but are less sure about their capacity to actually solve discipline problems. The figures for referrals suggest as much.

With this impact in mind, Christine and her team try to figure out if they can plausibly explain the pattern by looking at their process data. Given that they are a relatively large co-design team responsible for only one central intervention, data collection was detailed and spread over a number of team members. So the group has fairly detailed notes from all meetings and audio records for clarification. The process data indicate that the first four sessions of the intervention (hope, purpose, self-organizing) unfolded as intended:

- The intervention tapped into a strongly felt need.
- Novice teachers were ready to come together and connect on this burning issue.
- Deliberately selecting senior teachers created a sense of hope and progress for the GLTs.
- Group self-organizing techniques were embraced by both GLT leaders and novice teachers at the school level.

As mentioned earlier, senior teachers, by the time they were in the fourth session, already flagged uncertainties and discomfort associated with their role as enforcers. In hindsight, Christine's team recognizes the significance of these data and decides to see how this discomfort played out in subsequent sessions. The introduction of PBIS at the midpoint of the intervention was meant to strengthen technical competence, but the responses from the novices during the PBIS follow-up session, as reported by the GLT leaders, clearly show that the PBIS training occurred at the wrong time. The training did not answer the felt needs of the novices, who rejected it as violation of their expectations that their voices would be heard.

The subsequent two sessions on "burning issues for the team" were interjected as a response to this situation and show a curious pattern. In the first session, GLT leaders discussed and practiced the protocol for processing a burning issue. In the second session, they reported from the GLT meetings that the activity was a success: novices showed much appreciation and participation. But actual problem solving was an issue. Some GLTs had chosen to address relatively easy tasks: how to make sure that teachers do their hallway duty, for example. Others had chosen minor issues (e.g., should they allow chewing gum?) but had ended in disagreement and division. Still others had chosen really difficult issues, such as communication with the administration or the counseling office—issues that needed more processing time and good ideas than were available. The GLT leaders had guarded the formal protocol, but reported little by way of giving substantive advice.

The session on managing productive conflict came just in time for many GLTs. It allowed the leaders to reframe their GLT's squabbles as a necessary stage in the development of the group and to understand that the disagreements would be overcome in time. The session on the role of senior leaders, according to the process data, came too late. Even though the GLT leaders had fastidiously implemented what they had learned in the leadership workshops, uncertainty and discomfort erupted again, as they had at the beginning, in this last segment of the intervention. Senior teachers said that it was difficult to simultaneously have a formal role as team leaders, an informal role as givers of advice, and the status of a colleague.

Sifting through the data, Christine's co-design team concludes that the impact data make sense in light of the process data. The intervention was strong on group processing and relationships and weak on processing the task, that is, the participants only marginally improved their competence in handling student behavioral problems. Next the designers revisit their initial theory of action. They had initially assumed that five drivers would produce the powerful learning they considered necessary to advance the work of GLTs:

- Shared understanding of the GLTs' purpose
- Basic group functioning and self-organizing
- Expert leadership by senior teachers, which would fulfill a socializing function for novices
- Productive conflict
- New competence in behavioral management through the PBIS training

In interpreting impact and process data, the co-design team is ready to affirm the importance of the first four drivers. They are uncertain about the dimension of new competence. Since they had banked on PBIS as a program that would enhance technical competence and would structure the conversation about behavior management in the GLTs, and since the novices had balked at learning the program when it was presented, the intervention turned out to be inconclusive about this dimension. The team is ready to recommend the activities organized for six of the twelve sessions since the process data suggest that these sessions worked as intended and the impact data show growth on dimensions related to the session content.

Weighing strengths and weaknesses, the designers conclude that the design and the theory of action would have to be revised in two places for the next iteration: senior teachers' socializing role and the idea that training in a packaged program such as PBIS could be the main vehicle for enhancing technical competence. Developing and cultivating leadership by senior teachers in deliberate ways (i.e., organizational socialization) was definitely needed in these schools, which suffer from high turnover of novices. Without this leadership base, the GLTs would have foundered. But Christine's team had not anticipated the vexing ambiguities associated with this function. For a next iteration, her team therefore suggests that these ambiguities be addressed right at the beginning of the intervention, perhaps even before the GLT work starts, with more targeted activities.

It is also now clear to Christine and her team that they have overestimated the leaders' spontaneous advice giving. The team had assumed that the senior teachers needed support in managing groups, but that they knew what to do about student discipline. The theory of action had anticipated that novice teachers needed strategies, such as PBIS, but the team now realizes that senior teachers would have needed support in strategizing solutions for their schools. For the next iteration, Christine's team therefore makes two recommendations:

- Before taking up burning behavioral management issues named by GLT members, GLT leaders will be given the opportunity to brainstorm solutions in the district-level leadership group so that they can run more structured and effective problem-solving processes.
- Overall, senior leaders need ongoing support in strategizing a given school's approach to behavior management issues. This requires the deliberate phasing-in of conversations with the school administration as part of the design.

As to the second area for revision, the designers would need to thoroughly rethink the role of programs or packages in enhancing technical competence. In an intervention that has as one of its core features work-team development by giving voice to the burning concerns of novice teachers, competence should perhaps come about through more organic problem-solving activities structured by GLT leaders and launched from teachers' articulated burning concerns.

In sum, Christine's team states the following as design principles:

If one wants to improve on teachers' individual and collective competence in managing student behavior in a context characterized by tenuous orderliness, high numbers of novice teachers, and a climate of distress, systematic development of leadership on the part of senior teachers is a promising approach. One should train senior teachers in ways to help grade-level teams self-organize and deliberately address issues of distress, disagreement, and conflict to strengthen collective responsibility for student discipline. Promising activities to do this are listed in the report. Another iteration is required to find out how to better combine work-team development with more effective task processing. Activities aimed at preparing senior teachers for their dual role as grade-level team leaders and informal socializing agents went in the right direction, but need to be strengthened.

MICHELLE'S DESIGN PRINCIPLES

There are seven volunteers in Michelle's culturally relevant pedagogy (CRP) group. They have met after school for nine sessions that were planned and a couple of sessions added at the end, at the request of the participants. After one of the principals retreated from the project, Michelle worked with another colleague as collaborator. This principal has had five teachers in his group. This group did not extend its schedule of sessions. Michelle analyzes the impact data first. When she assesses the lesson sketches and the accompanying explanations with her rubric, she finds that most teachers in her group grew substantially. Among her seven participants, two already started with a top score at baseline. So their growth could not be captured by the instruments. Her collaborator's group did not produce any lesson sketches, so she has no way of assessing impact.

The process data show that in both Michelle's group and her collaborator's group, the sessions that they called CRP for Adults, during which the participants interpreted a rich adult text and then made connections between the text and their own lives, were quite powerful, as indicated by participants' reflective writings that were collected. Looking at the filled-in worksheets and her notes from the meeting, Michelle confirms her earlier impressions: the participants found it surprisingly easy to transfer the programs' reading skills, taught through program texts, to the richer texts that the teachers substituted. But this task was also facilitated by the up-front vetting of the children's stories by the equity committee, which considered the material's fit with the literacy program.

It was more challenging for the participants to shift from interpreting adult text to teaching interpretation skills to students. Originally, the design team had imagined that the teachers themselves would develop prompts for students in a more exploratory fashion. But this turned out to be too difficult. Even the volunteers had been disabused of thinking about their own lessons for so long that they needed Michelle's direct instruction on how to teach children how to interpret rich text. After this direct support, the participants in Michelle's group began experimenting. In her colleague's group, this step was skipped. Michelle believes that this lack of direct instruction in her colleague's group may have been one reason that his participants balked at the performance task.

When Michelle considers so-called must-retain and should-discard activities, as well as which parts of her theory of action are corroborated, she knows she must include the enormous context challenges and the much stronger role that her expertise directly played in the intervention. She settles on the following design principles:

> If you want to integrate new and rich culturally relevant texts into an established "prescription and coverage" mind-set, you should build from powerful adult experiences; reduce fears by showing how both the literacy program and the rich texts can be taught without losing sight of required reading skills; enhance choice by making teachers cover the curriculum conceptually, not procedurally; directly expose them to new instructional formats; and then experiment with these formats. The report lists the main elements of the activities that created solid learning among participants. The effect of these main elements depends on

the willingness of groups of volunteers to bring some curiosity about culturally relevant pedagogy and to experiment and take risks.

Michelle is actually still convinced, though she has no data to go on, that for the average nonvolunteering teacher in her district, her intervention would not work unless and until more organizational supports would be built into the design up front.

EXCURSION INTO THEORY

Output of Design Research

The output of design development research has three main purposes. Researchers want to distill from the design effort what worked and why, given their chosen problem of practice. In doing so, they aim at so-called design principles. Given that design research is iterative, researchers want to make suggestions for subsequent design iterations. Ultimately, design principles should be robust enough to be transferable from one user to another who encounters a similar problem of practice in a similar context.

Design Principles

The goal of design development research is both practical and theoretical. Researchers want to know what worked and what did not, that is, which elements, activities, or parts of an intervention ought to be retained for the design and which may be discarded in future iterations, keeping in mind that what worked is always context-specific. But researchers also want to know if the more abstract (i.e., the less context-bound) theory of action that undergirds the intervention is sound and can be transferred to other contexts. Van den Akker uses the term "design principles" for this dual purpose of design studies. He formulates the logic of design principles in this way (slightly interpolated with our terminology): "If you want to design intervention X for the problem of practice Y in context Z, then you are best advised to give that intervention the characteristics A, B, and C [substantive emphasis], and to do that via procedures K, L, and M [procedural emphasis], because of arguments P, Q, and R derived from the theory of action that informed the design."[2]

Iteration

In each iteration, various elements of the intervention are manipulated. Meanwhile, formative and summative evaluation data are collected and analyzed, and a theory of action is tested and reformulated until the effects of an intervention come close enough to the changes envisioned by the designers. Multiple iterations in similar contexts may corroborate the design principles. Once designs are tested in a greater variety of contexts, design principles that are less context specific may be distilled. The design principles (i.e., what worked and why it worked, according to a theory of action) become transferable to a variety of work settings encountering similar problems of practice. The theory of action becomes validated—that is, it advances validated causal claims about a connection between an intervention and an outcome. Thus, at a certain stage of reiteration in multiple contexts, design principles may be generalized to broader theory.[3] But this standard of generalizability requires a sustained research program.

Transferability

For the many problems of practice encountered by practitioners in educational settings and addressed by design development, a lesser standard than generalizability, as the ultimate aim of research, seems appropriate. This standard is transferability. A design becomes more transferable when contexts are clearly specified so that users in other contexts can assess what adjustments need to be made, and when design principles spell out what types of learning activities, formal organizational arrangements, resource allocations, tools, instruments, and so on, worked and why, according to a plausible theory of action. Transferable designs contribute to the field's practical design knowledge that professionals can usefully apply to recurring problems of practice. Transferable interventions resulting from design development studies are not aiming at replication, prescription, or implementation fidelity. Rather, these types of studies suggest guided reinvention by subsequent users along the distilled design principles.[4]

NORA'S DESIGN PRINCIPLES

Nora and her school-based leadership team designed an intervention to reduce racial and homophobic slurs, a pervasive problem in many high schools, where using slurs is part of adolescent culture. The team's school is located in an inner-city neighborhood with large numbers of economically disadvantaged people of color. The setting was conducive for the design because of the school's explicit social-justice theme that presumably attracted a certain type of teacher to the work there. Nora's team identified as the problem of practice the lack of response by adults when they hear slurs. The design challenge was to create an intervention that would increase teachers' disposition to intervene. We described a dramatic implementation story associated with Nora's intervention. Nora rose to the occasion and became her school's transformative and intellectual leader and, by doing so, enabled the intervention to be carried out.

When Nora's team analyzes the impact data, the group is puzzled. For its impact data, the team tallied the number of slurs heard in the school's hallways and cafeteria and the number of times adults in the school intervened when they were within earshot. Data were collected at the beginning and the end of the intervention. The team also gave a brief survey to students, asking about the frequency of slurs and the frequency of adult intervention. The two indicators show that slurs decreased, but that adults did not intervene more often. So in some sense the design worked, because slurs are reduced, but in reality, it didn't, because the intervention was about adult proactive behavior. And little seems to have changed in this regard, if the impact data can be trusted.

So what is going on? Nora and her team look at their process data. First they discover that during the "N-word drama," as they call it, the team stopped collecting process data. Nobody thought of collecting data during those trying moments, when they were afraid that their intervention may have prompted conflicts that they could not handle. When Nora went back and recast the "Why Do Slurs Hurt?" session and made it directly applicable to the experience her staff had just had about this topic, she did not dare to ask anybody to produce any artifacts that she could use as data. So she and her team had to rely on their collective memory.

For the following session, originally titled "Are We Ready to Act?" they did not think that an audio recording was appropriate. But they do have meeting notes that a couple of team members jotted down independently. And these notes help the team reconstruct what had happened. There was a lively discussion. Teachers tried to figure out if there were circumstances under which slurs could be tolerated (e.g., reading Mark Twain) or ignored and circumstances that would need a proactive response. The dividing line was this: slurs could not be ignored when they hurt. But when do they hurt? was the next question. What if the teacher thinks one thing and the students shrug it off? The discussion ended somewhat inconclusively.

For the next session, the team has an audio record. As the team members listen to their colleagues making suggestions about what to say or do when they hear slurs, it becomes clear that hesitation prevailed in this session of the intervention. In the end, the teachers agreed that they would use a standard comment: "Ladies/Gentlemen, this is not language we use at our school."

Nora's team goes back to its original theory of action. The lack of an increase in the teachers' response to slurs makes sense in light of the team's theorizing. Cognitive dissonance arose and created awareness, tension, and ferment for change. The teachers seemed to have gained a firsthand understanding of why slurs hurt (though the data the team relies on for this assertion is admittedly sparse). But the discussion about the situation-dependent meaning of slurs ended with confusion. In the end, the team concludes, teachers did not feel a sufficient sense of efficacy to proactively intervene. Yet, slurs used by students decreased in frequency. This could not have been a *direct* response to the intervention since the intervention targeted adults.

One team member suggests that the reduction of slurs could be *indirectly* related to the intervention. He says that at least for himself, he has become more aware of slurs in his classroom and he has talked with his students about it. The team decides to use one more informal round of conversations with colleagues to find out if this response may have been more widespread. They ask, "Has anything happened or changed as a result of our faculty conversations about slurs?" In many instances, teachers report that indeed they made slurs a subject in their classrooms. So while the teachers have not become more proactive in the hallways, they have become so in their classrooms, an environment in which they presumably feel more secure and can assess the situation-dependent nature of slurs with more confidence.

In interpreting the impact and process data, Nora's team believes that its theory of action is sound. Cognitive dissonance, psychological safety, appeal to shared values, deep understandings of the issue, learning new action strategies, and sense of efficacy explain both the strengths and the weaknesses of the intervention. While she and the team believe that the theory of action is sound, they are convinced that the activities need overhauling in a next iteration.

Nora believes that when she tackled the N-word confrontation, she inadvertently latched on to a powerful activity that may have made the adults personally aware that slurs hurt. She obviously would not wish the controversy on anybody, but she imagines that a discussion may be quite powerful that asks a hypothetical: "What if I, or another teacher, would use the N-word or F-word (as racially or sexually derogative terms, respectively) in their full pronunciation in this conversation? How would you feel? Should we do it?"

The team's recommendations for the next iteration is to add better preparation for the kind of courageous and skillful leadership that a controversial topic such as theirs demands. This preparation should be built into the design up front. Moreover, the activities that followed the controversy about the N-word had been redesigned at the last minute and now need careful retooling. But then again, Nora is not sure that her staff, after the N-word controversy, "had it in them" as she phrased it, to go further than they did. This may have been their next level of work.

From the start, Nora has been thinking in terms of transferring her design to other contexts. She herself is a high school principal, but she wants to develop a design that can make it at the district level. So she plans to try out the design in another school, where an interested colleague of hers is the principal. This school, however, has a science and technology profile and lacks the explicit commitment to social justice. Trying out the design in two schools reduces the effect of unique school-site factors. It was the iteration in Nora's school that yielded very preliminary design principles: must-retain and should-discard design elements backed up by a theory of action. Then her colleague's school will inherit Nora's design and insights on what to do better next time.

A design may become transferable if it shows verifiable impact under specific conditions. It is up to the next users to learn from the practical design knowledge that one, two, or several more iterations have generated, to improve the design, and to adjust it to new contexts. In sum, transferability of a design from one context to another is enhanced when the relevant behaviors are represented with data (visibility), when the metrics of growth are linked with evidence of process effectiveness (verifiability), and when contexts for implementation are specified and feasibility is considered.

ITERATIONS, SMALL-SCALE INTERVENTION, AND SCALE-UP

Designers are not aiming at getting it right on the first trial. But at the end of one, two, or more iterations, the designers may have learned that certain activities related to the focal problem of practice are definitely not useful, while others appear to be good candidates for a design prototype. It is these prototypical activities, rather than a packaged design, that are candidates for scale-up and are most useful for others who want to transfer a design to a different context. Undoubtedly, the designs will not be identical from one context to another, but may have some similarities or underlying design principles.

Design development pivots on outcomes. There is no question that deep professional learning and deep refection are worthy undertakings in their own right, but educators are designing interventions because they want to improve the services provided to students. In thinking about impact, educators distinguish between direct and indirect outcomes.

Let's return to Eric. We have skipped his data analysis and distillation of design principles here. Suffice it to say that Eric's ultimate goal is increasing student achievement. This is, after all, the metric on which his own performance as an instructional leader is evaluated and on which he himself evaluates his success.

But Eric also knows that administrators do not have a direct impact on student learning, but have an indirect one by supporting the services provided by teachers, counselors, and other adults. A new concept introduced to his principals will have to travel a distance to affect student learning. Student achievement is an indirect goal. But he has a more direct goal as well: enabling the participating principals to understand academic engagement and to conduct effective conferences around it. The time horizon for the direct goal is shorter, the direct goal's achievement can be measured close to the end of the intervention, and the desired behaviors or states relate to a focal group of actors. Impact data show that Eric was successful in his outcome measures and that, except for the instructional rounds, all activities contributed to the positive impact of the intervention. So Eric could be satisfied.

In actuality, Eric has broader ambitions when he imagines that the intervention could affect the whole district. For this to happen, student academic engagement, his focal concern, would have to become a central concern of everyone in the schools. And that in turn means that the concept needs to break out of the principal-teacher conversation. It needs to become a topic of teacher-teacher conversations and an object of teacher inquiry. Alas, he would also have to make his schools more inquiry-based. The issue would no longer be micro, but would become meso, perhaps even macro, because he would now face a cultural and managerial change in all the schools and his entire district. Academic engagement would need to be communicated as an organizational vision and goal in the whole district. Conversations in all the faculties and collegial work teams would have to be reinforced or created from scratch in some schools. Leadership at the district and school levels would have to create the technical know-how and cultural synergy for the idea of academic engagement to take off.

Short of that, Eric concludes, the concept and its attendant practices would lack the strong effect on student achievement that he desires and that the literature documents. It pains Eric to realize that even if his designed intervention were successful in terms of his direct goals in the short run, he might not obtain the effects that he really desires—student achievement gains in the longer run— unless his design became embedded into a bigger picture and scaled up. So why even bother?

Eric's pains are familiar to most social reformers. Most big social problems of practice are systemic, and only systemic solutions make a big difference. Social reformers know that small incremental programs are not a systemic fix. Yet these programs do make a difference on a smaller scale. Individuals who run through them successfully become more competent actors, and these new competencies may radiate out to larger social networks. Small-scale interventions have more power if they are embedded into a broader strategic agenda of change for a whole district or similar educational unit. So it behooves professionals to search for the systemic and strategic connections of every design or intervention they engage in. But designs and interventions on a small scale are most powerful as test beds for practices that can be spread and scaled up if proven successful.

CHAPTER SUMMARY

Design development research is appropriate when educational leaders face problems of practice for which clear practical remedies are not available. Leaders design and conduct research in uncertain territory. This means that their design iterations sometimes work and sometimes do not, or work partly and must be improved on in the next iteration.

Designers feel exhilarated when, after carefully thinking about the theory of action, painstakingly designing an intervention, and sometimes enduring an anxiety-provoking implementation, they realize that their design has actually worked. Similarly, senior teachers like those in Christine's school district feel rewarded when they become leaders in their GLTs and eventually help novice teachers tackle behavior management problems with a sense of cooperative agency. How can elementary school teachers like those in Michelle's schools not feel satisfaction when, after an effective professional development sequence, they are able and willing to teach culturally relevant texts to their students or to cultivate their students' authentic voice in the midst of tight curricular controls? And principals like those in Eric's school, after being involved in an intervention on student engagement with academic content, can be proud of improving instructional supervision and providing better feedback to teachers. Principals in other schools who experiment with an intervention like the one at Nora's school will no doubt sense great satisfaction when a faculty embarks on a proactive response to rampant racial and homophobic slurs. But educational leaders should feel no less satisfaction when a design goes astray because of some unforeseen learning complexities, conflicts, or unintended consequences, and the designers have the wherewithal to share their lessons with the next users in a systematic and research-based fashion.

Conclusion

The logic of design development that we have presented in this book lends itself to projects of varying ambition and scale. At a basic level, becoming familiar with this logic helps reflective practitioners engage in a structured process of problem solving and a rigorous way of evaluating whether their assumptions about a solution hold true. Design development logic enhances intellectual leadership. Using this logic, intellectual leaders think deeply through urgent problems of practice for which powerful solutions do not exist, or do not exist in a form that works in their own situation. Intellectual leaders communicate their insights to colleagues so that everyone, collectively, can mobilize to improve the organization, making it more efficient, more learner-centered, and more equitable.

Equity-relevant changes are difficult because they often go against the grain of how people understand and carry out their work together. When it comes to fairness and justice, people do not start from a blank slate. Rather, they usually maintain that what they are currently doing is at least adequate. Sometimes they defensively cling to "the way we do things around here." So the change process is not about filling an empty vessel with new information. Nor is it simply about confronting people about "immoral" behavior and its causes. People do change when they feel threatened or sanctioned, but the change is often defensive. When equity-minded leaders, guided by their ideals and committed to their solutions, apply a simplistic understanding of the change process and define their problem as the absence of their preferred solution, the leaders often perceive that they are surrounded by "resisters," whose unwillingness they are supposed to overcome.

Design-based thinking, we've shown, starts from a different assumption, namely, that adults, not unlike the children in their care, want to be respected, stimulated, and satisfied in their need for competence, autonomy, and belonging. Adults are usually willing and able to learn within the bounds of their capacity to stretch, that is, within the zone of development where the *next level of work* can be carried out. Equity-relevant changes are about sparking this next level of work. Work at the next level aims at collective mobilization as well as technical improvement. The design development logic laid out in this book helps educators understand this complexity of the change process.

Because equity-relevant changes are complex and emergent, they are often considered unmanageable or unpredictable. "Let's try something and then see where we end up" seems a legitimate way to respond. This approach is unfortunate because the attempt inevitably comes up short on results, wasting people's energy in the process. Design development, in contrast, pivots on results, but it does not expect results on the first or even second try. Its iterative nature is suited to the unpredictability of complex organizational change. Its rigorous, evidence-based methodology enables systematic and deliberate learning that helps equity-minded and reflective leaders link what they value to what works. We believe that our field is in great need for such a methodology.

When design development is applied at a larger scale, it can become an important mode of innovation for a school district or similar administrative unit. Even at this large scale, the underlying logic, explained in this book, remains the same, though it may now become embedded in a wider co-design partnership, which is capable of carrying out multiple iterations in multiple organizational subunits. Ambitions are greater. Now the search is on for an intervention related to a focal problem of practice that might work for a whole district. Design iterations may begin small, but the goal is to distill design principles that can be robustly applied across multiple organizational subunits (e.g., schools) of a given system.

Design development studies have the potential to make important contributions to the body of practical design knowledge for the profession as a whole.

We believe that our field needs to build up such knowledge, especially related to widely shared and vexing problems of practice for which we lack powerful ideas for intervention. This is especially true for complex equity-relevant problems for which educators, all too often, fail to produce evidence-based records. Practical design knowledge emerges when co-design partnerships pair up intellectual leaders at the school and district levels with applied researchers based at a university or similar knowledge-producing organization. We have shown in this book that a design development study undertakes several steps. Ill-structured problems of practice are framed and defined, needs and assets are assessed, a theory of action that draws from the professional and research knowledge base is formulated, intervention activities are carefully planned and evaluated, impact and process data are collected and analyzed, and, finally, designers' biases are checked. The process results in the derivation of design principles and recommendations for subsequent iterations. When all of this becomes codified in a document that can be shared with a community of practitioners and applied researchers, design studies can be inherited and practical design knowledge accumulates.

The evidence base for this book comes mainly from smaller-scale studies conducted within the Leadership for Educational Equity Program at the University of California, Berkeley. Our four featured designers engage in attempts at real and tangible change at a modest scale that nevertheless makes a difference for equity today. Our experience in the last couple of years with a district co-design partnership has shown us that design development for school improvement is promising on a larger scale as well. This book has introduced the basic logic. A sequel to this book would address co-design efforts at a larger scale.

There are many ways to advance toward more equitable schooling. One way is activism, charging ahead with determination, commitment, and aplomb while accepting the uncertainty of outcomes. There is no question that this kind of activism is essential: changing organizations against the grain can rarely work without visionary and evangelizing social-justice leaders who engage in struggle against the odds. Although it cannot replace the need for activism, design development is an approach to this struggle in its own right. It takes vision and creativity as well as determination and commitment into account. And it hitches them to a systematic query on results and impact. We have taken our inspiration from critical scholarship on schooling inequities, learning and improvement sciences, and the many school-improvement design studies that we have been involved in or read about. We believe that leaders for equity should take seriously the charge of transforming what they value into what works in the here and now. We believe that design development studies put us in the transformative space.

Getting Started
Key Sources Consulted by the Designers Featured in This Book

Christine: Behavior Management in Schools Staffed by Novice Teachers

Achinstein, Betty. "Conflict Amid Community: The Micropolitics of Teacher Collaboration." *Teachers College Record* 104, no. 3 (2002): 421–455.

Cherubini, Lorenzo. "Reconciling the Tensions of New Teachers' Socialisation into School Culture: A Review of the Research." *Issues in Educational Research* 19, no. 2 (2009): 83–99.

Cohen, Susan G., and Diane E. Bailey. "What Makes Teams Work: Group Effectiveness Research from the Shop Floor to the Executive Suite." *Journal of Management* 23, no. 3 (1997): 239–290.

De Dreu, Carsten K. "When Too Little or Too Much Hurts: Evidence for a Curvilinear Relationship Between Task Conflict and Innovation in Teams." Journal of Management 32, no. 1 (2006): 83–107.

Eaker, Robert, Richard DuFour, and Rebecca DuFour. *Getting Started: Reculturing Schools to Become Professional Learning Communities.* Bloomington, IN: National Education Service, 2002.

Jehn, Karen A., and Elizabeth A. Mannix. "The Dynamic Nature of Conflict: A Longitudinal Study of Intragroup Conflict and Group Performance." *Academy of Management Journal* 44, no. 2 (2001): 238–251.

Kardos, Susan. M., Susan Moore Johnson, Heather G. Peske, David Kauffman, and Edward Liu. "Counting on Colleagues: New Teachers Encounter the Professional Cultures of Their Schools." *Educational Administration Quarterly* 37, no. 2 (2001): 250–290.

Louis, Karen Seashore, Helen M. Marks, and Sharon Kruse. "Teachers' Professional Community in Restructuring Schools." *American Educational Research Journal* 33, no. 4 (1996): 757–798.

Osher, David, George G. Bear, Jeffrey R. Sprague, and Walter Doyle. "How Can We Improve School Discipline?" *Educational Researcher* 39, no. 1 (2010): 48–58.

Stoll, Louise, Ray Bolam, Agnes McMahon, Mike Wallace, and Sally Thomas. "Professional Learning Communities: A Review of the Literature." *Journal of Educational Change* 7 (2006): 221–258.

Michelle: Cultural Relevance of Instruction

Blanc, Suzanne, Jolley Bruce Christman, Roseann Liu, Cecily Mitchell, Eva Travers, and Katrina E. Bulkley. "Learning to Learn from Data: Benchmarks and Instructional Communities." *Peabody Journal of Education* 85, no. 2 (2010): 205–225.

Gay, Geneva. *Culturally Responsive Teaching: Theory, Research, and Practice*, 2nd ed. New York: Teachers College Press, 2010.

Hawley, Willis D., and Linda Valli. "The Essentials of Effective Professional Development." In *Teaching as the Learning Profession: Handbook of Policy and Practice,* edited by Linda Darling-Hammond and Gary Sykes, 127–150. San Francisco: Jossey-Bass, 1999.

Ladson-Billings, Gloria. "Toward a Theory of Culturally Relevant Pedagogy." *American Educational Research Journal* 32, no. 3 (1995): 465–491.

Mintrop, Heinrich. *Schools on Probation: How Accountability Works (and Doesn't Work)*. New York: Teachers College Press, 2003.

Pearson, P. David, Barbara M. Taylor, and Anamarie Tam. "Epilogue: Effective Professional Development for Improving Literacy Instruction." In *Learning to Write, Writing to Learn: Theory and Research in Practice,* edited by Roselmina Indrisano and Jeanne R. Paratore, 221–234. Newark, DE: International Reading Association, 2005.

Sleeter, Christine E. "Restructuring Schools for Multicultural Education." *Journal of Teacher Education* 43, no. 2 (1992): 141–148.

Valencia, Richard R., ed. *The Evolution of Deficit Thinking: Educational Thought and Practice*. Abington, Oxon: RoutledgeFalmer, 1997.

Valencia, Sheila W., Nancy A. Place, Susan D. Martin, and Pamela L. Grossman. "Curriculum Materials for Elementary Reading: Shackles and Scaffolds for Four Beginning Teachers." *Elementary School Journal* 107, no.1 (2006): 93–120.

Villegas, Ana Marie, and Tamara Lucas. *Educating Culturally Responsive Teachers: A Coherent Approach*. Albany: State University of New York Press, 2002.

Eric: Instructional Supervision for Student Academic Engagement

Ancess, J. "The Reciprocal Influence of Teacher Learning, Teaching Practice, School Restructuring, and Student Learning Outcomes." *Teachers College Record* 102, no. 3 (2000): 590–619.

Blase, Jo, and Joseph Blase. *Handbook of Instructional Leadership: How Successful Principals Promote Teaching and Learning.* Thousand Oaks, CA: Corwin Press, 2004.

Borko, Hilda. "Professional Development and Teacher Learning: Mapping the Terrain." *Educational Researcher* 33, no. 8 (2004): 3–15.

City, Elizabeth A., Richard F. Elmore, Sarah E. Fiarman, and Lee Teitel. *Instructional Rounds in Education: A Network Approach to Improving Teaching and Learning.* Cambridge, MA: Harvard Education Press, 2009.

Hattie, John. *Visible Learning: A Synthesis of Over 800 Meta-Analyses Relating to Achievement.* Abingdon, Oxon: Routledge, 2009.

Knight, Jim, ed. *Coaching: Approaches & Perspectives.* Thousand Oakes, CA: Corwin Press, 2009.

Mangin, Melinda M. "Capacity Building and Districts' Decision to Implement Coaching Initiatives." *Education Policy Analysis Archives* 22, no. 56 (2014): 1–25.

Marsh, Julie. A., Kerri A. Kerr, Gina S. Ikemoto, Hilary Darilek, Marika Suttorp, Rob W. Zimmer, and Heather Barney. *The Role of Districts in Fostering Instructional Improvement: Lessons from Three Urban Districts Partnered with the Institute for Learning.* Santa Monica, CA: RAND Corporation, 2005.

Newmann, Fred M., ed. *Student Engagement and Achievement in American Secondary Schools.* New York: Teachers College Press, 1992.

Tschannen-Moran, Megan, and Peggy McMaster. "Sources of Self-Efficacy: Four Professional Development Formats and Their Relationship to Self-Efficacy and Implementation of a New Teaching Strategy." *Elementary School Journal* 110, no. 2 (2009): 228–245.

Nora: Shaping a Respectful School Climate by Reducing Slurs

Abrams, Jennifer. *Having Hard Conversations.* Thousand Oaks, CA: Corwin Press, 2009.

Diaz, Elizabeth M., and Joseph G. Kosciw. *Shared Differences: The Experiences of Lesbian, Gay, Bisexual, and Transgender Students of Color in Our Nation's Schools.* New York: GLSEN, 2009.

Diem, Sarah, Nazneen Ali, and Bradley W. Carpenter. "'If I Don't Use the Word, I Shouldn't Have to Hear It': The Surfacing of Racial Tensions in a Leadership Preparation Classroom." *Journal of Cases in Educational Leadership* 16, no. 4 (2013): 3–12.

Ladson-Billings, Gloria. "Fighting for Our Lives: Preparing Teachers to Teach African American Students." *Journal of Teacher Education* 51, no. 3 (2000): 206–214.

Lawrence, Sarah M., and Beverley Daniel Tatum. "Teachers in Transition: The Impact of Anti-Racist Professional Development on Classroom Practice." *Teachers College Record* 99, no. 1 (1997): 162–178.

McKenzie, Kathryn Bell, and James Joseph Scheurich. "Equity Traps: A Useful Construct for Preparing Principals to Lead Schools That are Successful with Racially Diverse Students." *Educational Administration Quarterly* 40, no. 5 (2004), 601–632.

Schein, Edgar H. "A Conceptual Model for Managed Culture Change." In *Organizational Culture and Leadership,* 4th ed., 299–313. San Francisco: Jossey-Bass, 2010.

Shields, Carolyn M. "Dialogic Leadership for Social Justice: Overcoming Pathologies of Silence." *Educational Administration Quarterly* 40, no. 109 (2004): 109–32.

Singleton, Glenn. *Courageous Conversations: A Field Guide for Achieving Equity in Schools*, Second Edition. Thousand Oaks, CA: Corwin Press, 2014.

Theoharis, George. "Social Justice Educational Leaders and Resistance: Toward a Theory of Social Justice Leadership." *Educational Administration Quarterly* 43, no. 2 (2007): 221–258.

NOTES

INTRODUCTION

1. Oakes, Jeannie, "Can Tracking Research Inform Practice? Technical, Normative, and Political Considerations," *Educational Researcher* (1992): 12–21; Riehl, Carolyn J., "The Principal's Role in Creating Inclusive Schools for Diverse Students: A Review of Normative, Empirical, and Critical Literature on the Practice of Educational Administration," *Review of Educational Research* 70, no. 1 (2000): 55–81; Theoharis, George, "Social Justice Educational Leaders and Resistance: Toward a Theory of Social Justice Leadership," *Educational Administration Quarterly* 43, no. 2 (2007): 221–258.

2. Perry, Jill A., "To Ed.D. or Not to Ed.D.," *Phi Delta Kappan* 94, no. 1 (2012): 41–44; Perry, Jill A., and David T. Imig, "A Stewardship of Practice in Education," *Change* 40, no. 6 (2008): 44–49. For the Carnegie Project consortium, see Carnegie Project on the Education Doctorate, home page, accessed August 21, 2015, http://cpedinitiative.org.

3. Brown, Ann L., "Design Experiments: Theoretical and Methodological Challenges in Creating Complex Interventions in Classroom Settings," *Journal of the Learning Sciences* 2, no. 2 (1992): 141–178; Cobb, Paul, et al., "Design Experiments in Educational Research," *Educational Researcher* 32, no. 1 (2003): 9–13.

4. I am grateful for insightful conversations with Louis Gomez, who made this point clear to me.

5. Plomp, Tjeerd, and Nienke Nieveen, eds., *An Introduction to Educational Design Research* (Shanghai: East China Normal University and Netherlands Institute for Curriculum Development: SLO, 2010); van den Akker, Jan. "Principles and Methods of Development Research,"in *Design Approaches and Tools in Education and Training*, edited by Jan van den Akker et al. (Norwell, MA: Kluwer Academic Publishers, 1999), 1–14. See also the Netherlands Institute for Curriculum Development: SLO website, http://international.slo.nl.

6. Coghlan, David, and Teresa Brannick, *Doing Action Research in Your Own Organization* (Thousand Oaks, CA: SAGE Publications, 2014).

7. Bryk, Anthony S., Louis M. Gomez, and Alicia Grunow, "Getting Ideas into Action: Building Networked Improvement Communities in Education," in *Frontiers in Sociology of Education*, edited by Maureen T. Hallinan (New York: Springer Science+Business, 2011), 127–162; Bryk, Anthony S., Louis M. Gomez, Alicia Grunow, and Paul G. LeMahieu, *Learning to Improve: How America's Schools Can Get Better at Getting Better* (Cambridge, MA: Harvard Education Press, 2015). See also the Carnegie Foundation for the Advancement of Teaching website, www.carnegiefoundation.org.

8. City, Elizabeth A., et al., *Instructional Rounds in Education: A Network Approach to Improving Teaching and Learning* (Cambridge, MA: Harvard Education Press, 2009).

9. Brown, Tim, *Change by Design: How Design Thinking Transforms Organizations and Inspires Innovation* (New York: HarperCollins, 2009); Kelley, Tom, and David Kelley, *Creative Confidence: Unleashing the Creative Potential Within Us All* (New York: Crown Business, 2013).

10. Brown, *Change by Design*; Kelley and Kelley, *Creative Confidence;* Martin, Roger L. *The Design of Business: Why Design Thinking Is the Next Competitive Advantage* (Cambridge, MA: Harvard Business Press, 2009).

11. Ryan, Richard M., and Edward L. Deci, "Self-Determination Theory and the Facilitation of Intrinsic Motivation, Social Development, and Well-Being," *American Psychologist* 55, no. 1 (2000): 68–78.

12. Brown, *Change by Design*.

13. Schön, Donald A., *The Reflective Practitioner: How Professionals Think in Action* (New York: Basic Books, 1983).

14. Martin, *The Design of Business*, 6.

15. Kelley and Kelley, *Creative Confidence*, 25.

16. Martin, *The Design of Business*.

17. Brown, *Change by Design*, 16.

18. Kelley and Kelley, *Creative Confidence*, 25.

19. Martin, *The Design of Business*, 10.

20. I acknowledge a creative and inspiring conversation I had with Stan Pogrow about the importance of creativity in the design process.

21. Argyris, Chris, and Donald A. Schön, *Organizational Learning II* (Reading, MA: Addison-Wesley, 1996).

22. Boaden, Ruth J., "What Is Total Quality Management . . . and Does It Matter?" *Total Quality Management* 8, no. 4 (1997): 153–171.

23. For improvement science in health care, see Berwick, Donald M., "The Science of Improvement," *Journal of the American Medical Association* 299, no. 10 (2008): 1182–1184; Langley, Gerald J., et al., *The Improvement Guide: A Practical Approach to Enhancing Organizational Performance* (New York: John Wiley & Sons, 2009); Parry, Gareth J., "A Brief History of Quality Improvement," *Journal of Oncology Practice* 10, no. 3 (2014): 196–199. For education, see Bryk, Anthony S., Louis M. Gomez, and Alicia Grunow, "Getting Ideas into Action: Building Networked Improvement Communities in Education," in *Frontiers in Sociology of Education*, edited by Maureen T. Hallinan (New York: Springer Science+Business, 2011), 127–162; Bryk, Anthony S., et al., *Learning to Improve*; Marshall, Martin, Peter Pronovost, and Mary Dixon-Woods, "Promotion of Improvement as a Science," *Lancet* 381, no. 9864 (2013): 419–421; Park, Sandra, et al., *Continuous Improvement in Education* (Stanford, CA: Carnegie Foundation for the Advancement of Teaching, 2013).

24. Moen, Ronald D., and Clifford L. Norman, "Circling Back," *Quality Progress* 43, no. 11 (2010): 22–28.

25. Berwick, "The Science of Improvement"; Deming, William Edwards, *The New Economics: For Industry, Government, Education* (Cambridge, MA: MIT Press, 2000); Langley, et al., *The Improvement Guide*.

26. Parry, "A Brief History of Quality Improvement."

27. Harry, Mikel J., and Richard R. Schroeder, *Six Sigma: The Breakthrough Management Strategy Revolutionizing the World's Top Corporations* (New York: Broadway Business, 2005); Harry, Mikel J., and Reigle Stewart, *Six Sigma Mechanical Design Tolerancing* (Schaumburg, IL: Motorola University

Press, 1988); Pyzdek, Thomas, and Paul Keller, *The Six Sigma Handbook* (New York: McGraw Hill Education, 2014).

28. Berwick, "The Science of Improvement."

29. Batalden, Paul B., and Frank Davidoff, "What Is 'Quality Improvement' and How Can It Transform Healthcare?" *Quality and Safety in Health Care* 16, no. 1 (2007): 2–3; Berwick, "The Science of Improvement"; Bryk, Gomez, and Grunow, "Getting Ideas into Action"; Marshall, Pronovost, and Dixon-Woods, "Promotion of Improvement as a Science."

30. Park et al., *Continuous Improvement in Education*.

31. Bryk et al., *Learning to Improve*.

32. Ibid., 13.

33. Bransford, John D., and Barry S. Stein, *The Ideal Problem Solver: A Guide for Improving Thinking, Learning, and Creativity*, 2nd ed. (New York: Worth Publishers, 1993).

34. Schön, *The Reflective Practitioner*.

35. Schön, Donald A., and Martin Rein, *Frame Reflection: Toward the Resolution of Intractable Policy Controversies* (New York: Basic Books, 1995).

CHAPTER 1

1. City, Elizabeth A., et al., *Instructional Rounds in Education: A Network Approach to Improving Teaching and Learning* (Cambridge, MA: Harvard Education Press, 2009).

2. Ibid.

3. Senge, Peter M., *The Fifth Discipline: The Art and Practice of the Learning Organization*, rev. ed. (New York: Doubleday/Currency, 2006), 114.

4. Thornton, Bill, Gary Peltier, and George Perreault, "Systems Thinking: A Skill to Improve Student Achievement," *Clearing House: A Journal of Educational Strategies, Issues and Ideas* 77, no. 5 (2004): 222–230.

5. Bourdieu, Pierre, *Outline of a Theory of Practice* (Cambridge, England: Cambridge University Press, 1977); Bourdieu, Pierre, and Jean-Claude Passeron, *Reproduction in Education, Culture and Society* (London: Sage Publications, 1977).

6. Leithwood, Kenneth A., and Karen Seashore Louis, *Linking Leadership to Student Learning* (New York: John Wiley & Sons, 2011).

7. City, *Instructional Rounds in Education*, 124–127.

CHAPTER 2

1. Newell, Allen, and Herbert A. Simon, *Human Problem Solving* (Englewood Cliffs, NJ: Prentice-Hall, 1972); Jonassen, David H., "Instructional Design Models for Well-Structured and Ill-Structured Problem-Solving Learning Outcomes," *Educational Technology Research and Development* 45, no. 1 (1997): 65–94.

2. Jonassen, "Instructional Design Models."

3. Newell and Simon, *Human Problem Solving*.

4. Pretz, Jean A., Adam J. Naples, and Robert J. Sternberg, "Recognizing, Defining, and Representing Problems," in *The Psychology of Problem Solving*, edited by Janet E. Davidson and Robert J. Sternberg (Cambridge, England: Cambridge University Press, 2003), 3–30.

5. Ibid., 6.

6. Ibid., 3–30.

7. Newell and Simon, *Human Problem Solving*, 149.

8. Lortie, Dan C., *Schoolteacher: A Sociological Study* (Chicago: University of Chicago Press, 1975).

9. Newell and Simon, *Human Problem Solving*.

10. Pretz, Naples, and Sternberg, "Recognizing, Defining, and Representing Problems."

11. Newell and Simon, *Human Problem Solving*.

12. Hallinger, Philip, Kenneth Leithwood, and Joseph Murphy, eds., *Cognitive Perspectives in Educational Leadership* (New York: Teachers College Press, 1993); Leithwood, Kenneth and Rosanne Steinbach, *Expert Problem Solving: Evidence from School and District Leaders* (Albany, NY: SUNY Press, 1995).

13. Jonassen, "Instructional Design Models"; David H. Jonassen, "Toward a Design Theory of Problem Solving," *Educational Technology Research and Development* 48, no. 4 (2000): 63–85; Pretz, Naples, and Sternberg, "Recognizing, Defining, and Representing Problems."

14. Copland, Michael A., "Problem-Based Learning and Prospective Principals' Problem-Framing Ability," *Educational Administration Quarterly* 36, no. 4 (2000): 585–607; Jonassen, "Toward a Design Theory"; Timperley, Helen S., and Viviane M. J. Robinson, "Collegiality in Schools: Its Nature and Implications for Problem Solving," *Educational Administration Quarterly* 34, no. 1 suppl. (1998): 608–629.

15. Mumford, Michael D., Roni Reiter-Palmon, and Matthew R. Redmond, "Problem Construction and Cognition: Applying Problem Representations in Ill-Defined Domains," in *Problem Finding, Problem Solving, and Creativity*, edited by Mark A. Runco (Westport, CT: Ablex Publishing, 1994), 3–39.

16. Jonassen, "Instructio nal Design Models."

17. Ibid.; Schön, Donald A., and Martin Rein, *Frame Reflection: Toward the Resolution of Intractable Policy Controversies* (New York: Basic Books, 1995).

18. Schön and Rein, *Frame Reflection*.

19. Ibid.

20. Coburn, Cynthia E., "Framing the Problem of Reading Instruction: Using Frame Analysis to Uncover the Microprocesses of Policy Implementation," *American Educational Research Journal* 43, no. 3 (2006): 343–379.

CHAPTER 3

1. March, James G., "Theories of Choice and Making Decisions," *Society* 20, no. 1 (1982): 29–39.

2. Simon, Herbert A., *Administrative Behavior* (New York: Free Press, 1997), 88.

3. Davis, Stephen H., and Patricia B. Davis, The Intuitive Dimensions of Administrative Decision Making (Lanham, MD: Scarecrow, 2003); Simon, Administrative Behavior (1997).

4. Simon, Herbert A., *Administrative Behavior* (New York, NY: MacMillan, 1957).

5. Chaiken, Shelly, and Yaacov Trope, eds., *Dual-Process Theories in Social Psychology* (New York: Guilford Press, 1999); Kahneman, Daniel, *Thinking, Fast and Slow* (New York: Farrar, Straus and Giroux, 2011).

6. Davis, Stephen H., and Patricia B. Davis, *The Intuitive Dimensions of Administrative Decision Making* (Lanham, MD: Scarecrow, 2003).

7. Gilovich, Thomas, Dale Griffin, and Daniel Kahneman, *Heuristics and Biases: The Psychology of Intuitive Judgment* (Cambridge, England: Cambridge University Press, 2002), 3.

8. Davis and Davis, *The Intuitive Dimensions of Administrative Decision Making*.

9. Ibid.
10. Tversky, Amos, and Daniel Kahneman, "Availability: A Heuristic for Judging Frequency and Probability," *Cognitive Psychology* 5, no. 2 (1973): 207–232.
11. Ibid., 208.
12. Davis and Davis, *The Intuitive Dimensions of Administrative Decision Making*.
13. Ibid.
14. Ibid., 59.
15. Ibid., 102.
16. Ibid., 59.
17. Ibid., 66.
18. Kahneman, *Thinking, Fast and Slow*.

CHAPTER 4

1. Witkin, Belle R., and James W. Altschuld, *Planning and Conducting Needs Assessments: A Practical Guide* (Thousand Oaks, CA: Sage Publications, 1995).
2. Witkin, Belle R., *Assessing Needs in Educational and Social Programs*, Jossey-Bass Social and Behavioral Science (San Francisco: Jossey-Bass, 1984), ix.
3. Rossett, Allison, *Training Needs Assessment* (Englewood Cliffs, NJ: Educational Technologies Publications, 1987); Witkin and Altschuld, *Planning and Conducting Needs Assessments*.
4. Altschuld, James W., and David D. Kumar, *Needs Assessment: An Overview* (Thousand Oaks, CA: Sage Publications, 2010); Kaufman, Roger A., Alicia M. Rojas, and Hanna Mayer, *Needs Assessment: A User's Guide* (Englewood Cliffs, NJ: Educational Technology Publications, 1993); Watkins, Ryan, Maurya W. Meiers, and Yusra Visser, *A Guide to Assessing Needs: Essential Tools for Collecting Information, Making Decisions, and Achieving Development Results* (Washington, DC: World Bank Publications, 2012).
5. Watkins, Meiers, and Visser, *Guide to Assessing Needs*.
6. For needs defined as gaps in results, see Kaufman, Rojas, and Mayer, *Needs Assessment: A User's Guide*; and Altschuld and Kumar, *Needs Assessment: An Overview*. For needs defined as discrepancies between current and desired conditions, see Watkins, Meiers, and Visser, *A Guide to Assessing Needs*.
7. Watkins, Meiers, and Visser, *A Guide to Assessing Needs*.
8. Witkin and Altschuld, *Planning and Conducting Needs Assessments*.
9. City, Elizabeth A., et al., *Instructional Rounds in Education: A Network Approach to Improving Teaching and Learning* (Cambridge, MA: Harvard Education Press, 2009), 83–98.
10. Ascribed to an unnamed professor at Yale University, not Albert Einstein, to whom it is often attributed.

CHAPTER 5

1. Lewin, Kurt, *Field Theory in Social Science: Selected Theoretical Papers*, edited by Dorwin Cartwright (New York: Harper & Row, 1951).
2. Argyris, Chris, "Actionable Knowledge: Design Causality in the Service of Consequential Theory," *Journal of Applied Behavioral Science* 32, no. 4 (1996): 390–406.
3. Ibid.
4. Ibid., 402.
5. Ibid.

6. Little, Judith Warren, "The Persistence of Privacy: Autonomy and Initiative in Teachers' Professional Relations," *Teachers College Record* 91, no. 4 (1990): 509–536.

CHAPTER 6

1. Giroux, Henry A., "Teachers as Transformative Intellectuals," *Social Education* 49, no. 5 (1985): 376–379; Giroux, Henry A. *Teachers as Intellectuals: Toward a Pedagogy of Learning*, Critical Studies in Education (Westport, CT: Bergin & Garvey Publishers, 1988).
2. Giroux, *Teachers as Intellectuals*, 27.
3. Lave, Jean, and Etienne Wenger, *Situated Learning: Legitimate Peripheral Participation* (New York: Cambridge University Press, 1991).
4. Coburn, Cynthia E., William R. Penuel, and Kimberly E. Geil, "Research-Practice Partnerships: A Strategy for Leveraging Research for Educational Improvement in School Districts" (New York: William T. Grant Foundation, 2013); Cohen-Vogel, Lora A., et al., "Implementing Educational Innovations at Scale: Transforming Researchers into Continuous Improvement Scientists," *Educational Policy* 29, no. 1 (2015): 257–277.
5. Coburn, Penuel, and Geil, "Research-Practice Partnerships."
6. Ibid.
7. Lee, Yanki, "Design Participation Tactics: Involving People in the Design of Their Built Environment," PhD dissertation (Hong Kong: Hong Kong Polytechnic University, 2007); Lee, Yanki, "Design Participation Tactics: The Challenges and New Roles for Designers in the Co-Design Process," *Co-Design* 41, no. 1 (2008): 31–50.
8. Lee, "Design Participation Tactics."
9. Sanders, Elizabeth B.-N., and Pieter J. Stappers, "Co-Creation and the New Landscapes of Design," *Co-Design* 4, no. 1 (2008): 5–18.
10. Ibid., 16.
11. Ibid.
12. Steen, Marc, Menno A. J. Manschot, and Nicole De Koning, "Benefits of Co-Design in Service Design Projects," *International Journal of Design* 5, no. 2 (2011): 53–60.
13. Coburn, Cynthia E., and Mary Kay Stein, *Research and Practice in Education: Building Alliances, Bridging the Divide* (Lanham, MD: Rowman & Littlefield, 2010); Penuel, William R., Jeremy Roschelle, and Nicole Shechtman, "Designing Formative Assessment Software with Teachers: An Analysis of the Co-Design Process," *Research and Practice in Technology Enhanced Learning* 2, no. 1 (2007): 51–74.
14. Coburn, Penuel, and Geil, "Research-Practice Partnerships"; Penuel, William R., Cynthia E. Coburn, and Daniel J. Gallagher, "Negotiating Problems of Practice in Research-Practice Design Partnerships," *National Society for the Study of Education Yearbook* 112, no. 2 (2013): 237–255.
15. Coburn, Cynthia E., Soung Bae, and Erica O. Turner, "Authority, Status, and the Dynamics of Insider-Outsider Partnerships at the District Level," *Peabody Journal of Education* 83, no. 3 (2008): 364–399; Lee, "Design Participation Tactics: The Challenges"; Penuel, Coburn, and Gallagher, "Negotiating Problems of Practice."

CHAPTER 7

1. Gilovich, Thomas, Dale Griffin, and Daniel Kahneman, *Heuristics and Biases: The Psychology of Intuitive Judgment* (Cambridge, England: Cambridge University Press, 2002).

2. Johnson-Laird, Philip N., "Mental Models and Probabilistic Thinking," *Cognition* 50, no. 1 (1994): 189–209.

3. Ibid.

4. Kahneman, Daniel, *Thinking, Fast and Slow* (New York: Farrar, Straus and Giroux, 2011).

5. Ratcliffe, John W., "Notions of Validity in Qualitative Research Methodology," *Science Communication* 5, no. 2 (1983): 147–167.

6. Argyris, Chris, "Action Science and Intervention," *Journal of Applied Behavioral Science* 19, no. 2 (1983): 115–135; City, Elizabeth A., Richard F. Elmore, Sarah E. Fiarman, and Lee Teitel, *Instructional Rounds in Education: A Network Approach to Improving Teaching and Learning* (Cambridge, MA: Harvard Education Press, 2009); Senge, Peter M., *Schools That Learn: A Fifth Discipline Fieldbook for Educators, Parents, and Everyone Who Cares About Education* (New York: Doubleday, 2000).

7. Argyris, "Action Science and Intervention."

8. Coburn, Cynthia E., and Erica O. Turner, "The Practice of Data Use: An Introduction," *American Journal of Education* 118, no. 2 (2012): 99–111; Ratcliffe, "Notions of Validity"; Spillane, James P., and Amy F. Coldren, *Diagnosis and Design for School Improvement: Using a Distributed Perspective to Lead and Manage Change* (New York: Teachers College Press, 2015).

9. King, Gary, Robert O. Keohane, and Sidney Verba, *Designing Social Inquiry: Scientific Inference in Qualitative Research* (Princeton, NJ: Princeton University Press, 1994); Nisbett, Robert, and Lee Ross, *Human Inference: Strategies and Shortcomings of Human Judgment* (Englewood Cliffs, NJ: Prentice Hall, 1980).

10. Spillane and Coldren, *Diagnosis and Design for School Improvement*; Spillane, James P., and David B. Miele, "Evidence in Practice: A Framing of the Terrain," in *Evidence and Decision Making*, edited by Pamela A. Moss (Cambridge, MA: National Society for the Study of Education, 2007), 46–73.

11. Kassirer, Jerome P., John B. Wong, and Richard I. Kopelman, *Learning Clinical Reasoning* (Philadelphia: Wolters Kluwer/Lippincott Williams & Wilkins, 2009); Patel, Vimla L., José F. Arocha, and Jiajie Zhang, "Thinking and Reasoning in Medicine," in *The Cambridge Handbook of Thinking and Reasoning*, edited by Keith J. Holyoak and Robert G. Morrison (Cambridge, England: Cambridge University Press, 2005), 727–750.

12. Lundberg, Craig C., "Organizational Development Diagnosis," in *Handbook of Organization Development*, edited by Thomas G. Cummings (Thousand Oaks, CA: Sage Publications, 2008), 137–150.

13. Rebell, Michael A., and Jessica R. Wolff, "We Can Overcome Poverty's Impact on School Success," *Education Week*, January 18, 2012, www.edweek.org/ew/articles/2012/01/18/17rebell.h31.html.

14. Jonassen, David H., "Toward a Design Theory of Problem Solving," *Educational Technology Research and Development* 48, no. 4 (2000): 63–85.

15. Mishra, Punya, and Matthew Koehler, "Technological Pedagogical Content Knowledge: A Framework for Teacher Knowledge," *Teachers College Record* 108, no. 6 (2006): 1017–1054; Shulman, Lee S., "Those Who Understand: Knowledge Growth in Teaching," *Educational Researcher* 15, no. 2 (1986): 4–14.

16. Leithwood, Kenneth A., and Carolyn J. Riehl, *What We Know About Successful School Leadership* (Nottingham, England: National College for School Leadership, 2003).

17. Copland, Michael A., "Problem-Based Leadership Development: Developing the Cognitive and Skill Capacities of School Leaders," in *Reshaping the Landscape of School Leadership Development*, edited by Philip Hallinger (Lisse, Netherlands: Swets and Zeitlinger, 2003), 101–118; Fullan,

Michael G., *Successful School Improvement* (Bristol, PA: Open University Press, 1992); Leithwood, Kenneth A., and Karen Seashore Louis, eds., *Linking Leadership to Student Learning* (San Francisco: Jossey-Bass, 2012); Tichy, Noel M., and Mary A. Devanna, "The Transformational Leader," *Training & Development Journal* 40, no. 7 (1986): 27–32.

18. Steele, Claude M., "A Threat in the Air: How Stereotypes Shape Intellectual Identity and Performance," *American Psychologist* 52, no. 6 (1997): 613–29.

19. Alexander, Jeffrey C., et al., eds. *The Micro-Macro Link* (Berkeley: University of California Press, 1987).

CHAPTER 8

1. Au, Wayne, "High-Stakes Testing and Curricular Control: A Qualitative Metasynthesis," *Educational Researcher* 36, no. 5 (2007): 258–264; Mintrop, Heinrich, and Gail Sunderman, "Predictable Failure of Federal Sanctions-Driven Accountability—and Why We May Retain It Anyway," *Educational Researcher* 38, No. 5 (2009): 353–364.

2. Tyack, David B., and Larry Cuban, *Tinkering Toward Utopia: A Century of Public School Reform* (Cambridge, MA: Harvard University Press, 1997).

3. Metz, Mary H., "Real School: A Universal Drama Amid Disparate Experience," *Journal of Education Policy* 4, no. 5 (1989): 75–91.

4. Tyack, David B., *The One Best System: A History of American Urban Education* (Cambridge, MA: Harvard University Press, 1974).

5. Schein, Edgar H. *Organizational Culture and Leadership* (San Francisco: Jossey-Bass, 2010), 15.

6. Singleton, Glenn, and Curtis Linton, *Courageous Conversations* (Thousand Oaks, CA: Corwin Press, 2006).

7. Burnes, Bernard, "Kurt Lewin and the Planned Approach to Change: A Re-appraisal," *Journal of Management Studies* 41, no. 6 (2004): 977–1002; Pettigrew, Andrew, Ewan Ferlie, and Lorna McKee, "Shaping Strategic Change: the Case of the NHS in the 1980s," *Public Money & Management* 12, no. 3 (1992): 27–31.

8. Fullan, Michael, *Change Forces with a Vengeance* (New York: Routledge, 2003).

9. Burnes, "Kurt Lewin."

10. Louis, Karen Seashore, and Viviane M. J. Robinson, "External Mandates and Instructional Leadership: School Leaders as Mediating Agents," *Journal of Educational Administration* 50, no. 5 (2012): 629–665; Mintrop, Heinrich, *Schools on Probation: How Accountability Works (and Doesn't Work)* (New York: Teachers College Press, 2004); Scheurich, James J., and Linda Skrla, "Continuing the Conversation on Equity and Accountability: Listening Appreciatively, Responding Responsibly," in *Educational Equity and Accountability: Paradigms, Policies, and Politics*, edited by Linda Skrla and James J. Scheurich (New York: Routledge Falmer, 2004), 39–47.

11. Whelan-Berry, Karen S., and Karen A. Somerville, "Linking Change Drivers and the Organizational Change Process: A Review and Synthesis," *Journal of Change Management* 10, no. 2 (2010): 175–193.

12. Burke, W. Warner, and George H. Litwin, "A Causal Model of Organizational Performance and Change," *Journal of Management* 18, no. 3 (1992): 523–545.

13. Huy, Quy Nguyen, "Time, Temporal Capability, and Planned Change," *Academy of Management Review* 26, no. 4 (2001): 601–623.

14. Bryk, Anthony S., Louis M. Gomez, and Alicia Grunow, "Getting Ideas into Action: Building Networked Improvement Communities in Education," in *Frontiers in Sociology of Education*, edited by Maureen T. Hallinan (New York: Springer Science+Business, 2011), 127–162; Langley, Gerald J., et al., *The Improvement Guide: A Practical Approach to Enhancing Organizational Performance* (New York: John Wiley & Sons, 2009).

15. Bryk, Gomez, and Grunow, "Getting Ideas into Action."

16. Ibid.

17. Argyris, Chris, and Donald A. Schön, *Organizational Learning II* (Boston: Addison Wesley, 1996); Leithwood, Kenneth A., and Karen Seashore Louis, *Linking Leadership to Student Learning* (New York: John Wiley & Sons, 2011).

18. Argyris, Chris, and Donald A. Schön, *Organizational Learning: A Theory of Action Perspective* (Reading, MA: Addison-Wesley, 1978); Hanson, Mark, "Institutional Theory and Educational Change," *Educational Administration Quarterly* 37, no. 5 (2001): 637–661; Leithwood, Kenneth A., Robert Aitken, and Doris Jantzi, *Making Schools Smarter: Leading with Evidence* (Thousand Oaks, CA: Corwin Press, 2006); Scribner, Jay P., et al., "Creating Professional Communities in Schools Through Organizational Learning: An Evaluation of a School Improvement Process," *Educational Administration Quarterly* 35, no. 1 (1999): 130–160.

19. Schein, Edgar H., *Organizational Culture and Leadership* (San Francisco: Jossey-Bass, 2010).

20. Cobb, Paul, et al., "Design Experiments in Educational Research," *Educational Researcher* 32, no. 1 (2003): 9–13.

CHAPTER 9

1. Csikszentmihalyi, Mihaly, *Flow: The Psychology of Optimal Experience* (New York: HarperPerennial, 1991).

2. Argyris, Chris, and Donald A. Schön, *Organizational Learning II* (Boston: Addison-Wesley, 1996).

3. Argyris, Chris "Actionable Knowledge: Design Causality in the Service of Consequential Theory," *Journal of Applied Behavioral Science* 32, no. 4 (1996): 390–406.

4. Blanc, Suzanne, et al., "Learning to Learn from Data: Benchmarks and Instructional Communities," *Peabody Journal of Education* 85, no. 2 (2010): 205–225.

5. See, for example, San Francisco Unified School District, School Health Programs Department, Student Support Services, "Responding to Anti-Gay/Homophobic Slurs," accessed September 8, 2015, www.healthiersf.org/LGBTQ/InTheClassroom/docs/Responding%20to%20Homophobia.pdf.

CHAPTER 10

1. Creswell, John W., and Vicki L. P. Clark, *Designing and Conducting Mixed Methods Research* (Thousand Oaks, CA: Sage Publications, 2010).

2. Yin, Robert K., *Case Study Research: Design and Methods* (Thousand Oaks, CA: Sage Publications, 2013).

3. Netherlands Institute for Curriculum Development: SLO, "International Activities," accessed September 8, 2015, http://international.slo.nl/activities/.

4. Plomp, Tjeerd, "Educational Design Research: An Introduction," in *An Introduction to Educational Design Research*, edited by Tjeerd Plomp and Nienke Nieveen (Enschede, Netherlands: Netherlands

Institute for Curriculum Development, 2010), 9–36.

5. Ibid.

6. Barab, Sasha A., and Kurt Squire, "Design-Based Research: Putting a Stake in the Ground," *Journal of the Learning Sciences* 13, no. 1 (2004): 1–14.

7. Plomp, "Educational Design Research," 13.

8. Ibid., 14; Reeves, Thomas C., "Design Research from a Technology Perspective," *Educational Design Research* 1, no. 3 (2006): 52–56.

9. Plomp, "Educational Design Research," 16.

10. Benedict, Elizabeth A., Robert H. Horner, and Jane K. Squires, "Assessment and Implementation of Positive Behavior Support in Preschools," *Topics in Early Childhood Special Education* 27, no. 3 (2007): 174–192.

11. Plomp, "Educational Design Research," 22.

CHAPTER 12

1. Creswell, John W., and Vicki L. P. Clark, *Designing and Conducting Mixed Methods Research* (Thousand Oaks, CA: Sage Publications, 2010).

2. van den Akker, Jan, "Principles and Methods of Development Research," in *Design Approaches and Tools in Education and Training*, edited by Jan van den Akker et al. (Norwell, MA: Kluwer Academic Publishers, 1999), 1–14.

3. Creswell, John W., *Qualitative Inquiry and Research Design: Choosing Among Five Approaches* (Thousand Oaks, CA: Sage Publications, 2012).

4. Miles, Matthew B., and A. Michael Huberman, *Qualitative Data Analysis: An Expanded Sourcebook* (Thousand Oaks, CA: Sage, 1994).

5. Plomp, Tjeerd, and Nienke Nieveen, eds., *An Introduction to Educational Design Research* (Shanghai: East China Normal University and Netherlands Institute for Curriculum Development: SLO, 2010).

6. Schön, Donald A., *The Reflective Practitioner: How Professionals Think in Action* (New York: Basic Books, 1983).

7. Schön, Donald A., and Martin Rein, *Frame Reflection: Toward the Resolution of Intractable Policy Controversies* (New York: Basic Books, 1995).

8. Fullan, Michael G., *Leading in a Culture of Change* (San Francisco: Jossey-Bass, 2007).

CHAPTER 13

1. Coghlan, David, and Teresa Brannick, *Doing Action Research in Your Own Organization* (Thousand Oaks, CA: SAGE Publications, 2014), 65.

2. Ibid., 21.

3. Ibid., 33.

4. Ibid.

5. Ibid.

6. Plomp, Tjeerd, and Nienke Nieveen, eds., *An Introduction to Educational Design Research* (Shanghai: East China Normal University and Netherlands Institute for Curriculum Development: SLO, 2010).

7. Bang, Megan, et al., "Innovations in Culturally Based Science Education Through Partnerships and Community," in *New Science of Learning*, edited by Myint Swe Khine and Issa M. Saleh (New

York: Springer Science+Business, 2010), 569–592; Gutiérrez, Kris, Patricia Baquedano-López, and Carlos Tejeda, "Rethinking Diversity: Hybridity and Hybrid Language Practices in the Third Space," *Mind, Culture, and Activity* 6, no. 4 (1999): 286–303; Gutiérrez, Kris, and Shirin Vossoughi, "'Lifting Off the Ground to Return Anew': Mediated Praxis, Transformative Learning, and Social Design Experiments," *Journal of Teacher Education* 61, no. 1–2 (2010): 100–117.

8. Gutiérrez and Vossoughi, "Lifting Off the Ground," 111.

9. Ibid.

CHAPTER 14

1. U.S. Department of Education's Office of Special Education Programs, Technical Assistance Center on Positive Behavioral Interventions and Supports, home page, accessed September 8, 2015, www.pbis.org.

2. Slavin, Robert E., "Evidence-Based Education Policies: Transforming Educational Practice and Research," *Educational Researcher* 31, no. 7 (2002): 15–21.

3. Olson, David R., "The Triumph of Hope over Experience in the Search for 'What Works': A Response to Slavin," *Educational Researcher* 33, no. 1 (2004): 24–26.

4. Correnti, Richard, and Brian Rowan, "Opening Up the Black Box: Literacy Instruction in Schools Participating in Three Comprehensive School Reform Programs," *American Educational Research Journal* 44, no. 2 (2007): 298.

5. Pressman, Jeffrey L., and Aaron Wildavsky, *Implementation: How Great Expectations in Washington Are Dashed in Oakland; or, Why It's Amazing That Federal Programs Work at All*, 3rd ed. (Berkeley: University of California Press, 1984).

6. Cohen, David K., and Susan L. Moffitt, *The Ordeal of Equality: Did Federal Regulation Fix the Schools?* (Cambridge, MA: Harvard University Press, 2010).

7. Honig, Meredith I., *New Directions in Education Policy Implementation* (Albany: State University of New York Press, 2006).

8. Elmore, Richard F., and Milbrey W. McLaughlin, "Steady Work: Policy, Practice, and the Reform of American Education" (Washington, DC: National Institute of Education, 1988); McLaughlin, Milbrey W., "Implementation as Mutual Adaptation: Change in Classroom Organization," presented at the American Educational Research Association Annual Meeting (Washington, DC, 1975).

9. Cohen, David K., "A Revolution in One Classroom: The Case of Mrs. Oublier," *Educational Evaluation and Policy Analysis* 12, no. 3 (1990): 311–329.

10. Coburn, Cynthia E., "Beyond Decoupling: Rethinking the Relationship Between the Institutional Environment and the Classroom," *Sociology of Education* 77, no. 3 (2004): 211–244; Spillane, James P., *Standards Deviation: How Schools Misunderstand Education Policy* (Cambridge, MA: Harvard University Press, 2006).

11. Hess, Frederick M., *Spinning Wheels: The Politics of Urban School Reform* (Washington, DC: Brookings Institution Press, 1999).

12. Meyer, Heinz-Dieter, and Brian Rowan, eds., *The New Institutionalism in Education* (Albany: State University of New York Press, 2006).

13. Meyer, John W., and Brian Rowan, "Institutionalized Organizations: Formal Structure as Myth and Ceremony," *American Journal of Sociology* 83, no. 2 (1977): 340.

14. Cuban, Larry, "Reforming Again, Again, and Again," *Educational Researcher* 19, no. 1 (1990):

3–13; Payne, Charles M., *So Much Reform, So Little Change: The Persistence of Failure in Urban Schools* (Cambridge, MA: Harvard University Press, 2008).

15. Shields, Carolyn M., "Dialogic Leadership for Social Justice: Overcoming Pathologies of Silence," *Educational Administration Quarterly* 40, no. 1 (2004): 109–132.

CHAPTER 15

1. Reeves, Thomas C., "Enhancing the Worth of Instructional Technology Research Through 'Design Experiments' and Other Development Research Strategies," presented at the American Educational Research Association Annual Meeting (New Orleans, 2000); Reeves, Thomas C., "Design Research from a Technology Perspective," *Educational Design Research* 1, no. 3 (2006): 52–56; van den Akker, Jan, "Principles and Methods of Development Research," in *Design Approaches and Tools in Education and Training,* edited by Jan van den Akker et al. (Norwell, MA: Kluwer Academic Publishers, 1999), 1–14; van den Akker, Jan, et al., *Educational Design Research* (New York: Routledge, 2006).

2. van den Akker, Jan, "Principles and Methods of Development Research," 1–14.

3. Yin, Robert K., *Case Study Research: Design and Methods* (Thousand Oaks, CA: Sage Publications, 2013).

4. Berlin University of the Arts, Design Research Lab, "Transferability, Case Transfer & Rip+Mix," accessed September 8, 2015, www.design-research-lab.org/projects/transferability/.

ACKNOWLEDGMENTS

This book would not be complete without the intellectual commitment of the educational leaders who have inspired my colleagues and me and who labored alongside us. We are particularly indebted to the professionals who have engaged in doctoral studies in the Leadership for Educational Equity Program (LEEP) at the University of California, Berkeley. Students and alumni associated with this program have contributed substantially to our understanding of design development. We are grateful for their determination, creativity, analytical skill, and intellectual leadership. Together, we are part of an intellectual community that has learned collaboratively over the past eight years, developing and supporting transformative, innovative, and equity-focused leaders.

The following individuals conducted design development studies (titles of studies in italics) that served as sources for Christine, Michelle, Eric, and Nora, the composite characters that animate this book (please see the website of the Leadership for Educational Equity Program for more information and copies of complete dissertations: http://leep.berkeley.edu/):

Cindy Acker, Principal, The Child Unique Montessori School (*Montessori Education: Attaining Common Ground with Public Schools*)

Sondra Aguilera, Network Superintendent, Oakland Unified School District (*Developing Principal Leadership through Instructional Rounds*)

Daniel Allen, Executive Director of School Renewal, Santa Ana Unified School District (*Socialization Circles: Using Site Based Teacher Leaders to Socialize New Staff in Urban Schools*)

Judy Jaramillo Argumedo, Director of Academic Supports, Palo Alto Unified School District (*Responding to Disproportionality of Special Referrals through Addressing Teacher Practice*)

Liz Baham, Faculty, Research and Development, Reach Institute for School Leadership (*School Capacity and Overload Review (S.C.O.R.E.): Measuring School Capacity to Maximize School Improvement*)

Dennis Caindec, Instructor, UC Berkeley CalTeach (in progress)

Brenda Carrillo, Director of Student Services, Palo Alto Unified School District (*Building Successful Student Study Teams*)

Cheryl Cotton, Human Resources Director, West Contra Costa Unified School District (*"They Don't Teach This in Prep Programs": Training Principals to Negotiate School and District Politics*)

Nina D'Amato, Deputy of Academics and Programs, Naval Postgraduate School (*Improving the Capacity of Online Instructors in Online Learning Environments*)

Brent Daniels, Principal, Piedmont Unified School District (*Co-teaching to Support Special Education Students' Success in Math*)

Jivan Dhaliwal, Director of Curriculum and Instruction, Campbell Union High School District (in progress)

Jamila Dugan, Assistant Principal, Yu Ming Charter School (*Underprivileged Families in a Privileged School: Designing Productive Communication Centered on Student Needs*)

Will Dunford, Assistant Principal, Pittsburgh Unified School District (*Building Capacity for the Implementation of Culturally Sustaining Pedagogy*)

Itoco Garcia, Principal, Hayward Unified School District (*Accelerating Literacy Development Through Hip-Hop Pedagogy*)

Elizabeth Guneratne, Assistant Superintendent, Diocese of Oakland (*Integrating Technology into Teacher Practice*)

Jeremy Hilinski, Principal, San Francisco Unified School District (*Beyond Compliance: Toward Effective Principal Leadership of English Language Development Instruction*)

Anya Hurwitz, Deputy Director, Sobrato Family Foundation (*Transforming the Learning Experiences of Elementary School English Learners and Their Teachers*)

Brian Inglesby, Director, Contra Costa Special Education Local Plan Area (*Principals Utilizing Leadership for Special Education: The PULSE Workshop Model for Improving the Practice of Instructional Leadership for Special Education*)

Julia Kempkey, Director of Secondary Education, Novato Unified School District (*Integrating Mobile Devices into Constructivist Classroom Practices*)

Gerry Lopez, Migrant Education Program Manager, Santa Clara County Office of Education (*Developing the Effectiveness of Parent Liaisons for Parent Empowerment*)

Samuel Martinez, Elementary Math and Science Coordinator, Fresno Unified School District (in progress)

John Melvin, Principal, Hayward Unified School District (*Collective Responsibility Through Peer Observation in "Instructional Rounds"*)

Grace Morizawa, Consultant, National Writing Project (*Nesting the Neglected "R": A Design Study: Writing Instruction Within a Prescriptive Literacy Program*)

Jason Murphy, Vice Principal, Antioch Unified School District (*Development of a Measure to Evaluate District's Local Control and Accountability Plans*)

Karin Navarro, Director of Child Development Center Lab, Mission College (in progress)

Micaela Ochoa, Chief Business Officer, Santa Clara County Office of Education (*Building Communication and Accountability Between the Business Office and Academic Departments in a Public School District*)

Peter Ivano Parenti, Director of Curriculum and Instruction, Albany Unified School District (*In progress*)

Kafi Payne, Director of Talent Development, Oakland Unified School District (*Developing Skill and Expertise in Coaches' Discourse with Beginning Teachers*)

Barbara Penny-James, Principal, West Contra Costa Unified School District (*Introducing Culturally Relevant Literary Content Into an Established Skills-Based Literacy Program*)

Thomas Reinhardt, Secondary Science Coordinator, Oakland Unified School District (in progress)

Brooke Soles, Coordinator, Los Angeles County Office of Education, Charter School Office (*The SHU:SH Project Slurs Hurt Us: Safety and Health—Lesbian, Gay, Bisexual, and Transgender Students at School*)

Chin Song, Director of Technology, Milpitas Unified School District (in progress)

Brandee Stewart, Principal, Oakland Unified School District (*Leading Through the Use of Productive Conflict: Professional Development for Principals to Use Productive Conflict Among Teachers for Organizational Learning and Growth*)

Erik Swanson, Superintendent, St. Hope Public Schools (*Developing a Culture of "Warm Demand" in Secondary Schools*)

Julie Valdez, Director of Special Education, Piedmont Unified School District (in progress)

Pam VandeKamp, Principal, San Lorenzo Unified School District (*Insights and New Horizons: Creating the Context for Effective Feedback for Teachers*)

Matt Wayne, Assistant Superintendent, Hayward Unified School District (*Visiting Classrooms: A Design Study to Support Principals' Instructional Leadership*)

Linda Wells, Supervisor for Secondary Programs, San Francisco Unified School District (*RENEW: Revitalizing Educators Through a New Experience of Work*)

Sarah Williams, Director of Assessment and Achievement, Napa Valley Unified School District (in progress).

ABOUT THE AUTHOR
AND CONTRIBUTORS

AUTHOR

RICK MINTROP, currently on the faculty at the University of California, Berkeley, was an educator at the school level in various capacities in both the United States and Germany before he entered into an academic career. He received an MA in political science and German literature at the Freie Universität Berlin and a PhD in education from Stanford University.

He was the faculty co-director of the Principal Leadership Institute at UCLA and has been the director of the doctoral program in Leadership for Educational Equity (LEEP) at Berkeley since 2006. LEEP aims to prepare strong leaders for high-need urban schools, and design development studies are the signature pedagogy of this program.

As a researcher, he explores school change and improvement at the nexus of educational policies, teachers' work, and broader institutional changes. He examined these relationships, first, in East German schools that underwent fundamental changes after the collapse of authoritarian socialism. A number of articles and a book, *Educational Change and Social Transformation* (with Hans Weiler and Elisabeth Fuhrmann, 1996), resulted from this work. He coauthored (with Bruno Losito, CEDE, Italy) *The Teaching of Civic Education* (2001), which looks at the conditions of civic education teaching in twenty-eight countries. His interest in design-based thinking began in a project that was inspired by the work of the late Ann Brown and produced, among other publications, an article, "Educating Student and Novice Teachers in a Constructivist Manner: Can It All Be

Done?" (*Teachers College Record*, 2002), which was the Top Featured Article in the 2002 volume.

He has written various publications about his research on school accountability; these include *Schools on Probation: How Accountability Works (and Doesn't Work)* (2004); "The Practical Relevance of Accountability Systems for School Improvement" (with Tina Trujillo, *Educational Evaluation and Policy Analysis*); "Predictable Failure of Federal Sanctions-Driven Accountability for School Improvement—And Why We May Retain It Anyway" (with Gail Sunderman, *Educational Researcher*, 2009); and "Bridging Accountability Obligations, Professional Values, and (Perceived) Student Needs with Integrity," (*Journal of Educational Administration*, 2012), which was named Commendable Paper for the 2012 volume.

CONTRIBUTORS

MAHUA BARAL is a doctoral student in the Policy, Organizations, Measurement, and Evaluation Program (POME) and an instructor in the Leadership for Educational Equity Program (LEEP) in the Graduate School of Education at the University of California, Berkeley. Her research focuses on examining how research and practice partnerships facilitate innovation and school improvement. Before entering the doctoral program, Mahua worked as a research associate at the American Institutes for Research, where she managed a variety of projects reporting assessment data, improving social and emotional learning climates, and developing teacher evaluation systems. Mahua received a BS in psychology and child development from Syracuse University and an MsEd in teaching, learning, and curriculum from the University of Pennsylvania.

JOHN HALL is an assistant professor in the College of Education at Temple University. John studies the relationships between school systems, school leaders, and the broader social, cultural, and political environment. Previously, John led a redesign team focused on leadership development in the Oakland Unified School District, and before that, he helped launch a charter school network serving disadvantaged populations in the Bay Area. He has been a teacher and an administrator in district schools, charter schools, independent schools, and international schools. He began his career as a research scientist, studying cellular responses to nervous system trauma. John received a BS in biology from the University of Washington and an MA and a PhD in education policy from the University of California, Berkeley. While conducting his doctoral studies, John was an instructor in and coordinator of LEEP for many years.

ELIZABETH ZUMPE is a doctoral student in the Policy, Organizations, Measurement, and Evaluation Program (POME) and an instructor in the Leadership for Educational Equity Program (LEEP) in the Graduate School of Education at the University of California, Berkeley. Her research focuses on the cognitive, social psychological, and organizational dimensions of school improvement. Before graduate study, she taught for over a decade in several urban school districts serving large proportions of disadvantaged students. She holds National Board Certification in Teaching for English Language Arts for Early Adolescence. Elizabeth earned a BA in English from Oberlin College.

INDEX

action research
  biases and, 191, 194
  bolstering validity in, 194–195
  combining with design development, 195
  cycle of, 194
  distance between participants and researchers in, 192–193
  insider perspectives and, 193
  internalizing control and distance in, 193
  passion and dispassion of leaders and, 196–198
  questions to consider, 191–192
  rigor in studies and, 193
  summary, 198–199
asset maps, 119–120, 121
assistant superintendent's design development. *See* Eric

biases
  action research and, 191, 194
  collecting impact and process data and, 169
  considerations of blind spots, 79–80
  decision making and, 48
bounded rationality and decision making, 47

Carnegie Foundation for the Advancement of Teaching, 91
CDPs. *See* co-design partnerships
Christine (middle school principal)
  asset map, 121
  challenges of unforeseen complexities (*see* Christine's intervention implementation)
  co-design partnerships (*see* Christine's co-design team)

decision to use design development, 11
defining and framing problems of practice, 33–34, 42
derived design principles (*see* Christine's design principles)
exploratory needs assessment, 59
filtering of ideas, 78–79
impact data selection, 169–171
initial steps in developing her research-based project, 159
intervention design (*see* Christine's intervention design)
intuitive theory of action used by, 49–50, 58
iterations in her level of understanding of the problem, 77
needs assessment, 64–65
passion and dispassion for the work, 197
preliminary design challenge formulation, 67–68
problem identification, 77
professional knowledge base use, 76–80
unit of analysis for the intervention, 167
validity of the impact metrics, 184–185
Christine's co-design team, 89
  acquired understanding of PLCs, 136
  decision on the focus of the intervention, 137–138
  expectations for the plan, 138–139
  identification of dimensions of work-team development, 136–137
  intervention design details, 138–139
  mini-experiments use, 149
  selection of the main drivers of change, 137
  training plan, 138
Christine's design principles
  final design principles, 225
  intervention design and assessment, 220–221

Christine's design principles, *continued*
   revision of the original design, 224–225
   revisiting of the original theory of action, 223–224
   search for a pattern in the process data, 221–223
Christine's intervention design
   acquired understanding of PLCs, 136
   decision on the focus of the intervention, 137–138
   expectations for the plan, 138–139
   identification of dimensions of work-team development, 136–137
   intervention design details, 138–139
   mini-experiments use, 149
   selection of the main drivers of change, 137
   training plan, 138
Christine's intervention implementation
   changes in feedback as the sessions progress, 205–207
   changes made by the task force, 206–208
   context for the intervention, 205
   main elements of the intervention, 204
   process plan, 205
co-design partnerships (CDPs)
   co-design relationships, 89–91
   co-design teams described, 88, 90–91
   co-design versus cocreation, 92
   consultative, 94–95
   examples of, 93–94
   integrated, 96–98
   meaning of interaction in, 135
   mediated, 95–96
   types overview, 94
   used by Christine, 136–139, 149
   used by Eric, 90, 157
   used by Michelle, 89, 111–112, 140–143, 149–150
   used by Nora, 90, 112–113
consultative co-design partnerships, 94–95
continuous quality improvement, 13–15, 135
culturally relevant pedagogy (CRP), 34, 46, 141–143

decision making
   biases in heuristics and, 48
   bounded rationality and, 47
   choices and, 46
   heuristics defined, 47–48
   intuition defined, 48–49

   intuition's role in, 47–49
deficit thinking, 34, 63
Department of Education, US, 91
design-based thinking
   assumptions made about, 13
   basic questions in a design mode of innovation, 16
   characteristics of design thinking, 12–13
   continuous quality improvement and, 13–15
   defining and framing problems of practice (*see* problems of practice definition and framing)
   described, 11–12
   disciplined inquiry and, 14
   leaders and, 13
   principles of improvement science and, 15–16
   questioning of the intuition and heuristics surrounding a problem (*see* needs assessment)
   rationality and intuition and, 12–13
   reality of designing, 19–20
   selecting problems of practice (*see* problems of practice selection)
design development
   applying research rigor to (*see* research-based intervention design)
   assumptions made about participants, 238
   challenge of equity-relevant changes, 237–240
   common approach to innovation and problem solving, 4–5
   complexities of equity-relevant improvement, 1
   core challenges of equity in education, 2
   defined, 4
   design-based thinking and (*see* design-based thinking)
   design mode of innovation, 6
   examples of leaders' application of the concept (*see* Christine; Eric; Michelle; Nora)
   excursions into theory, 9
   key principles and approach of the LEEP, 6–8
   limitations of the available knowledge base, 2–3
   logic model, 19, 237
   making it research based (*see* professional knowledge base)
   need for practical design knowledge, 3
   potential of, 238–239
   power of applying on a large scale, 238
   power of its iterative nature, 238
   purpose of, 219

questions to ask when designing a program, 16
relationship to innovation, 93
summary, 69–70
design principles derivation
analytical steps in, 220
basis of design principles, 220
Christine's final design principles, 220–225
design development's reliance on outcomes, 232
Eric's final design principles, 232–234
inevitability of adaptations, 219–220
iterations' role in, 228
logic of design research, 227–228
Michelle's final design principles, 225–227
Nora's final design principles, 229–232
purpose of design development, 219
purposes of design research, 227
summary, 234–235
transferability and, 228
usefulness of small-scale interventions, 234
design research methodology
applicability to education, 161
educational design research defined, 161
formative and summative data collection, 162–163
iterative nature of the process, 162
methodology defined, 160
preliminary phase, 162
process of research, 160
uniqueness of methodologies, 161
domain knowledge, 104, 108–110
double-loop learning, 123
dual-process models, 47

elementary school principal's design development.
    See Michelle
empty-vessel intuition, 45–46
ERIC, 80
Eric (assistant superintendent)
asset map, 121
a challenge to viewing the outcome as successful,
    157–158
co-design relationships, 90
data collection, 212–213
decision to use design development, 11
defining and framing the problem of practice,
    35–36, 42

design principles derivation, 232–234
direct and indirect outcomes sought, 232–233
ease of losing track of the criteria of success, 156
exploratory needs assessment, 60
impact data selection, 172
initial results of the intervention, 213
initial steps in developing his research-based
    project, 159
intervention design (see Eric's intervention design)
intuitive theory of action used, 51–53, 58
lessons learned from the intervention, 158
macro-level changes needed for effective impact,
    233
original goal versus actual outcome, 156–157
passion and dispassion for the work, 197–198
preliminary results of the multi-step program,
    154–156
process data collection strategy, 175–177
process data problems, 213–214
theory of action, 212
unit of treatment for the intervention, 167
Eric's intervention design
evaluating the success of the outcome, 157–158
initial steps in developing a research-based
    project, 159
intervention design details, 146
mini-experiments use, 150
original goal versus actual outcome, 156–157
preliminary results of the workshop-based
    program, 154–156
re-thinking of original drivers of change, 146–147
selection of the main drivers of change, 144–145
understanding the problem, 143–144
exploratory needs assessments, 59–60, 63–64

framing a problem of practice. See problems of
    practice definition and framing

Google Scholar, 80

high-inference statements, 60
high school principal's design development. See
    Nora

IDEAL model of design, 19
IES (Institute for Education Sciences), 91
impact and process data collection
    biases and, 169
    distal actors' perceptions and, 168
    identifying and selecting the pieces of process
        data, 174–175
    impact data described, 168–169
    outcome selection decision matrix examples,
        169–173
    process data described, 173–174
    questions to consider, 165–166
    strategy for a multi-session intervention, 175–177
    strategy for unobtrusive data collection, 177–180
    summary, 180
    unit of analysis and unit of treatment, 166–168
implementing interventions
    challenges in, 203–204
    institutional context of education and, 211
    leadership element, 214–218
    logistics of data collection and, 212–214
    policy implementation complexities, 210–211
    summary, 218
    trade-offs in design fidelity, 209–210
    unforeseen complexities in adult learning and,
        204–208
    unstable organizational context and, 208–209
improvement science principles, 14–16
Institute for Education Sciences (IES), 91
institutionalized environment, 211
instructional rounds, 25
integrated co-design partnerships, 96–98
intellectual leadership
    co-design teams and (see co-design partnerships)
    design-based thinking and, 13
    design development logic and, 237–238
    design development's relationship to innovation,
        93
    domain knowledge needed by an education
        leader, 109–110
    equity-relevant problems in education, 2, 89
    intellectuals described, 88
    leadership element in Nora's implementation,
        214–218
    leaders' need for actionable knowledge, 75
    leaders' role in design work, 88

leaders' role in enacting change, 118–119
leaders' use of the knowledge base (see
    professional knowledge base)
passion and dispassion of leaders and action
    research, 196–198
questions to consider, 87
research-practice partnerships, 87, 91–93
summary, 99
intervention design
    aim of a design, 135
    applying research rigor to (see research-based
        intervention design)
    for a behavior management problem (see
        Christine's intervention design)
    characteristics of a well-designed lesson, 134
    for a culture-change issue, 147–149, 150
    interventions defined, 133
    meaning of interaction in a co-design team, 135
    patterns of learning, 134–135
    for a process improvement goal (see Eric's
        intervention design)
    qualities of research-based design development,
        135–136
    questions to consider, 133–134
    quick trials or mini-experiments use, 149–150
    for a societal change issue (see Michelle's
        intervention design)
    summary, 151
intuitive theories of action
    applied to a school discipline problem, 49–50, 58
    basis of intuition, 43–44
    bringing focus to the problem (see understanding
        the problem)
    decision making and (see decision making)
    defining a problem as the absence of a solution,
        50–51
    development of the understanding of a problem,
        53–54
    empty-vessel intuition, 45–46
    heuristics defined, 44, 47–48
    intuition defined, 48–49
    intuition's role in decision making, 47–49
    leaders' reliance on shortcuts, 46
    PD heuristic, 44–45
    process for making them explicit, 49
    questions to ask about, 44

shifting of the frames around a problem of
      practice, 51–53
   summary, 55
iSeek, 80

JSTOR, 80

knowledge base. *See* professional knowledge base

Leadership for Educational Equity Program
      (LEEP), 6–8, 239
leadership in design development. *See* intellectual
      leadership
*Learning to Improve: How America's Schools Can Get
      Better at Getting Better*, 15
low-inference observations of behaviors, 60, 62–67

mediated co-design partnerships, 95–96
Mendeley, 81
Michelle (elementary school principal)
   asset map, 121
   broadening of her understanding of the problem,
      111–112
   co-design relationships, 89, 111–112
   conclusion about how to address the problem, 112
   dealing with unstable organizational context,
      208–209
   decision to use design development, 11
   defining and framing the problem of practice,
      34–35, 42
   design principles derivation, 226–227
   exploratory needs assessment, 59
   findings from the knowledge base, 110–111
   impact data analysis, 225
   impact data selection, 171–172
   initial steps in developing her research-based
      project, 159
   intellectual leadership of, 110
   intervention design (*see* Michelle's intervention
      design)
   intuitive theory of action used by, 50–51, 58
   needs assessment, 65–67

observed behavior seen through societal factors,
      105
   passion and dispassion for her work, 197
   preliminary design challenge formulation, 68
   process data results, 225–226
   understanding the problem, 102–104
   unit of treatment for the intervention, 167
Michelle's intervention design
   blocks for the intervention, 142–143
   framing of the problem, 140
   quick trials use, 149–150
   selection of the main drivers of change, 140–142
middle school principal's design development. *See*
      Christine

needs assessment
   assumptions analysis, 59
   attitudes discernment and, 62–63
   exploratory, 59–60, 63–64
   formulation of the preliminary design challenge,
      67–68
   high versus low-inference statements, 60
   low-inference observations of behaviors, 62–64,
      65–67
   principles of, 61
   problem statements and, 60
   purpose of, 61
   questions designers need to ask, 57
   reframing of a problem, 64–65
   scope of approaches taken after, 57–58
   steps in a design challenge, 67–68
   summary, 68
No Child Left Behind (NCLB), 117
Nora (high school principal)
   benefit of context, 126
   co-design relationships, 90, 112–113
   consideration of indirect impacts, 230–231
   decision to use design development, 11
   defining and framing the problem of practice, 36,
      42
   design principles derivation, 229–232
   exploratory needs assessment, 60
   identification of the problem of practice, 229
   impact data analysis, 229
   impact data selection, 172–173

Nora (high school principal), *continued*
    initial steps in developing her research-based
        project, 159
    intervention design, 147–149, 150
    intuitive theory of action used by, 53–54, 58
    leadership in her implementation (*see* Nora's
        leadership in the implementation)
    low-inference observations of behaviors, 64
    passion and dispassion for her work, 198
    process data collection strategy, 177–180
    process data results, 229–230
    recognition of suitable drivers of change, 124–125
    rethinking of the process sequence, 231
    transferability of her design, 231–232
    understanding of the change process, 123–124
    understanding of the problem, 112–113
    unit of treatment for the intervention, 167–168
    use of the knowledge base, 112, 126–127
    validity of the impact data, 185
Nora's leadership in the implementation
    conflicts among the faculty, 215–216
    data collection and presentation, 215
    embracing of her role as a leader, 216–218
    theory of action, 214

operationalizations, 63
organizational change
    change dynamics, 122
    drivers of change, 120, 122–123
    single- and double-loop learning and, 123

plan-do-study-act (PDSA), 14, 92
problems of practice
    defining and framing (*see* problems of practice
        definition and framing)
    scope of approaches taken after determining, 57–
        58
    selecting (*see* problems of practice selection)
    theories about solving (*see* problem solving
        theory)
problems of practice definition and framing
    frame for a problem, 41–42
    identifying a core skill needed by principals, 35–
        36

identifying who should act to address a problem
    with slurs, 36
process of picturing the problem of practice, 31–32
in a school with an achievement gap, 34–35
in a school with a student-behavior problem, 33–
    34
shifting of the frames around a problem of
    practice, 51–53
summary, 42
problems of practice selection
    actionable problems determination, 27–28
    identifying core practices, 24–26
    organizational-level focus for, 26–27
    practicality and sensitivity to context and, 29–30
    problems of practice defined, 23, 25
    questions used to identify problems of practice,
        23–24
    scope of the term "practice," 26
    strategic orientation requirement, 28–29
    summary, 30
problem solving theory
    defining the problem, 40–41
    framing the problem, 41–42
    ill-defined problems, 38–40
    problem and solution spaces, 37
    task environment and, 37–38
    well-defined problems, 38
procedural fidelity, 210
process data collection. *See* impact and process data
    collection
professional development (PD) heuristic, 44–45
professional knowledge base
    classification of genre, 81
    considerations of blind spots in, 79–80
    consistency considerations, 83–84
    filtering of ideas for the specific situation, 78–79
    identification of relevant concepts, 79
    identifying the topic, 81–82
    iterations in understanding the problem, 77
    lack of consistency in the knowledge base, 77–78
    main parts of a theory of action, 74
    moving from intuition to analysis, 74
    problem identification and, 77
    questions to ask, 73–74
    results of research into culturally relevant
        instruction, 110

results of research into PLCs, 76–80
results of research into understanding a culture
    problem, 112–113
robustness considerations, 82–83
strategies for searching for sources, 80–81
summary, 85
professional learning communities (PLCs), 78, 84,
    136

research-based intervention design
    Christine's (see Christine's intervention design)
    criteria for being a researchable intervention
        design, 163–164
    ease of losing track of the criteria of success, 156
    Eric's (see Eric's intervention design)
    Michelle's (see Michelle's intervention design)
    purpose of procedures, 154
    qualities of, 135–136
    questions to consider, 153–154
    research methodology (see design research
        methodology)
    summary, 164
    visibility and verifiability of the intervention and,
        159
research-based theories of action. See theory of
    action development
research-practice partnerships
    categories of partnerships, 92
    characteristics of, 91
    co-design versus cocreation and, 92
    participants' roles, 92
rigor in design development
    connection between intervention and results and,
        185
    construct validity, 184, 188
    context sensitivity, 189–190
    high external validity and, 185–186, 188
    high internal validity and, 187–188
    importance of instruments and metrics, 183–185
    methods and data and, 186–187
    questions to consider, 181
    reliability and, 187
    researcher bias considerations, 187–189
    research functions compared to courts of law,
        181–182

steps in effective data collection procedures, 183
summary, 190
ways to ensure rigor, 182–183

single-loop learning, 123
social design experiments, 195
social theory and domain knowledge, 109–110
stereotyping, 63

theories of action
    derived from intuition (see intuitive theories of
        action)
    developing through rigor (see professional
        knowledge base)
    main parts of, 74
    preliminary phase of design research and, 162
    research-based (see theory of action development)
    summary, 199
    testing with rigor, 186–189
theory of action development
    definition of concepts, 75
    leadership's role in (see intellectual leadership)
    leaders' need for actionable knowledge and, 75
    main parts of a theory of action, 74
    professional knowledge base use (see professional
        knowledge base)
    role of science in generalizations, 75–76
    summary, 128–129
    uncertainty and unpredictability and, 84
    understanding the change process and (see
        understanding the change process)
    understanding the problem and (see
        understanding the problem)
transactional dynamics, 122
transferability of a design, 228, 231–232
transformational dynamics, 122

understanding the change process
    activities and, 125
    asset maps, 119–121
    challenge of implementing change, 115–116
    change dynamics, 122
    contexts and, 126

understanding the change process, *continued*
  design-relevant specifics of the change process, 126
  dimensions of human action and, 119
  drivers of change, 120, 122–123
  leaders' role in enacting change, 118–119
  learning about how to facilitate change, 123–124
  learning and unlearning and change, 120
  nature of change in educational organizations, 117–118
  questions to ask in the change process, 117
  requirements for changing behaviors, 118
  selecting suitable drivers for the situation, 124–125
  single- and double-loop learning and, 123
  summary, 128
  treatment of participants in equity-minded designs, 116
  unintended consequences of a mandated learning model, 117
  use of the knowledge base, 126–127
understanding the problem
  analyzing behavior with respect to societal factors, 105
  broadening of the understanding of a problem, 111–112
  core practices and context considerations, 106
  deepening of needs assessments, 106–107
  diagnosis of a behavior problem, 102–104
  inferences and, 107–108
  intellectual leadership and, 110
  parallels with a doctor diagnosing a malady, 102
  questions for bringing focus to the problem, 101
  root causes of behavioral patterns, 104–105
  social theory and domain knowledge and, 109–110
  spheres of society where actions are carried out, 104–105
  summary, 113–114
  understanding the problem diagnosis, 108–109
unit of analysis and unit of treatment, 166–168

Zotero, 81